The Strange World of Willie Seabrook

Books by Marjorie Worthington

Novels

Spider Web
Mrs. Taylor
Scarlet Josephine
Come, My Coach
Manhattan Solo
House on the Park
The Enchanted Heart

Biographies

Miss Alcott of Concord
The Immortal Lovers

For Children

Bouboukar, Child of the Sahara

Marjorie Worthington

The Strange World of Willie Seabrook

Harcourt, Brace & World, Inc., New York

Dedicated:
To our friend, Snow

The Strange World of Willie Seabrook

Chapter One

I've never really understood what Gertrude Stein meant by calling us "the lost generation." She said a lot of things that were true, no doubt, but it is hard to think of her in the role of Delphic Oracle, as some did, or even as a very profound philosopher. When we visited her at Belley, France, she seemed to be an extremely practical, intelligent, literary woman, fully aware of her own importance and also of the value of success. She could be as easily dazzled by a celebrity as anyone else, and from the company she kept one suspected that she would have nothing to do with the *really* lost.

However, no matter what the term "lost generation" meant, I guess I was part of it. I left my own country in April, 1926, and, except for periods when I returned to sanity and New York, I lived in France, on and off, until 1934. I was not an expatriate, though, and my reasons for living abroad had nothing to do with those set forth in a manifesto that explained why artists and writers could not create in the United States. I could write anywhere, and I firmly believed that the United States was the most wonderful place in the world. I set sail on that April day because I had earned and saved up enough money to pay my passage on the *De Grasse* and wanted to see Paris—and also because I was completely, unreasonably, idiotically in love—and, as the song goes, my love was there!

During those years abroad with Willie Seabrook, I met and became friends with many members of the "lost generation." Now that I have come to rest after the turbulent years, I would like to tell about some of those people, the lost and the not lost, as I remember them—and before I forget. It may turn out to be a patchwork quilt. It may show a pattern, I hope, like those wonderful quilts in museums. The pattern, come to think of it, may only be "my life with Willie." But, then, that was as much a part of the scene as anything else.

Perhaps the first prominent author I met in Paris was Ford Madox Ford. It was not long after I arrived, and Willie and I were walking in the Luxembourg Gardens. The trees were awakening and the daffodils and hyacinths were out in the formal gardens before the Palace. We watched the children sail toy boats in the pond, and we stopped to admire the statues of the Queens of France and the Medici Fountain where, a long time later, I was to sit and watch the gold and russet leaves of autumn fall, with my tears.

We left the gardens and walked to the rue de Veaugirard. We entered the courtyard of what had once been a private mansion in a day when homes were about as intimate as castles, and we climbed three flights of stone stairs with indentations made by centuries of human footsteps.

I don't remember how we got into the apartment; perhaps a maid let us in, though I doubt it, because Ford was always too poor to hire servants. But I do remember walking into a small, dark stuffy room, untidy and filled with books and papers, and seeing Ford, massive and uncomfortable-looking, seated in an armchair that was too small for him. Before him was a small, inlaid antique table on which, with his hamlike hands, he was playing solitaire with the smallest deck of cards I had ever seen.

During the conversation I gathered that he was in the thinking and planning stage of a new book. He explained the game of solitaire by saying that while he kept his hands occupied, and the top of his brain, his mind could dwell on the subject of his book serenely and without interruption.

It was difficult to understand what Ford was saying unless you knew him well and heard him daily. It was not only his British accent that made things difficult for American ears; it was also a slight impairment due to a wound to his jaw he had received in the First World War. If one listened carefully, the

4

words that came were brilliant. He was an accomplished raconteur, who told not always the truth but something much more interesting and amusing.

We remained not more than half an hour, I think. It was long enough for me to perceive that there was no love lost between Ford Madox Ford and Willie. Ford had a deep-rooted contempt for popular success, and Willie's *Adventures in Arabia* and *The Magic Island* had both been best sellers. Willie admired Ford as a novelist and critic, but, sensing his contempt, he built up a wall of his own that manifested itself in an amused disdain for Ford's "artiness."

Somehow, in spite of all that, we maintained a friendship with Ford, and in odd ways our paths often crossed, over there in France and when we came back to the United States.

Ford's ex-wife was Stella Bowen, an Englishwoman and a painter, and one of the finest women I've ever met. Stella lived in a large studio apartment with their little daughter, Julie, a strangely quiet child who, at an early age, had asked that she be allowed to become a Roman Catholic. Julie had been raised in the shadow of the church of St. Sulpice; there seemed to be no other explanation for her sudden request. Ford and Stella had respected Julie's wishes and did what they could to help her become a good little Catholic. Whenever her mother gave a party—which was fairly frequent, because Stella liked people, and her parties would often include such disparities as Edith Sitwell and Willie Seabrook—Julie remained in her narrow ascetic room, studying her catechism and the Lives of the Saints. And almost everyone in the artistic and literary world of Paris in the middle 1920's had attended Julie's First Communion.

Stella also had a studio in the South of France that she used very rarely and often lent to Ford. When Willie told her he was looking for a place in the Midi, Stella Bowen, with typical generosity, offered us hers.

2 bis Quai du Parti. Toulon. Var. France. That was our address for seven years, more or less. The core of my life, really.

The best and the worst years, and surely the most exciting.

The studio was on the second floor of a warehouse on the Toulon waterfront. Beneath us, on the ground floor, was a furniture maker who filled the atmosphere with the smell of glue and wood shavings from eight in the morning until five-thirty every weekday afternoon. Then he would lock up and leave the whole empty building to us. The top floor belonged to Othon Friez, a landscape painter who as far as I knew was never in residence. However, we would refer to him when people wanted to know how we managed to live in such an unlikely place. We could always say, "Our studio belonged to Stella Bowen, and Othon Friez paints there." That seemed to give it some sort of cachet, because it *was* a crazy place to live in—which is why we loved it, I guess. It was, in a way, what the beatnik of today might call a pad, but we were not beatniks in any sense. Willie admired success and was a dyed-in-the-wool Republican, and among his dearest friends in France was Princess Murat and the Honorable Daisy Fellowes and a wonderful old aristocrat with the beautiful name of Tranchant de Lunelle.

It is impossible not to "drop names" in writing all this, because part of the excitement of living with Willie was the people we met, at the top and the bottom. He had no use for anything at the middle. In the middle were solid respectable citizens who slept in safe beds. None of them would have slept on the dirty floor of a crowded third-class compartment on a night trip from Paris to Arles, as Willie did, and none of them would have slept the night through on the icy sands of the Sahara Desert, as I did. At least, that's what Willie thought about the Middle Class, which he dismissed as if it were non-existent.

The room we lived in on the Quai du Parti was very long and fairly wide, with one enormous window at the end overlooking the *Rade*, a basin where a large part of the French fleet was anchored. The floor of our studio was of paving brick, unevenly laid. We cleaned it at intervals by strewing moist tea leaves on the ground and sweeping them and litters of dust up into a bin with a bundle of twigs like the besoms witches go riding about on.

There was no running water and no electricity or gas. For light we had an acetylene lamp suspended from the ceiling, and for cooking a primus stove that Willie had used on his first African trip, when he gathered the material for *Jungle Ways*. With unusual patience he had shown me how to light it, but it scared me to death every time I did. First you poured kerosene into a cup that surrounded the wick. Then you lit the kerosene with a match, and while it was blazing you pumped a lever like mad and suddenly there would be an explosion—and then there was calm, and the wick was lit, and you could cook whatever you wanted without danger. Sometimes, when we grew tired of the rich food served in the restaurants, I would boil up a few fresh vegetables and we would dine, with relief, on them. But it was Willie who used the stove to make morning coffee. He would always bring me a cup, sometimes with a flower in the saucer. The fact that I usually got the coffee at five A.M., before he went up to the studio he later rented on the third floor, didn't seem important. Taking a lot of other things into consideration, I appreciated the thoughtfulness.

Our furnishings were of the simplest, and mostly as Stella Bowen had left them. There was a large double couch in the upper corner to the left of the window, and a long refectory table made of planks on trestles on the other side of the room. There was a round table in the middle of the brick floor, and against one wall was a pot-bellied stove in which we burned fagots of wood during the cold damp months of December and January.

At the lower end was a dry sink with a bowl, a pitcher, and a slop jar. For many years this was the only bathroom we had. I would go down twice a day with an enormous tin pitcher to a sort of fountain that trickled out of the wall of one of the buildings that lined the Quai du Parti. I would enjoy waiting in a queue with the women of the *quartier*, who were

7

good-natured and joked with us—and about us—and accepted us as good neighbors. They thought we made books for a living (that is, actually bound them and sold them), and that was a trade, and so we were proper and honest working people like themselves.

The fetching of water was romantic, but there was another chore which presented more of a problem, and that was the emptying of the slop jar! The *Rade* was filled with pleasure craft as well as the French navy, and all their refuse, naturally, was pumped out into the already dark and oily waters of the port, although there was a city ordinance to the effect that nothing was to be thrown into the water.

The people of Toulon were an independent lot when I knew them. They were not to be intimidated by a little thing like a city ordinance. We had seen them dumping whatever they chose into the harbor—but discreetly, after dark. And so Willie and I did as the Romans did. When night had come on, with its velvety blackness disturbed by no more than a lamp or two on our deserted quay, we would descend the stairs carrying our slop pails and empty them between two small yachts that were usually anchored in front of our house.

No matter how late it might be, whether we came home from a party on one of the yachts, or a visit uptown to the Grand Hotel, or a movie, or just from an evening of drinking at a café on the Quai Cronstadt, we would empty our jars before we went to bed. In the morning I would watch from the window as the clean-up man passed by, dragging what looked like a huge butterfly net along the edges of the quays, and I knew we were not the only Toulonnais with the slops problem. It gave us a sense of belonging.

Later, when Ann Watkins sold *Jungle Ways* to the *Ladies' Home Journal* for $30,000, a large sum in those days, Willie felt rich enough to install plumbing and electricity in the stone-walled room. It was never quite the same to us after that.

One of the reasons for the bad feeling between Ford Madox Ford and Willie Seabrook was the fact that Stella had offered us her Toulon studio and Ford had planned to live in it with

Janice, his third wife. In fact, they were using it when they were notified about us. They moved out hastily and in a way to show Ford's displeasure, and took a cottage at Cap Brun, where Ford planted an English garden and cooked wonderful meals—to which he occasionally invited us. Perhaps he enjoyed the arguments he and Willie had, interminably, about some little thing such as the way Ford pronounced the Latin phrase *Summa spes* as if it were summer's peas, or the origin of some superstition, or whether there actually were foxes in the South of France to eat up Ford's carefully tended grapes, as he claimed! They certainly had a rare fight over that one.

When we had disposed of the things Ford and Janice left behind in the studio on the Quai du Parti, Willie arranged a lot of objects on the long trestle table: heavy brass bracelets and anklets from the African jungles, silver bracelets and belts from his travels in Arabia, and a collection of daggers with Damascus blades. The remembrance of those daggers brings back an incident which still surprises me when I think of it but for which I must first supply the background.

At right angles to the rather short Quai du Parti, with its pale yellow warehouses converted into living quarters for a considerable part of the population of Toulon, was the long Quai Cronstadt, lined with shops, sidewalk cafés, and restaurants, all facing the water where the French navy's corvettes landed sailors at all hours of the day and evening, and fishing boats returned with their nets wriggling with silver sardines, and the little boats flying a Swiss flag (for no reason I could ever find out) bobbed up and down, waiting to take passengers to Les Sablettes, the white-sanded beach across the harbor.

There was always excitement on the Quai Cronstadt, always good food and drink and ways to spend hours and hours of beautiful time. Sometimes, especially when we were entertaining visitors from Paris or America, we would take our *apéritifs* at the Café de la Rade, the most elegant of the cafés and one frequented largely by naval officers and their families. Or we would lunch and dine at the Restaurant de l'Europe for the same reason. But the place that we frequented most of the time

9

was the café of M. and Mme. Ripperte, on the corner of the Quai Cronstadt and the Cours Lafayette, where the wonderful market began. It was at this café that we ate our breakfast almost every day, stopping at one of the colorful stalls to buy a melon from Africa, which Willie would cut in half with his pen-knife and which we would then eat with our *café au lait* and *croissants* at a marble-topped table on the small terrace.

We became very good friends with the Rippertes. They were of Italian descent as were most of the real Toulonnais, and they talked French with the broad thick dialect of the Marseilles district, stressing each syllable evenly and pronouncing the last letter even if it was an *e*. Although I had studied French for years before my first visit to France, I really learned to talk it when I lived in the Midi, and my accent always retained something of the Marseilles-Toulon-Italianized French, plus, I suppose, something American. *Quel dommag-e!*

Madame Ripperte was a big handsome woman with coarse black hair and quizzical dark eyes. Her husband was a fine strong man who had once been a prize fighter. They were tough, they were hard as nails, and they could be, I found out, both sentimental and kind. Willie and I were very fond of them. We would listen to Madame's complaints about her husband and his about her, and to their joint complaints about business in general and at their café, and about the government and the world. We sympathized at the appropriate times, but we never dared agree, because they were fiercely in love with each other, fiercely proud, and fiercely patriotic. They complained only because it added spice to conversation.

One day I drifted alone into the Rippertes' café and sat at a table in the corner, where it was dark and I could weep into my drink without being observed—or so I thought.

Willie liked women, in spite of a deep-rooted hostility to his mother, Myra, that compelled him to make them miserable. He liked all kinds of women, young, old, pretty, beautiful, and even intellectual. And they liked him. And I, in spite of a rather mild disposition, was jealous to the point of sickness. But it was a fact that any woman Willie decided to charm, he did! He just had the combination of ingredients, apparently, that most women found irresistible. Author, traveler, celebrity, he could still look wistful and sort of small boy, and he had a way of making a nice woman feel that he needed her, that she alone could help him get rid of the demons that beset him, his drinking and his sadism. Women are either very kind or extremely vain. A little of both, I suppose.

While I think he was good-looking, he was no Apollo. He was about six feet tall, with broad shoulders and narrow hips. He dressed in a style of his own: in winter he wore brown corduroys or heavy tweeds, made to order by Lloyds of London, with a red bandanna handkerchief tied around his neck; in summer he wore blue denim pants or red-orange ones from Brittany, with short-sleeved tricot shirts and bare-foot Capucine sandals.

He had blue eyes, a rather pudgy nose, a smallish mouth with a brush mustache, and a cleft chin. And he had curly brown hair, except for a brief period when he shaved it off completely, à la Gourdjieff. What was more important, he had a tremendous amount of personal magnetism. Somehow one was always aware of him in a room, even if it was filled with people. And when he left, the company went flat, like champagne with the bubbles gone.

It is almost impossible to describe the person one loves unless one is a poet, and I am no longer a poet. So, with the addition that he walked like—and, in a way, resembled—a large friendly brown bear, this will have to do.

To get back to Toulon, there I was, sitting in the darkest corner of the Rippertes' bar on a late summer afternoon. I was wearing my usual costume, a colorfully printed cotton dress with tight bodice and full skirt that I had bought from a rack in the department store on the rue d'Alger, as did most of the young women of Toulon. I wore rope espadrilles and no stockings, and on my almost black hair I wore a bandanna handkerchief that covered my forehead and was tied in the back. On my arms were heavy bracelets, tons of them, some of copper and some of silver. This was the way

I dressed in Toulon because this was the way Willie liked me to dress, morning, noon, and night, no matter what our plans might be.

It was too early for the *apéritif* hour and too late for after-luncheon liqueurs. I didn't really want anything to drink, just something that would knock me over the head and make me unconscious and unable to think—or something that would make the world seem beautiful again. I was suffering from acute and galloping jealousy. I was angry. I was miserable. And I was, or so it seemed, at the edge of an abyss that I didn't know whether to attempt to jump over, or into.

A few weeks before we had been at St.-Tropez, visiting at Jeannot Duranty's. She was the French wife of Walter Duranty, *Times* correspondent in Moscow for many years, unofficial host to all visiting celebrities to the Soviet Union, and subsequent author of several books on the U.S.S.R. He had just achieved the first interview with Stalin granted to any Western journalist, and his account of it in the *Times Magazine* section had appeared the weekend of our visit.

Walter was enjoying a brief vacation from the Kremlin news front and had invited a few friends, with or without Jeannot's knowledge. At any rate, another guest was George Seldes, a correspondent who had been expelled from Italy and who had written a book about Mussolini called *Sawdust Caesar*. George had just arrived from America with a beautiful, fashionable, left-wing blonde whom I shall call Donna, and he brought her to St.-Tropez.

I don't know whether George was in love with Donna or had just gallantly escorted her across the Atlantic and paid her passage. But over that weekend Donna and Walter Duranty became extremely interested in each other. I don't remember all that happened, but there was a lot of drinking and basking in the sun, and eating delicious meals, and listening to brilliant conversation, and reading the article on Stalin and congratulating Walter Duranty.

But suddenly, or so it seemed, Jeannot rose up in wrath, like

12

Hecuba or another of the Trojan women, and ordered everyone from her house, especially Donna. I remember all of us dispersing, I with Willie to return to Toulon, Donna with Walter to a nearby hotel—and George Seldes to a bench outside the walls of Jeannot's property, where he sat looking bewildered and possibly relieved.

A few days later we received a message from W.D. He was compelled to return to Moscow and would we mind looking after Donna? It was Willie who answered immediately, "Of course we'd be glad to."

That, then, was the background to the story of why I was sitting in a dark corner of the Rippertes' Bar du Monde et des Cyclistes, weeping into my rum. Donna had moved in with us that morning, complete with trunk and expensive hand luggage. She was at that moment sharing the big couch in our stone-walled room with Willie. Our couch!

Opposite me was the *zinc* bar, with the bottles arrayed on a shelf behind it and the cash register at the left. There were no customers and Madame Ripperte was standing behind the bar, next to the register, with her elbows on the *zinc* and her chin cupped in her hands. She was staring over at me. Suddenly she said, *"Et, alors, qu'est-ce que c'est?"*

I stared back numbly and shrugged my shoulders, too sick to utter words.

She nodded her head, understandingly and asked, *"Cette blonde?"* with an accent on each last *e*.

I nodded. She snorted. And then she invited me to come up to the *zinc* and have a drink on the house. We clicked glasses . . . very tiny glasses . . . and then she filled them up again.

"Look," she said to me, "I will give you some advice. You march yourself right back home. Get yourself a knife with a good sharp blade, and tell this blonde that if she does not leave, at once, you will cut her throat!"

I stared at Madame Ripperte. She had run her finger across her neck to illustrate her point, but I didn't need the illustration. I grasped the idea, and it seemed a very good one. I finished the rum and thanked her politely, and we bade each other good day.

I walked resolutely over the rough cobbles in my espadrilles. I turned the corner of the two quays and went into the little alley to the entrance of 2 bis, and I walked upstairs. The massive door of our atelier was unlocked. I pushed it open, walked in, and went to the long table where all of Willie's souvenirs of his journeys were arrayed, the brass and silver bracelets, the leather amulets, the carved African masks and fetishes—and the daggers from Damascus, their blades concealed in ornate silver sheaths. I chose one of them at random and walked to the couch, unsheathing the blade as I walked.

Willie and Donna were smoking cigarettes and staring at me. When I reached the edge of the couch, I said, not raising my voice:

"Donna, I happen to be a very jealous person. If you are not out of here, with your trunk, within ten minutes, I will cut your throat."

I am not sure I would have done it, but I am not sure I wouldn't. What is more important, they believed me. Within not ten but thirty minutes, Donna had departed from 2 bis Quai du Parti in a taxicab hastily summoned from the Grand Hotel in town, with a driver who obligingly carried her trunk down the stairs for her.

I was sure Willie would be furious and was prepared for the worst. Instead, the whole incident seemed to amuse him enormously. We celebrated with a good dinner at the Restaurant de l'Europe, accompanied by my favorite wine, Chateauneuf du Pape. Come to think of it, I believe that for just one moment Willie had been afraid of me.

Chapter Two

Life in Toulon during those years was rich and pungent. Each day and night was crowded with sights and sounds and scents and people, with hard work, swimming, sunshine, laughter, and pain. And all of it was dulled or heightened by Three Star Hennessy, Courvoisier, Rhum Négrite, and Pernod—or *pastis,* a local product that resembled absinthe.

In the morning, at five, Willie went up to work in an atelier on an upper floor of the building at 2 bis, and I got up at a more reasonable hour and made my ablutions in the wash-bowl. (We did take a daily swim at the Lido Beach in Mouril-lon, not far away.) When Willie came down at half past eight or nine, we went out for breakfast on the terrace of the Rip-pertes' café. Then we returned, to work until noon.

I was writing a book, too, but it was frequently interrupted because when Willie finished a chapter he would bring it down to our studio and I would read it aloud to him and he would change a word here and there, although for the most part his first copy would stand. I was so sure that his writing was much better and stronger than mine that this reading would throw me off my own work for days.

Lunch, whether we ate at the Restaurant de l'Europe on the Quai Cronstadt, or at Charley's, a smart bistro on the rue d'Alger, or a cheaper place on a back street behind the port, was always excellent, and it lasted at least two hours. After that, Willie took a siesta for an hour or two and I used the uninterrupted time to get on with my own writing.

Late in the afternoon we left the studio to join the crowds making their daily promenade on the Quai Cronstadt. Unless we had arranged to meet friends at some particular place, we usually started out with an *apéritif* at the Rippertes' and then at another café down the line, to say a few words to Boubou, the little brown monkey Willie had brought from the Ivory Coast and given to the café owner, who was better able to take care of a monkey than he was.

Boubou was a darling when he was young, and he adored Willie. During the sunny days he was kept on a long chain attached to one of the awning posts in front of the small, not very successful café which was down near the naval end of the quay. He would spot us before we had gone half the distance and would chatter something in his own language until we arrived. Then he would leap on Willie's shoulder and hug him and scold him and love him. I felt a poignant sorrow for Boubou and wished Willie had left him where he belonged, on the Ivory Coast.

We walked the length of the quay, mingling with whole families of Toulonnais, and with French sailors in their tight blue pants, neat blouses, and beguiling hats with fluffy red pompons on top (and only a few sous in their pocket to spend on their night off); and with the vendors of peanuts or thick sandwiches or *la cade,* a kind of hot custard served and eaten on a slip of paper; and with "les girls" from the brothels, out for fresh air and to advertise their wares, and with a few friends here and there in the crowd. Then we usually ended up at the Café de la Rade, to sit and drink until dinnertime.

There were often visitors to be entertained: Harrison Smith, Willie's editor at Harcourt, Brace, or his English publisher, Jonathan Cape, or even Alfred Harcourt himself; or the sculptor Paul Manship and his family, or Grace Hegger Lewis, a charming woman, who apparently still loved Sinclair Lewis and could talk about it to Willie, who also loved him. And there were countless others.

Usually we took them in our stride, offering an *apéritif,* lunch, or dinner, and sometimes a trip in one of the little boats across the harbor to Les Sablettes. But when Carl Van Vechten and his vivacious wife, Fania, arrived, they expected more than that. At least, Carl did. For all his sophistication there was a streak of naïveté in Carlo that was perhaps part of his charm.

We took him and Fania to Charley's, where we enjoyed our dinner, and then Carl announced that he wanted to visit a Toulon brothel. I am quite sure he would never have asked to visit one in New York or any other American city, but because he was in France and because Marseilles had a certain reputation and Toulon, actually, was not far from Marseilles, he expected Toulon to be filled with houses of ill fame, all of them very exciting and special.

The truth was, Willie and I were the last people to act as cicerones in the area of commercialized vice. When Willie wanted excitement he had his own ways of creating it, and the synthetic stuff likely to be found in brothels would have bored him to death.

However, since all our friends expected us to show them the sights, we walked with the Van Vechtens to a part of the town that was almost as unfamiliar to us as it was to them. As I remember it, there was a row of houses over near one of the gates in what remained of the wall that had surrounded Toulon in medieval times. Over each house, on the glass transom, was written in elaborate lettering, a name: Adele, Nanette, Mignon, etc. And over the name was a naked light bulb, painted red.

We went along the row and came back to the first one, Adele's house, because it was the largest and therefore promised the most elaborate entertainment. We rang a bell and the door was opened for us after a while by a rather drab female whom we took to be a servant. She led us into a large square room, and to a wooden table along a wall. She took our order for drinks, and disappeared.

We looked around. Anything less like a house of joy would have been hard to find. The floor and walls were bare. In a corner was an upright piano and a bench but no piano player. In fact, a lugubrious silence filled the room, and we waited for our drinks with the hope they would brighten things up, at least for us. They took a long time coming and when they ar-

17

rived were served by a short squat little man with handlebar mustaches, wearing sloppy trousers and carpet slippers.

Carlo asked him where everyone was and he shrugged his shoulders. Adele was not working tonight, he said, and her regular customers had the delicacy to stay away. It appeared that Adele's father had just died, and the house was in mourning.

However, he added, as we started to leave, there was one girl on duty, *"une brave jeune fille,"* and he would send her to us immediately. In the meantime, since the "girls" were permitted to drink only champagne, would we not like to order a bottle? Of the very best? It was obvious that he disapproved of our *marc,* the local *eau de vie,* which Willie had ordered for all of us in a vain effort to show we were not tourists. The French were always great sticklers for form, and in the circumstances champagne was the proper thing to drink, even the sweet, sickening stuff he opened for us with a pop and a flourish. It didn't make us feel any gayer.

Pretty soon a young woman entered the room and came up to our table. She was wearing a plain dark skirt and blouse and she looked vaguely familiar. It was the little slattern who had opened the door for us, only now her dark hair was brushed and she looked cleaner. She sat down with us and accepted a glass of wine. Then she looked at us expectantly.

Willie spoke to the girl, using the patois of the region, and Carlo listened as if he understood, and I grew very nervous. I looked at Fania and she looked at me and we didn't need words in any language to understand each other. We made an excuse and asked the girl to show us where the powder room was, just as though we were at "21" or the Colony, and if the girl looked puzzled it was only for a moment. She caught on quickly enough that we wanted to talk to her.

When we got out of sight, Fania took a handful of francs from her bag and I found fifty of my own to add to them. "Say no to the Messieurs," I managed to say. She understood, *parfaitement,* and thanked us. After all, with a death in the family . . . you understand . . . and the funeral tomorrow . . . one didn't feel exactly like . . . It was understood. And she thanked us.

Carlo and Willie were as relieved as we were to be out on the street again. The hour was late, and the Van Vechtens were catching a train for Italy early in the morning. We took them back to the Grand Hotel, still good friends in spite of the fact that we, as well as Toulon, had failed to live up to our reputation.

One morning, while Willie was working in his granary on an upper floor and I was busily putting flea powder on a new little kitten I'd found in the streets and adopted, there was a knock on the heavy wooden door.

I called, *"Entrez,"* and went on with what I was doing. I heard a few steps, and then there was silence and I turned. I saw a well-dressed youngish man, with a round face, slanting eyes, and an amused smile. I released the kitten and stood up.

"Paul Morand?" I asked, but I knew who it was. Willie had talked to me about him and I had seen pictures of him, and his *Fermez la Nuit* had enjoyed a tremendous success not only in France but in the United States.

He came farther into the room, and we began a discussion of cats and kittens, and I told him how difficult it had been to find a powder; when I told the tradespeople what I wanted it for, they shrugged their shoulders and said, "But all cats have fleas. It is good for them." And then suddenly I stopped talking and grew embarrassed. How could I be so stupid as to entertain one of the most brilliant members of the Parisian smart set with a dissertation on cats and fleas!

I apologized and flew upstairs to get Willie, who was delighted to see Paul Morand and came downstairs at once. I didn't open my lips again, but when we parted and Morand kissed my hand, I felt that I had a new friend.

Later, it was Morand who arranged for Willie's first trip to Africa to get material for *Jungle Ways,* pulling the right wires

19

and sending letters to Colonial VIP's and advising about equipment. In fact, when the book was ready for publication, Willie dedicated it: "To Paul Morand, who made it possible."

I met him again in Paris, when he gave a luncheon for us and for Blanche Knopf, who was my publisher as well as his. Morand had married a wealthy woman from, I think, some Central European country. They lived in a very elegant house in one of the most exclusive neighborhoods. Soon after we arrived, Paul showed us his studio, which was reached by way of a spiral staircase, and I remember wondering how anyone could write surrounded by so much luxury and elegance. I still had the idea, deeply rooted from Greenwich Village days, that the true writer or artist must live, if not exactly in direst poverty, at least with the minimum of creature comforts. It was a sort of reverse snobbishness that I don't believe I've ever quite outgrown.

I remember that luncheon, and Madame Morand, who was heavily bejeweled and dressed in black, and who never smiled. Willie sat at her right and Blanche at her left, and I sat next to Paul. I imagine the food and the wines were superb, but I was too busy talking to Paul Morand to notice. I've forgotten what we talked about, but I do know that it wasn't about fleas, and that we laughed a good deal, and that I was put at my ease by his charm and friendliness. Blanche Knopf ate almost nothing, as usual, but she smoked constantly, using a long cigarette holder and gesticulating with it as she talked. Encouraged by her example, I reached for a cigarette during the pause between the main course and dessert. Paul stopped me and whispered, "That is pardonable only when it is done by one's American publisher." I caught one cold glance from Madame Morand, and was grateful for the warning.

I saw a strange television program not long ago, in which someone had the idea of re-creating Marcel Proust by showing interviews with people, still alive, who knew him. There was his nurse and housekeeper who had been with Proust at the end, and there were friends, intimate and casual, who were asked to say a few words. Among these were Paul and Madame

Morand. He still looked a little like a Chinese schoolboy and she was still dressed in black, bejeweled and unsmiling.

Another French author who spent a lot of time in Toulon and who was one of our very good friends was Jean Cocteau. I remember a late afternoon when he came to see us alone, which was unusual, because he generally traveled with an entourage.

Willie was seated somewhere in the shadows and I was busy in the center of the room, at the round table, and Cocteau stood in front of the window and talked. His voice was mellifluous, and no matter what he talked about, it sounded like poetry, French poetry that is all cadence and fireworks. He used his hands as he talked, those beautiful hands of his that were like pale birds in flight. Behind him was the Toulon sunset, green and yellow, with the masts of ships, their sails draped around them, and the steel turrets of the naval destroyers visible. It was an unforgettable tableau and one for which I am still grateful. There was a great deal that was ugly and violent and shocking in our life in Toulon; there was also a great deal that was filled with beauty and glory. This was one of the glorified moments.

Very often, during the *apéritif* hour at the Café de la Rade, we would see Cocteau, followed by a group of disciples, some of them beautiful young men, but all of them talented and witty. Among the most talented and beautiful was a young American writer, George Davis.

He came from the Middle West, Ann Arbor, I think. He was intelligent and gifted. He was handsome. And he was, without any ambiguity or attempt to hide it, a homosexual. He spoke French fluently and without an accent, and he was, I am sure, of great use to Cocteau as a link with American writers and editors.

George and I became very friendly. We had this in common, that we were both young and both novelists. My first novel had been published, and George's first novel had just been accepted by Harper's and was said to be about to win the Harper Prize.

"It was said . . ." *"On dit . . ."* George's circle of friends was as gossipy, as full of rumors and private information, as any small clique. Perhaps more so. It was from one of them, Allan Ross MacDougall, that we heard about the Harper Prize, which George hadn't mentioned to us. But he walked with the dignity and importance of one who has already won a triple crown. In fact, next to Cocteau, George Davis at that moment was the most important literary figure to walk along the Quai Cronstadt or to sip a Cinzano *à l'eau* at the Café de la Rade.

I don't know exactly what happened or how it happened, but even as George walked in triumph, assured from whatever his source back home was that *The Opening of a Door* was to receive the Harper Prize, the Paris *Herald* and the Paris edition of the Chicago *Tribune* appeared on the kiosks in Toulon. That was how George Davis learned that the prize had gone to Robert Reynolds for *Brothers in the West*.

To me that has always seemed one of the cruelest of disappointments that could come to a young writer at the outset of his career. Knowing that group of sharp wits in Toulon, I could easily imagine what it must have been like to receive their commiseration.

George had a little apartment of his own at the end of the quay, near the arsenal and next door to the Hôtel du Port et des Négociants. We visited him there and I was amazed that for all the continental polish he had acquired, his rooms were furnished exactly as they might have been in a Michigan farmhouse. I remember a round oak table in the center of what could only be called a parlor, antimacassars on the overstuffed chairs, and a corner whatnot filled with ornate objects, including the shell boxes that were sold to sailors and tourists along the quay.

This is where he went to nurse his wounds, I think, while he played the phonograph continuously. We all had American records, and I remember my own favorite was one that Allan Ross MacDougall gave me: Duke Ellington's "Mood Indigo." When I was homesick—which was pretty often—I would go up to the granary I had now acquired on the second floor of the warehouse, and I would play that one record over and over. "You ain't been blue. No . . . No . . . No . . ."

Pretty soon George Davis was walking along with Cocteau and his entourage again, his handsome head held just as high and his place in Cocteau's affections firmer than ever, because Jean was truly understanding and compassionate. *The Opening of a Door* appeared under the Harper imprint and received good reviews. But it was the last novel George ever wrote.

Chapter Three

People came to Toulon for various reasons. Among them were deviates, and those who came to be nearer a source of opium. There were others who came to paint or to write, to make love, or just to steep themselves in the ways of a populous, foreign city. But they could have done that in any other city as crowded and dirty.

Toulon, in ways Willie and I knew not of—nor could we have cared less—was a place where opium could be obtained. And while there was always the fear of being caught at what was as illegal a traffic in France as it was anywhere else, there were fewer arrests, or perhaps more ways of avoiding collisions with the law.

Things were probably very different from the way they are now, just as Toulon itself, whose waterfront was totally destroyed during the war and then rebuilt with modern shop fronts and neon signs, is different from the one we knew and loved.

At any rate, some of the people we knew "smoked," and they weren't at all like the image I had brought with me from home of dope fiends, nor did they resort to opium dens. They smoked their pipes in their suites at the Grand Hotel up in the town, or on their yachts that were anchored in the *Rade*. And I remember being invited to an afternoon party at the home of a seventy-year-old aristocrat who asked us, quite casually, "Would you care for a cocktail or a pipe?"

Willie had experimented with drugs, just as he experimented with anything that would move life above or below the normal and respectable. But he was never drawn to any of them, finding in alcohol, which he consumed in Gargantuan potions,

24

sufficient release from whatever he was trying to escape. However, I do remember the time he tried smoking opium.

A very dear friend of his sent us a postcard saying she would be in Toulon on such and such a date, at the Grand Hotel, and would we both come to see her the night of her arrival because she would be alone, and she hated being alone. It was signed "The Toad." I shall call her Princess Telle, and try to describe her.

She was a short, round woman with dainty legs and feet, a face ravaged by all kinds of excesses, including grief, wonderful brown eyes that understood everything, and a beautiful speaking voice. She had learned English from a British governess, and spoke it fluently with a British accent.

Descendant of one of Napoleon's generals, she had married the great-grandson of another. She had led a conventional life with her husband, whom she loved deeply in spite of the fact that the marriage had probably been arranged by both families. When her husband died, and after her children were safely married, Princess Telle tried to find, by any means at all, a way to dull the pain of her loneliness.

About once a year, at the insistence of her doctor or her family, she would go to a spa for a "cure"—usually Vichy, sometimes Aix-les-Bains. She would install herself comfortably in one of the suites with a case of Scotch, a powder box on which was engraved the legend *Honi soit qui mal y pense,* and an array including pipes, a lamp, and a supply of opium. She would drink exactly one glass of the curative waters on her arrival, and upon leaving, after a few days or a couple of weeks, insist that she felt simply wonderful. "A new woman."

There was one period, and this was during the time we knew her, when Princess Telle lived as sedately, conventionally, and irreproachably as any dowager of the Faubourg St.-Germain. That was the season when her granddaughter was introduced to Parisian society. As soon as the young girl was safely launched and properly affianced, Princess Telle returned to her vices, comforted by the knowledge that she had done her duty.

On the evening mentioned in the postcard, Willie and I,

25

after dining on the quay, wandered slowly up to the center of the town by way of the winding rue d'Alger. Some bars were open and so were a few restaurants, but the shops were shuttered for the night. We passed a small plaza where a marine band was playing marches. It was like band night in one of the small towns at home, and we stopped to listen for a while with a mild attack of homesickness.

The Grand Hotel was on the Boulevard Strasbourg, Toulon's most impressive thoroughfare. To reach it we passed an open café where they had an all-girl orchestra, and I told myself— as I did every time I glanced at that collection of aging female musicians in seedy evening dress—that I would someday write a story about one of them. Only a Balzac or a Maupassant could have done it, but I was ambitious.

It was about ten o'clock when we reached the hotel. That was pretty early for Toulon, but the big yellow Victorian palace of a place, with ornate chandeliers and Brussels carpeting, seemed very quiet. We almost tiptoed to the door indicated to us, and knocked. A voice asked who was there, and when Willie answered, "Seabrook," there was a happy laugh and the command, *"Entrez."*

It was not a suite, but just one enormous bedroom, with lots of chairs around, a fireplace, and a bar set up on an ormolu cabinet. The princess had expensive tastes and an income much more modest than that of her friends, and she must have been in one of her economy streaks.

She was wearing a silk pajama suit, the kind that was worn for afternoon and evenings in the South of France at that time. Her bed was fully made, and she was lying on top of the creamy satin spread. At one side of the bed was a table on which was laid a lacquered tray containing all the paraphernalia for smoking opium: a small spirit lamp, a sticky lump of black stuff, and a long, ivory-colored pipe with a small cup-like thing near one end. The little lamp was lighted and she was rolling some of the black gum into a ball, or pill.

"Make yourselves drinks," she said, waving to the bottles and glasses with her free hand. "Then come and sit near me

26

and tell me what wonderful and scandalous things you have been doing. I am starving for news of you."

We did as we were told, and Willie talked, telling marvelous tales, some of them true, most of them not. I sat quietly drinking my drink and listening some of the time, and thinking my own thoughts; but mostly I watched the princess, who spent so much time preparing her pipe for what amounted to one deep puff. Being a rather lazy person, I wondered what there was in that puff to make it worth such a long and complicated process. I decided not to find out.

The room became filled with an acrid-sweet smell that mingled with the fumes of the cognac in the glass I held in my hand. Willie had joined the princess on the bed and she was teaching him to fill a pipe. I felt very drowsy. There was a chaise longue in the room, and I settled myself upon it and waited. A musical clock on the mantel chimed the hours of twelve . . . one . . . two . . . three. . . .

I remember making, or being asked to make, a pot of tea. I found what looked like a solid gold teapot and put it over the alcohol lamp I found near it, and lit the wick. When I remembered about the tea again, the whole beautiful little gold teapot had melted down into a nugget. Evidently I had forgotten to put any water in it. I was very sad about the teapot and told the princess so, but she was off in some exalted region with Willie tagging behind on his own cloud. And it didn't matter.

The clock went on ringing out the intervals of hours. Through the cracks in the venetian blinds I could see daylight. The murmur of voices had been going on forever: Princess Telle describing her childhood, then her marriage and her happiness, and then her sorrow. I slept through most of it, almost as drugged, by the fumes, as they were by their pipes. And then it was six o'clock, and Willie was standing up and telling me we must go.

We went out very softly; the hotel was not awake. But as we walked down through the city, people began to sweep the sidewalks before the shops and cafés, and some of them greeted us with a polite *"bon jour,"* to which we responded. We reached our studio somehow, I leading a remote Willie by the hand most of the way. I didn't know how many pipes he had smoked, but I knew they were too many for a neophyte. I was worried enough to become heroic and attack the primus stove by myself. I made a large pot of coffee and kept pouring cup after cup until he had drunk enough, I thought, to counteract the opium. Then we slept for a while, and then we woke up and went to our respective typewriters. Another Toulon day had begun.

I don't know whether it was during this same sojourn of Princess Telle, but we received a note one morning, telling us that she would pay us a visit at five that afternoon. Willie decided that because we lacked all the niceties for serving tea at five o'clock in the afternoon, the only possible substitute would be champagne and caviar.

After breakfast he went upstairs to write and I went in search of the old woman who sometimes cleaned the enormous stone room. She was much better than I at sprinkling wet tea leaves and sweeping them up with the accrued dust. Fortunately, I found her in her apartment at the top of another one of the warehouses on our quay.

Madame Tadadam, as we called her, not being able to understand the name she gave us through toothless gums, was a bent little gray-haired woman who always dressed in black because she was always in mourning for some remote cousin. She resembled a witch, and now I found that she lived alone with a black cat. She was a darling, and we both loved her, and since the one thing she wanted in the world before she died was to go on one of the seasonal pilgrimages to Lourdes from Toulon, Willie paid her expenses and we went to see her off on the train, with the priest and the other pilgrims. Willie did a lot of unexpected and understanding things of this sort. Perhaps they gained him entrance to Heaven, which he expected to explore one day. Because he believed it so strongly, I am sure he is there. With Madame Tadadam.

I set out then to do the marketing, with an oilcloth sack like all the Toulon women. I walked first to a liquor store on the Cours Lafayette to buy the champagne, and chose one of the finest from Rheims. Knowing how Willie filled a tumbler with whatever he was drinking, wine or rum or cognac, and drank it at one swallow, I bought two bottles and put them in my sack. I then went in search of the caviar, which was harder to find.

After combing our whole neighborhood, I went up as far as the Boulevard Strasbourg and found a store that sold a fairly large jar for a price that staggered me, because everything else, including champagne, had been so inexpensive. I bought a box of English biscuits to go with the caviar, and then I returned to 2 bis Quai du Parti, mad as a wet hen over losing a whole morning's work at my typewriter.

Besides all that, I had a sneaking and ignoble and utterly bourgeois feeling that our crazy stone-walled and -ceilinged and brick-floored room was no place to entertain a princess, whether merely Napoleonic or not! That bourgeois streak of mine was about a yard wide and was always showing at the wrong time, which is why I probably never entirely belonged to the "lost generation." Willie did his best to erase the streak, but he never quite succeeded. For which I am belatedly grateful, I think, because it meant I could continue living after the world collapsed. Our world, I mean.

We had lunch on the quay as usual, and afterwards Willie took his siesta, also on schedule, and then we got ourselves ready for the visit. The champagne was in a proper bucket, borrowed from the Rippertes and filled with ice from the same source. The caviar was in its own jar, with the lid pried off and disposed of, and the biscuits were arranged on the best dish I could find in our meager supply. And then we waited.

Five o'clock went by, and then six. By seven Willie decided our guest had forgotten the engagement, and he opened the first of the bottles, poured a wine glass for me and a tumbler for himself, and we drank. I spread some of the caviar on a biscuit and handed it to him. We were hungry. By eight o'clock the

29

bottles were empty and so was the jar of caviar, and we were feeling wonderful. And then we heard voices on the staircase. Voices and the laughter of lots and lots of people. And the cupboard was bare.

Willie threw open the door and ushered in the princess and her cousin and an indefinite number of attractive men and women, all thirsty and hungry. We served them gin and whiskey, and our guest of honor found a crust of bread and ran it around the inside of the caviar jar and ate it. We all laughed at the host and hostess who had eaten and drunk their own party, and then we started off, some in our Citroën convertible truck and the rest in a red Bugatti, on our way to have dinner at St.-Tropez.

I'll never know why, at such a late hour, we didn't settle for dinner at Charley's or the Restaurant de l'Europe on the nearby quay, but someone had heard of a famous restaurant at St.-Tropez that we simply had to try; and there we were, traveling as fast as the wind along the Mediterranean shore, with the stars bright overhead and the scent of mimosa in our nostrils and laughter in our ears.

The rest of that night is even dimmer in memory than other nights of that alcohol-and-love-bedimmed era, but out of it I remember two incidents. One was finding myself at a table being introduced to Emma Goldman. Of all places and seasons to meet the most publicized and possibly the most feared anarchist in the world! She was short and dark and plump and very mild, and she was wearing a summer evening dress and an embroidered Mandarin robe, and her companions were the divorced wife of a well-known multimillionaire and a very intelligent schoolteacher who may have been Emma's niece. I recall, hazily, that someone expressed surprise at seeing her, an anarchist, in one of the world's playgrounds, and that she replied, with a smile, "But that's what the fight has been for. So that everyone can play and be happy."

The second incident I remember was of finding myself, much

30

later, walking out into the water and getting into a small coral boat that was anchored in the little port. I was about to lift anchor when somebody—maybe it was Willie—came and stopped me and brought me back to shore. I'm not sure where I wanted to go. I only know it was . . . away.

Chapter Four

I suppose ever since man emerged from a cave, he has dreamed of being the master of his own castle. The dream that became a reality for knights in armor was shared by Willie, son of a Lutheran minister and a proud but impoverished gentlewoman named Myra. His childhood in Abilene, Kansas, and whatever other town his father was called to, was spent in ugly frame houses furnished with rejects from the houses of parishioners. When he married Katie Edmondson, during his reporting days on the Atlanta *Journal,* they lived in a small apartment on Peachtree Street. Then, after fighting with the French in the First World War, he and Katie lived in a series of apartments in Greenwich Village.

Now, although he had expanded his living quarters to include granaries on two other floors of 2 bis Quai du Parti, Willie was restless. When large sums of money began to arrive via his American agent, Ann Watkins, he pulled out his dream of owning a castle, and with typical determination set about doing something to make it come true.

He went off on several wild goose chases to the Dordogne, having a vague idea that a region still savage and filled with mysticism, would suit him. When these leads failed he discovered the Château d'Evenos in the hills behind Toulon, almost in his back yard.

Several roads led out of Toulon, and one of them went to a little village called Ollioules, situated in a gorge by that name, between two rocky mountains which were actually hills; but in Provence everything was exaggerated. We had driven along that road a number of times, and had noticed on top of one of the hills what looked like a mass of ruins surmounted by an iron stairway that led nowhere except to infinity. Those ruins were the Château d'Evenos, and it was for sale. No, not exactly for sale, because it was listed as a *monument historique* and could not be sold. But it could be rented—for a term of ninety-nine years.

There was some difficulty finding the heirs, but they were located at last way up in the north of France, in the city of Lille. Willie and I were in Paris when the end of the search arrived, and we took a long slow train that got us to Lille in the middle of a cold, wet November afternoon. He left me at a large café near the *gare* while he went to the lawyer's office.

I began by sitting outside on the terrace, at a table next to a charcoal *brasier*. I ordered a Pernod, perhaps because it was the kind of drink one could linger over and I didn't know how long Willie would be, buying his castle. Even next to the stove it was cold on the terrace, and damp with the penetrating damp of cold knives, and the people who passed by on the murky business street were drab, pinched, and uninteresting. I went inside, where it was warmer, and there were a few customers, some men at the bar and others at a table playing a card game —the same one, I gathered, that is played in almost every café in France where men gather. It reminded me, absurdly enough, of baseball, in which everything goes along quietly for a while, even boringly—and then, suddenly, all hell breaks loose. There would be a period of calm at the table in the rear, and the snapping of cards, and suddenly all the men were shouting at once and shaking their fists at each other.

An hour passed, and I ordered another Pernod. Through the windows to the terrace I could see the fog turning blacker. I have been alone often in my life, and sometimes in strange places where I didn't know a soul. But on that particular evening, drawn out into an infinity of time, I felt more alone than I ever had before. It was as though my one link with humanity had fallen off the brink of the world, leaving me in a strange city on a strange earth.

After my third Pernod I took out a scratch pad and pencil from my handbag and began writing a long poem. It was inspired a little by the *brume* and a little by the loneliness, but mostly by Pernod. It expressed, I believed, the loneliness of everything born. It was maybe the best thing I ever wrote; at least it felt that way as I was catching the words from my subconscious and putting them down on paper for posterity. I was almost finished when Willie arrived, threw some money down for the waiter, and grabbed me by the hand. A taxi was waiting and we had only a few minutes to make the train out of Lille for Paris. My poem was left behind, on the damp, cold marble-topped table of a nameless café. But Willie had signed a ninety-nine-year lease for his castle.

The Château d'Evenos had been a stronghold of one of the Kings of Var. It was built on a plateau overlooking the Gorge d'Ollioules on one side, but on the other side, at the end of the domain, it overlooked the Mediterranean Sea. On the first day of inspection we made exciting and wonderful discoveries. Underlying the whole structure of the chateau were Roman ruins, including fallen columns and a statue that Willie identified as Telemachus, the only son of Ulysses and Penelope. (It may have been a bust of someone much more obscure, but Willie went on referring to "Télémaque" and our French friends were nice about believing everything Willie told them.)

On top of the Roman foundations were the walls of rooms built during the Middle Ages. These included the beautiful blue slate window frames such as were to be found in the houses left standing in Les Beaux. Most of the rooms were as roofless as the topless towers of Ilium, their floors filled with debris over which I stumbled as I followed Willie on this first tour of his castle.

I never knew how many of those ruined chambers there were because we never counted them, but there were at least two, on the side nearest the entrance, that had been fully restored by the eccentric count who had last lived there. They had roofs and tiled floors, and in one there was a perfectly intact marble fire-place. The windows were without panes, but that, we decided, could be easily remedied. In fact we could begin living in the chateau, in these two rooms, as soon as we found a glazier. The rest of the rooms could be restored one at a time. After all, we had ninety-nine years to complete the restoration.

We locked the big gate at the entrance with an enormous key that Willie had obtained from the mayor of the tiny village. Evenos consisted of about a dozen peasant houses, built in the Middle Ages around the chateau, as they were in all the small hill towns of Provence. Many of the houses had fallen to ruin, like the major part of the chateau, and goats wandered in and out of them, and countless scrawny chickens. A few children were playing in the roadway as we drove down the hillside, and we waved to them. They stared at us, but didn't wave back.

I still have these few pages from a diary I kept spasmodically at the time:

Avril. 27 Dimanche 1930. Went to Evenos. Took Boubou the *singe* with us, and a mason. Sunshine. Willie and the mason put up a sign near the gate, warning tourists to keep out. I sat on one of the terraces reading a new Simenon that has just come out. Boubou climbed a tree and ate green almonds. We lunched in one of the little houses that is huddled against walls of chateau. The Corrozzos, most important people of village. Papa Corrozzo, his son and son's beautiful little wife, and a neighbor woman who helped with the cooking on a flat charcoal stove in dark but clean kitchen. Good dinner, very garlicky, of course. Then more work on chateau. The children of village gathered around Boubou and me all day, bringing us gifts of flowers and fruit. Lovely day.

A week later we returned with a workman from Toulon who was to take measurements for the windows in the two livable rooms. We were in high spirits, and I had overcome my apprehension (as I so often had to do) and was trying to imagine myself as chatelaine of a medieval castle.

As we drew up to the gate we noticed some additional writing on the board we had posted there. We got out of the car and went closer to read it. In bright red crayon someone had scrawled the following message, in English:

GO BACK TO CHICAGO   YOU PORK BUTCHER

If someone had slapped Willie's face while he was extending a hand in friendship he could not have been more astonished or hurt. His relationship with people of all walks of life and in all parts of the world had always been of the friendliest. This rebuff, where he had least anticipated it, was a great shock to him. Then the humor of the thing hit us. Nothing less like a pork butcher from Chicago could one imagine than Willie Seabrook! He went at once to pay a visit to Papa Corrozzo, the mayor of Evenos.

We might have been able to discover who the perpetrator of the insult was, because not many of the people who lived in those airless, sunless, crazy little houses could possibly have had enough knowledge of English to have written it—much less to have read Carl Sandburg.

But we never tried to find out. What we did learn was the very good reason for resentment against us. Ever since the last owner of the chateau had died, the gates had been left open and the village had used the grounds as grazing land for their livestock, their goats, sheep, cows, and donkeys. The terraces within the gate were covered with grass, while the rest of the terrain in and around the village was barren and hard, caked dirt or stubbly rocks. Our locking of the gates to the chateau grounds meant a real hardship to the villagers, who must have hated us, sight unseen.

Willie settled all this at once by handing over the key to the mayor, and telling him the villagers could continue to graze their livestock within the castle grounds whenever we were not "in residence." He also explained carefully that we were not American millionaires, but writers who had to work for a living, like everyone else in Evenos.

We were all friends after that. Willie was asked to join the "Cercle d'Evenos," the men's club, which met in one of the low yellow houses on the square below the chateau. He actually

36

spent a few Sunday afternoons there, playing *boules* with the men of the village, and drinking *pastis* with them, and even the warm beer they used to mix half and half with lemonade. The insulting legend was removed with a broad stroke of whitewash, and all was well.

The glazier who had come to measure the windows finally notified us that the panes were ready to be installed. And then came the day, a long time afterward it seemed, when we were told that the window panes were in and all was ready for our occupancy.

We drove up to Evenos that day with the keenest anticipation. We found the two rooms with the tiled floors and fireplace in perfect repair. We sat down on the cold floor and ate our lunch and made plans. One room would be to live in and the other to sleep in. We would furnish them in antiques, a mixture of Louis Quinze and French Provincial. We could get rugs from Morocco and china from Spain and Italy and linen from the Trois Quartiers department store in Paris.

We would soon make these two rooms livable and then we could take our time about restoring the ruins—the *donjon* and the other fascinating places. And having made our plans, we walked hand in hand to the end of the plateau, where there was a small structure like the gazebo or "summer house" in rural America, with domed roof and pillars and a bench running all around the interior, a place where old-fashioned sweethearts became engaged, and where, perhaps, troubadours sang to the ladies of the lords of Var.

We thought of ourselves moved back centuries in time and living like lords and ladies of the manor. I could already hear the keys jangling from the waist of my long, dove-colored gown, keys to dozens and dozens of rooms. In spite of an icy doubt or two, I began to enjoy the prospect.

The next time we drove up to Evenos we found the two restored rooms a mess of broken glass. Not one pane, so carefully and painstakingly installed, was left intact. At first, with sinking hearts, we believed that the hand that had scrawled the insult at the gates had thrown stones to break our windows. But eventually we learned the truth. For the last three days the Mistral, that fierce wind of Provence, had blown over the land, sweeping everything before it. Even on the Quai Cronstadt it had blown bottles off the tables on the terraces of the cafés. How much fiercer had been its force up here on the hill! Certainly no mere pane of glass could have withstood its onslaught.

Relieved, we placed a new order with the obliging glazier of Toulon, and waited. But after the panes were reinstalled, the Mistral blew again, and the glass was shattered as before. This may not have been an entirely unsurmountable problem if another and much more serious one had not arisen. That was the question of water.

We found that all the inhabitants of this little hill village got their water from the same well, halfway down the slope of the so-called mountain. They assured us we could do the same; the well had not yet been known to run dry. We walked down to the well. Donkeys and goats had been grazing on the dry yellow herb surrounding it, depositing their waste: little black pellets from the goats and ordinary droppings of dung from the donkeys. Nobody had troubled to keep the area around the well free of human refuse, either, and there were potato peelings, coffee grounds, and melon rinds strewn around. We had serious doubts that the well was artesian, and didn't even ask.

"We could buy a donkey," I said, trying to bring some hope to the situation because Willie looked so depressed. "And I could lead it down to Ollioules and back with two pails . . ."

"Two pails for a whole castle?" Willie said.

"We could buy cases of Perrier water to drink," I suggested, "and just use this for washing."

"Our guests will want baths," Willie said, in one of those contrary moods, so I gave up.

The next day, in Toulon, he consulted plumbers and then engineers. The result was that we learned it would cost more than a million francs to run a pipeline from Ollioules to the chateau. We decided not to try to live at Evenos, but to use it for picnics.

And what beautiful picnics we had there, especially in spring, when the almond trees were in bloom. We invited everyone we knew and carried great hampers of food from the Charcuterie on the Cours Lafayette, and even hot things in copper pans from Charley's. I am almost sure we brought Violette and her entourage, and possibly Cocteau, and Monsieur and Madame Ripperte, and the Greek owner of a coral boat, one of the Rippertes' customers.

One guest I remember affectionately. He was a beautiful young Swede whom we met one day as we were driving up to the chateau. He was scrambling over the rocks in bare feet. He wore faded blue denim pants and no shirt. We invited him to lunch and became good friends. We called him "Sunlit" because we couldn't pronounce his Swedish name, and because he was rather like a sun god in appearance and spirit.

Sunlit was a poet and he was very poor. He lived in a narrow little furnished room in one of the most squalid streets of Toulon. The house itself was old and dirty, with clotheslines strung from window to window across the narrow street. Waste ran in the gutters and mothers picked vermin off their children in plain daylight on the doorsteps.

But Sunlit's room was scrubbed clean and neat as a matchbox. He introduced us to the poetry of Rimbaud, reading to us, in French, "Bateau Ivre" and "Tête de Faune." And when I expressed rapture, he gave me his yellow-bound paper copy, and would not let me refuse it.

One morning he came to see me in the big room on the Quai du Parti. I was alone, working on a novel, and Willie was upstairs, working on *Jungle Ways*, I think. I noticed that Sunlit seemed unhappy and I asked him questions. His brother, who was the editor of a Swedish newspaper, had given him the money to come to France, but only enough for a one-way ticket and a little to live on while he tried to support himself by writing poetry. Now all the money was gone, he couldn't sell his poems, and he wanted to return to Sweden to go to work. For some reason, pride or maybe some inner family situation, he couldn't cable his brother for more money. Did I think, he asked me, that Seabrook would lend him the money, which he promised to return?

Willie gave away lots of money, to strangers as well as friends, and so I could have gone upstairs and asked him. But he was so delighted with Sunlit, so pleased to have found him scampering over the rocks of Evenos like a young faun, that I was afraid his feeling might change, as it did, sometimes unconsciously, when a question of money entered the picture. I had a little money of my own, and that morning I had cashed a check and hadn't yet had time to spend it all on a dress or a new pair of espadrilles. Fortunately it was just enough, added to the few francs he had left, to buy Sunlit a third-class ticket home.

I must add this footnote. Many years later, when Willie and I were living in Rhinebeck, N.Y., I received a letter from Sweden. It had traveled around a lot and finally caught up with me. Enclosed was a money order for the exact amount I had lent Sunlit, and the news that he was married, employed in a bank, and very happy. He said nothing about poetry.

Of all those who came with us to picnic on the grounds of the chateau, none had a better time than Boubou, Willie's little brown monkey. We would let him loose and he would sit on a branch of an almond tree, breaking open the green almonds and chattering away in ecstasy. I have often thought that Willie had paid a lot of money and gone to a lot of trouble just to give a day or so of happiness to a sad little displaced monkey from the Ivory Coast. In my own crazy way of reckoning, I believe it was worth it, and made sense.

For the rest, Willie had made a boyish dream come true, and later, when we were living in a villa in Sanary and no longer needed to picnic on the plateau, he would take friends and visitors for a ride along the Gorge d'Ollioules and point up to the mass of ruins and say, "See that castle up there? It's mine."

I often wondered whether the Nazis made use of that strategic position during the time they occupied France. And if, on top of the Roman, the medieval, the nineteenth-century relics, they added relics of their own brief period of infamy. Or is that strange iron staircase—erected on top of the ruins by that last

40

demented owner, the Count d'Evenos, who wanted to get a little closer to heaven when he prayed—still the most modern bit of restoration?

Perhaps, in some way I cannot recall, there are a few traces of its ownership by two writers from America. Maybe when the Cercle d'Evenos meets, in between the games of *boules* and the drinking of *pastis,* someone remembers Willie Seabrook and speaks of him.

Chapter Five

Willie decided one day that we would go to visit Gertrude Stein. Every once in a while he would get an idea that somebody could help him, whether the help was spiritual, intellectual, esoteric, or merely practical. Now he was taking himself very seriously as a writer, and the written word was sacred, and Gertrude Stein was the priestess of the written word.

Because of the sensational material in his books, the fact that Willie wrote very well was overlooked by most of the literary critics, and probably by most of the readers who had bought hundreds of thousands of copies of *Adventures in Arabia* and *The Magic Island* for their hair-raising tales about the Druses and whirling dervishes and the practice of voodoo in Haiti, and not for the brilliance and aliveness of Seabrook's prose.

Few people knew how hard he labored over every sentence, every word; but I did. Whenever he finished one of the long chapters of *Jungle Ways* on which he was working that summer in Toulon, he would bring down a batch of yellow copy paper on which he wrote the first draft and give it to me to read aloud to him.

There would be a bottle of rum or cognac on the round table in the center of the long stone room, and he would pour himself a tumblerful even before we got started. This was, however, his reward for hard work, because Willie, in those days, wrote only when he was cold sober. That was why he started to work so early—at five in the morning—and wrote only until noon. Once the meridian arrived he left his typewriter for the day and drank as much as he liked, which was more than he liked, actually.

Well, there we would be, facing each other across the table,

I reading aloud and Willie listening. Sometimes when I was turning a page or had started a new one he would ask me to go back and change a word that had been read ten lines or so before. And sometimes, when I had finished reading a passage on which I could tell he had worked hard, he would say with tears in his eyes, "That's beautiful, isn't it?" And I would answer, "Yes, it is," because I genuinely admired it and because I wanted to help Willie, and I believe that the only help any artist needs is the encouragement of praise.

And so now we were going to visit Gertrude Stein, to find out what she had to say about words. We had learned that she was at her country house in Belley, in the department of Ain, not far from Aix-les-Bains, straight north of us over the Basses- and Hautes-Alpes.

Willie's Citroën had been bought in Paris a couple of years before and it was still as good as new, in spite of the occasional trips we took back and forth to Paris on the Route Nationale. The Citroën was a good car in the middle-price field. Lots of people drove them, but not many in private life had the kind we had. For some unearthly reason I was never able to discover, Willie had bought a model that could be converted into a truck by taking out the back seats. If we had been the kind of people who move around a lot with all their worldly goods, there might have been some sense to it. But when we traveled, we traveled light, I with one suitcase and Willie with a blanket roll and sometimes a typewriter. Still, he had the seats removed almost at once, and from then on we drove in the front seats and whatever guests we had sat on the floor of the truck. This became even funnier when we lived in a villa between Bandol and Sanary and hired, along with three other servants, a uniformed chauffeur.

Comfortable or not, I always loved traveling anywhere with Willie. Somehow he managed to see more than anybody else ever did, and there were always adventures along the way; so small an adventure as sharing our lunch with a stray dog who adopted us and whom we named "Magali," from Mistral's poem in the Provençal language, *"O Magali, ma tant amado";* so big

43

an adventure as flying to Timbuctoo across the whole Sahara Desert.

This voyage by car up through the French Alps in summertime was a happy one. Willie was on his best behavior, charming, amusing, and full of enthusiasm because he was on his way to meet Gertrude Stein and was preparing a lot of questions to ask her.

We arrived at the small village of Belley towards evening, and registered at a hotel before Willie telephoned Miss Stein. She and Miss Toklas were at dinner, but Miss Stein knew about Willie and said she would be happy to see us if we would come early in the evening.

We stayed only a short while for that preliminary visit. Because of Picasso's portrait of Gertrude Stein, I had expected to see a Buddha-like figure with her hair in a bun on top of her head, but she was nothing like that. She was a stockily built middle-aged woman who wore tweeds and sensible shoes like an Englishwoman, and her iron-gray hair was cropped short, almost in the style of a modern crew cut. Her face was round and saved from homeliness by the intelligent dark eyes and a very occasional smile; and she had a deep contralto speaking voice of great beauty.

In her second autobiography, called *Everybody's Autobiography*, which it wasn't, she expressed surprise at our appearance. She wrote: ". . . he looked like a south European sailor and he looked American. She looked American, she looked like a college woman and together they looked different from anything that we saw around here."

Bilignin, their home, was attractively furnished. I looked for some of the Picassos and Braques and Matisses that should have been part of her famous collection, but when she showed us her paintings they were all by a young man named Francis Rose in whom she was at the moment interested.

It was the first time I had come across surrealism, and I liked it, especially since the painting was well done. Willie found the canvases filled with mysticism and a kind of black magic, and said so. Then he asked Miss Stein what she thought of

44

them. She answered, candidly, that she didn't know. That was why she had hung them up in her house, so that she could live with them for a while and make up her mind.

Then she and Willie went into another room to discuss art and literature and themselves. Alice B. Toklas sat down with me and discussed domestic things, such as the prices of this and that commodity in Belley compared with the prices in Paris, and the difficulty of keeping servants in the country.

I was deeply sympathetic with Miss Toklas. I knew it was her role to entertain the wives of celebrities who came to see Gertrude Stein, just as it was mine to do the same when famous men called on Willie. But I found it disappointing to be considered a "wife," because I was a writer, too, and my first novel had received good reviews. And I knew a lot more about painting than Willie did because I had studied painting before I began to write, and even if I no longer painted I went to all the exhibitions I could, and cared for pictures as much as books.

Besides, I really knew very little and cared less about the cost of meat and fruit; Willie did most of the marketing on the Cours Lafayette, and at that time we didn't have any servants, unless the old woman whom Willie had sent to Lourdes could be called one. I, too, had expected to sit at the feet of Gertrude Stein and absorb pearls of wisdom.

However, I liked Alice B. Toklas and did my best to act like a wife or a consort. And their huge white poodle, Basket, did a lot of tricks to entertain us while we waited for the séance to be over.

The next day Miss Stein and Miss Toklas had planned something nice for us. We were to drive with them to Aix-les-Bains and have dinner there with William Aspenwall Bradley, our literary agent in Europe, and hers.

First we had lunch at Bilignin, and then they showed us around the town of Belley; after we had admired the statue of Brillat-Savarin, who came from there, we started off for Aix, with Miss Stein at the wheel of her Ford.

I was not as nervous then about riding in cars as I was later, after our almost fatal accident in the South of France. But I was a little nervous because I couldn't help wondering if Gertrude Stein drove as she wrote, and if so, how would that be? With short starts and stops, perhaps? Straight through traffic lights, as she did through punctuation? I might have saved myself the worry. Gertrude Stein drove a car, as Willie remarked, like a bat out of hell, but she drove very well. With all her disregard for the laws laid down by literary craftsmen of preceding generations, she was obedient to the traffic laws of France. We relaxed, enjoyed the scenery, and arrived safe and sound at the restaurant in Aix-les-Bains where Mr. Bradley was waiting for us.

In all my life I have met at least two men who qualify for the old-fashioned attribute of "gentleman and scholar." Frank Crowninshield was one and William Aspenwall Bradley the other. They are both gone, and their kind has decreased, and I, for one, deeply regret their passing.

On this wonderful evening we were to enjoy a superb dinner with accompanying wines, ordered by Bradley. We sat at a table on a balcony overlooking the Lac du Bourget, and this time we were all together and I didn't have to miss the conversation between Miss Stein and Willie, although the passage of so many years has made me forget a lot of it, naturally, and unlike Boswell I didn't take notes.

But I do remember how startled Bradley and I were by Willie's suddenly turning to Gertrude Stein and asking her whether she thought that her close relationship to her brother Leo had had any effect on her sexual life. I fully expected the author of *Three Lives* and *Lucy Church Amiably*, the spinster of the rue de Fleurus and Bilignin, to ask him what business it was of his or the world's. But she didn't. She opened up like a wallflower who has just been asked to dance, and she told him.

Gertrude Stein had two brothers, one considerably older than herself and the other, Leo, only two years her senior. Since she was the youngest in the family, she said, everyone looked after her. But Leo, apparently, did the most, teaching and protecting her and pointing the way. She adored him. He was her hero and her right arm. When she went away to Radcliffe they wrote to each other, and this continued when she enrolled in Johns Hopkins Medical School. They were together constantly during vacations. Then Leo took a trip around the world with a wealthy cousin, and they were separated for more than a year. She crossed the ocean to meet him in Antwerp, and after that they were together almost constantly.

They both liked to talk, she said, and they argued a lot, as people who like to talk do. But it was always about abstract truths. About most things they were in complete accord. Then Gertrude began to write and Leo to paint. She gave up all idea of a medical career, and Leo abandoned his studies of biology and history. They lived together in Paris, on the rue de Fleurus, but he painted in an atelier somewhere else. They lived together until 1914. Everybody interesting came to see them, and they went on talking and painting and writing.

Gradually, Leo's younger sister began to be important. It was Leo who first admired her writing and attempted to explain it to others, and it was he who first insisted she was a genius. But when she began to believe in herself as a genius, and acted accordingly, Leo didn't like it. It is hard to lose the adoration of someone else, especially a younger sister. And when Gertrude Stein began admiring herself for being a genius, naturally she couldn't go on adoring her brother, who was not as much of a genius as she was!

Then, too, although she didn't mention it that night at Aix-les-Bains, Leo Stein was getting quite a reputation as an art critic, and for having discovered Picasso, Matisse, and others. Gertrude, who had been asked by Picasso to sit for a portrait, began to feel that she knew as much about cubism, futurism, vorticism, etc., as her brother did, and that she could become a collector, too.

One little thing that annoyed her was that Leo began to talk about his childhood as an unhappy one, and as she remembered it their childhood had been unusually happy—for geniuses.

Another thing was that he began to resent openly the fact that while he could talk better than he could paint, she could and did write even better than she could talk! A bitterness grew up

47

between them, and that was the beginning of the end. "Little by little," she has said, "they never met again."

Basically, I think, Miss Stein was a prude. I believe she honestly tried to answer Willie's question, but she could do so only indirectly. It was obvious that Leo Stein had filled the place of romantic love for her during the formative years of her life. She had never laid claims to beauty, and it is doubtful whether many men ever made passes at her in the ordinary physical sense, or asked for her hand in marriage. But in spite of the significance a Freudian might attach to that brother-sister relationship, it didn't leave her with any obvious hostility toward the male sex. On the contrary, I am convinced she preferred men to women, and as final proof of my theory, when American soldiers began swarming over the French countryside, after the liberation of Paris in 1945, Gertrude Stein fell in love with the whole young army and wrote a book to prove it.

I wish I could remember all the talk at the table by the lake on that wonderful evening. I do know that we were all very happy and that Gertrude Stein and Willie did most of the talking, and that whatever Willie expected of Gertrude Stein, she didn't disappoint him.

We left with very warm feelings for a warm and remarkable woman—whether or not she was a genius. In fact, I wouldn't be surprised if they had fallen a little in love with each other.

Somewhere, Gertrude Stein has written that she did not invent the term "lost generation," but that someone, perhaps the postman in Belley, referred to the war generation as lost. However it was intended, the phrase has a haunting quality, like the sound of a lot of banshees wailing down the corridor of Time.

Chapter Six

There are many ways of telling the truth. There is the obvious truth which everyone can easily see, hear, taste or feel. There are also shades of truth, which depend on the individual's capacity for seeing, hearing, and feeling. This varies a great deal and has many dimensions.

Willie's truth was something special to him. People called it exaggeration when they were being kind. When they weren't being kind they accused him of lying. In this they were wrong. Willie almost always told the truth: *his* truth.

I was struck by this talent of his for decorating fact when I first saw Timbuctoo. He had described it in purple, lush prose, giving it magnificence and color, while what I saw was a gray, sad mausoleum of a dead civilization.

What I am about to relate, with a number of digressions, deals with a passage in *Jungle Ways* wherein Willie described sharing with a tribe of cannibals a meal in which the main dish was human flesh, taken from a young warrior who had been killed in a tribal battle. It was a passage that caused a lot of discussion when the book was first published. Some critics said that what he had probably been offered was the flesh of a pig or a wild boar, or even a monkey. Some insisted that since the meat was described as pale gray it must have been veal. Some just called Willie Seabrook a liar.

But what he told was the truth—his kind. Only it happened in Paris, the most civilized city in the world, and not in Africa.

It was while he was writing the chapter about living with a tribe still supposed to be cannibalistic that he felt frustrated. How much stronger the chapter would be if he could include a first-hand description of what earlier travelers had called "long pig." And yet, with his own code of morals, he wouldn't go so far as to invent the incident. It was regrettable that he had missed the opportunity in Africa, but that didn't make the whole thing impossible. An idea came to him, and he acted upon it, and waited for an answer to a wire he had sent to a friend on a Paris newspaper.

I was blissfully unaware of all this until the morning a telegram was delivered to Willie at 2 bis Quai du Parti. He came downstairs from his studio holding it in his hand.

"We're catching the *Train Bleu* to Paris," he said. "Pack a few things while I go up to the station to make reservations and get time schedules."

"Why?" I asked, turning around from my typewriter.

"Because I have a date with X—," he mentioned the name of our journalist friend, "at noon tomorrow in the Place de l'Odéon."

The Blue Train, which carried only first-class passengers between the Riviera and Paris, was not only faster than other trains of that day but certainly the most luxurious of them. After living as we did, without plumbing or any of even the ordinary comforts of life, I was simply enthralled with my own separate compartment, adjoining Willie's. The *boiserie* looked like satinwood inlaid with mother-of-pearl, the upholstery was of gray velvet, and the commode had fixtures that could have been silver, with porcelain as fine as Sèvres.

One of the enchantments of life with Willie was that it was filled with contrast, and the reason I enjoyed my little compartment *de luxe* so much was that it contrasted not only with our room on the Quai du Parti, but also with the last time I had traveled by train with Willie. That time it was strictly third-class.

The reason for that other trip by train, so different from the *train de luxe,* was that Willie, during a sojourn in Neuilly, decided we would take a walking trip in the South of France, covering a route he had taken when he was a young man with his first newspaper job on the Augusta *Chronicle.* Fresh out of college, he had earned enough to pay his passage across the

Atlantic, steerage. He walked around Provence, settling down for a whole winter in Arles, where he lived with a shoemaker in the workingman's district, on the street where the brothels were when Van Gogh visited them.

Willie made friends that winter with several lovely Arlesian ladies who mended his clothes, took care of him when he had a cold, and taught him not only French but the Provençal of Mistral, their poet. He had not been back to Arles since then, and he was seized with a desire to return to see if any of those old friends were still alive and if they would remember him.

Characteristically, however, he wanted to return not as a well-known, successful author, but as one of them, a workingman. And so we first did some shopping in a department store in the poorer section of Paris where we could find "proletarian" clothes. Willie ended up looking somewhat like a mechanic, in khaki pants and jacket to match, and a horrid little cap with a visor. I bought a black gabardine skirt and blouse, cheap high-heeled leather pumps and black lisle stockings. I also carried a large black oilcloth sack in which were stuffed all we needed for the journey.

Bob Chanler gave a party for us at the Select the night of our departure. Almost everyone we knew in Paris was there. We wore our proletarian clothes, and they must have been pretty authentic, because the conductor on the bus we took down from Neuilly winked at me and the waiters at the Select treated us coldly.

We got to the station all right, and boarded the third-class train. The only compartment with room left for us was pretty crowded. We managed to squeeze into a place between a fat woman, with bundles at her feet and on her lap and on the rack over her head, and a drunken little sailor who was fast asleep. The rest of the occupants were a variation of these two. The air was hot and close, reeking of garlic, sour wine, and human bodies soaked in the sweat of fatigue and anxieties.

Willie had drunk a lot and needed sleep badly. He tried it sitting up, but his head would fall in the fat lady's lap, which was already full, or on me. At last, with apologies to those in

51

the compartment who were still awake, he borrowed my oil-cloth sack for a pillow and made himself comfortable on the floor, among the cigarette butts, the orange skins, the crusts of bread, the rinds of cheese, and the gobs of spit.

He fell asleep at once and slept the whole night through. I was still awake to see the first light of dawn and the red tiled roofs of the Midi. And then, at last, our journey by train was over and we were at Arles, stepping off into a fresh new world, for me at least—a world of white sunshine, plane trees, and men playing an early game of *boules*.

After so long a digression, there can be no additional harm in telling about that wonderful walking trip with Willie. It was one of the happy experiences, and there were many that were not so happy, and so I like to remember it.

It was a hot summer day when we started off to walk from Arles to Les Beaux, which Willie had visited in his youth. I wore a short cotton dress and espadrilles with thick rope soles, the kind that are impossible to find any more, that I bought at the same cobbler's shop over which Willie had lived. The old shoemaker had died, but the tradition of good workmanship was still being carried on. We had taken a room over a restaurant opposite the shoemaker's shop, on the same street with the brothels.

We soon left the cobbled, twisting streets of Arles and came out into the countryside, and, somehow, it was as familiar to me as it was to Willie. That was because every cypress tree recalled the ones Van Gogh had painted, and every distant hill was outlined with the blue of Cézanne's brush. Willie may have been walking through the haze of actual memory, but I was walking through the canvases of the French Impressionists I loved.

When we were thirsty, we stopped at farmhouses along the way, asking for water and being offered wine. When we got water they put sugar in it, because nobody in those days drank plain well water unless they were foolish. We lunched in the shade at the entrance to a farmer's barn, and we ate our *saucisson d'Arles,* bread, goat cheese, and black olives with a seasoning of perfume from the hay-and-manure piles that surrounded us. We even took our after-lunch siesta lying on the warm reeking hay in the barn.

I don't remember how many kilometers there were between Arles and Les Beaux, but it was a long day's walk and the Midi sun was mercilessly hot and gave me a deep and painful sunburn on bare arms, face, and neck. I remember how glad I was when we came within sight of Les Beaux, and then Willie insisted on taking the long way round, through the Valley of Inferno, so called because the landscape was of white stones and chalk pits and was a fitting place for the bones or ghosts of lost souls.

There was a long slope still to climb, and then there we were, in a medieval city, with a restaurant-hotel perched on the site of what had once been a stronghold of the Kings of Var. "If I were king," a poet had written long ago, "at Beaux I would make my capital."

We walked around the town during the sunset hour, exchanging *bon jours* with the old women in the Arlesian costume —wide white fichu crossed on bosom, tiny little cap perched on neatly brushed hair—that had been worn for centuries with pride. There was an air of quiet mystery about the women, just as there was about the crumbling houses of Les Beaux. One could almost hear the steps of the troubadours and the sound of their lutes. A belvedere, or the ruins of it, lay below in the valley.

Next day we set out on foot for St.-Remy, where Nostradamus came from. We started very early in the morning and before we had gone far up a mountain road we met a group of shepherds leading their flocks to new grazing ground. There was no way of walking around them, so we walked along with them—sharing our lunch with them, talking, singing their songs—for the whole long beautiful day, until we reached a crossroad and parted.

That was one of the pleasant memories, and this that I am about to recount is not, which, I suppose, is why I have made so many detours.

After the unexpected luxury of the Blue Train, the hotel, Place de l'Odéon, where we usually stopped on our short trips to Paris, seemed comfortably shabby. We said hello to the patron and his family, left our luggage, and hurried across the Place to the small café where Willie had his rendezvous.

The young French journalist arrived on time, with a package neatly tied up as only French packages seem to be. He laid it on the table. I remember we discussed Proust and Gide, after the polite questions about each other's health and families. We drank our Pernods. We discussed Sinclair Lewis and Theodore Dreiser. And then the journalist said he had to get back to his office, and we all shook hands.

As Willie and I were crossing the Place de l'Odéon to return to the hotel, I noticed the package in the pocket of his brown tweed jacket. I asked him about it. And he told me.

A healthy young workman had been killed in a traffic accident the day before. Our friend, who covered such items for his newspaper and whom Willie had asked to help him, rushed to the hospital, where he knew one of the interns. The result of all this was that Willie now possessed a pound of flesh wrapped in a surgical napkin. Other cadavers had been used to advance science. The anonymous young workman was to have the privilege of contributing to literature.

Willie went to telephone and I went up to our room and considered walking out on the whole thing. If I did, I would be walking out on Willie, I knew. And I couldn't.

One of the telephone calls Willie made was to Princess Murat, to ask if he could use the kitchen in her apartment for a half-hour that afternoon, and if she could send her servants away or keep them out of the kitchen for that length of time. Violette, who was very fond of Willie, asked him to call at five and she would see what she could do.

After he had hung up he rang another friend, a French writer who was a great admirer of Willie's books. He said he would be delighted and honored to receive us at six o'clock and to let Willie use his kitchen for as long as he pleased—and for whatever mysterious reason, especially since Willie explained it had something to do with the new book he was writing. Thus Willie, as usual, had an ace in the hole.

We arrived at Violette's apartment promptly at five. The butler looked dubious but let us in and ushered us into a small gray salon. We heard Violette's voice and then she entered, looking as if she had dressed hastily. She wore an old black silk dress, no stockings, and tiny black satin mules. She greeted Willie enthusiastically and was very gracious to me, and she talked all the time, as if she were nervous, walking about the room looking for something and then forgetting what she was looking for.

The disapproving butler came in to announce callers and he was quickly followed by a handsome, ultra-modish woman who was Violette's sister-in-law, and a man who turned out to be a well-known composer. Drinks were served by Violette, and then she said, abruptly, "Willie dear, I can't send the servants out of the kitchen. Especially not at this hour. They would talk."

Willie thanked her for even having considered it, but, he said, he had realized after their talk how inconvenient it would be, and so he had made other arrangements.

"But what on earth do you want a kitchen for?" she asked.

"To cook a piece of meat I have in my pocket," he answered.

Princess Murat looked disappointed. She said she thought it would be "something amusing, nothing so banal as that!"

For just a second I thought I would have hysterics, but fortunately we left before that happened. We taxied across Paris and up to Montmartre, and stopped before a dreary apartment house where the French writer lived. I shall call him Daniel Blanc, although that wasn't his name, of course. He had a small government job and did his writing on the side, and I suspect he had a hard time making both ends meet.

He opened the door for us, a frail man with a face like an Arab. He took us into a dark living room, crowded with fussy furniture. His little son, a child of about four, was there, playing with blocks. We had understood that his wife would be out. We hadn't counted on a child.

The little boy took a fancy to Willie and got out all his toys to show us. I thought of the surrealistic movie Dali and some other young Spaniard had just made, *Le Chien de Loup,* I think it was called. It opens with a child playing in the street with some horrible object, a combination of innocence and horror that is shocking.

I couldn't understand why Willie didn't just go into the kitchen and get the business over with. The Blancs had a servant, and we could hear her rattling things about in the kitchen. She was probably getting the child's supper ready. It was growing late and the talk was running down.

Finally our host said the only thing possible for him to say, which was, "Won't you stay to dinner?"

And Willie said, promptly, "Thank you. That would be very nice." Then he turned to me and asked me to find a wine shop in the neighborhood and buy a bottle of cognac and some dinner wine. And I left.

On the way I rather hoped that one of the wildly honking taxis that flew through the narrow, crowded streets at this busy hour would run over me so that I wouldn't have to be a witness to what would soon be happening in the Blancs' apartment.

When I returned, the three of us had a drink of brandy, and then Willie rose, with all the slowness of a figure in a nightmare, and said, "Now I would like to use the kitchen, if I may."

I remained in the stuffy living room, and had another drink. I heard voices from the kitchen: Daniel Blanc and the cook asking *"quelle espèce de viande?"* and Willie saying it was a kind of wild goat that no one had ever eaten before.

The cook obviously took a liking to Willie and offered to roast one little piece, broil another, and make a ragout of the rest. Willie sounded excited and pleased, and announced he would stand by and take notes while she did the cooking.

In the middle of all this, Daniel's wife came home. She was surprised and understandably annoyed to find she had guests. She was a tall Englishwoman with red hair and obviously the temperament to go with it. With icy politeness she introduced a woman accompanying her, who spoke with a

Cockney accent. They had been to a Bahai meeting. They were, it appeared, not only teetotalers but vegetarians, and we had brought not only cognac and wine into the house—but meat.

A table was set in the ugly dining room and the usual raw vegetables and salads that made up their evening meal were brought in disdainfully by the cook and placed in front of the family. Then, on her last trip, the cook brought in the three dishes she had prepared for Willie, and put them down in front of him with a look of pride.

To my consternation, the two Englishwomen looked coyly interested in the hot dishes, and decided to sample, just this once, the exotic African food.

I spoke up, begging them not to touch it because it was something utterly nasty. Evidently I was persuasive enough to stop them, but they both looked disappointed and envious as they watched Willie bite, chew, put his head on one side as he did when he was thinking, and then make notes.

Suddenly I had to excuse myself. The room was spinning. I rushed out to the bathroom down the hall, and was sick. When I returned they had all left the table and were sitting in the crowded living room and Willie was asking Madame Blanc how she came to be interested in Bahaism.

We left at ten o'clock. Willie was both exultant and silent, and I refused to talk to him. The next day we took the Blue Train back to Toulon, and Willie dictated his notes to me as I sat at the typewriter. He told exactly what human flesh tasted and looked like when it was cooked; but the repast, as he dictated it, was eaten in the heart of the African jungle with his black African hosts.

57

Chapter Seven

Willie decided he wanted to be in New York when *Jungle Ways* was published, and so we came over for the winter of 1930. We traveled by ship, tourist class; no matter how rich Willie might be—or feel—he spurned the first class because one had to dress for dinner every night and it was too much like stopping at a hotel. He preferred to roam the lower decks of a ship in his corduroys and beret. As a rule, however, first-class passengers came down to see us when they discovered his name on the passenger list. It was, I suppose, like having a trained bear or some other curious creature aboard.

We were traveling this time in a threesome. On a previous voyage by myself, I had met and become fond of a beautiful young White Russian émigrée, Natasha Galatzine. I ran into her again in Paris, just before we were leaving for our trip to the United States. Although her sister had married into the Vickers family in England and although Natasha always dressed well, she was broke, like most White Russians. When she said how much she would like to go to New York, Willie invited her to join us if she didn't mind traveling tourist class.

And so we arrived at the Port of New York with a genuine Russian princess in tow, to the delight of the photographers and of Willie, who had a keenly developed sense of publicity. Natasha was very good company, with a sense of humor and a good mind and, along with her striking beauty, another quality that might have been naïveté—though I am not sure.

Before we arrived in port, I saw Natasha staring at her customs-declaration form as if she were trying to understand it. I asked her if she had anything to declare and if Willie and I could help. She said she had nothing, and thanked us.

But after we had docked and our trunks and bags were arranged under our initials on the pier, I happened to glance over at the G's and saw Natasha surrounded by a small army of customs inspectors. We rushed over to see what was the trouble.

In those days people used wardrobe trunks that stood on one end and opened out, with a place to hang dresses on one side and a row of drawers on the other. All the drawers in Natasha's trunk were hanging open, and we could see the neatly stacked piles of hand-embroidered merchandise with price tags attached!

It was the first and last time I saw Willie angry at the beautiful Natasha. "What the hell did you mean by saying you had nothing to declare?" he asked.

Natasha shrugged her slim shoulders. "I didn't understand," she said. "These things are not mine. The Grand Duchess Xenia asked me if I would bring them over for all those darling people from Russia who are so poor they have not a crust of bread to eat, but their needlework is so beautiful, Xenia thought the relatives in America could sell it and then everybody would have enough money to buy bread."

I don't remember whether she was able to convince the customs inspectors of her innocence or not, but somehow we got her through, and soon we were on our way to the Hotel Brevoort on Eighth Street and Fifth Avenue.

Among the people waiting to greet us at the pier were Lyman and Katie, to whom, odd as it may seem, we were still married. Perhaps this is as good a time as any to explain what must seem a strange four-way relationship, even to those who, like us, lived in an era and an environment that did its best to be as unconventional as possible.

In the top layer of Greenwich Village society it was considered bad form to be seen out dancing, or at the theater, or even dining in restaurants with one's own wife or husband. Katie and Willie, before we met them, had other playmates, as it were, with whom they were more often seen than with each other. Lyman and I had not quite reached that point of liberation when we met the Seabrooks, but we were close to it. We had been married, a few years before all this, by John Haynes Holmes in the Community Church, of which Lyman was a member. We lived in the Village, in an apartment house on the corner of Waverly Place and Eleventh Street, a conventional enough building, but still of the Village. Lyman, tall, blond, handsome and a Dartmouth graduate, was a successful space seller in the advertising department of the *Daily News,* and at first I had a job on the *International Book Review,* put out by Funk & Wagnalls for a while as an adjunct of the *Literary Digest.* But when Lyman was earning enough I stopped going to work and stayed home to begin a novel.

One evening an actor friend of ours, Donald McKee, phoned to say he was trying to get up a bridge game for a friend who was at loose ends. Would we make a third and fourth? I told Donald that I was without any doubt the world's worst bridge player, but he said it didn't matter.

We went over to Donald's apartment, a few blocks away, and that is how we met William Seabrook. We had heard about him, and were pleased to meet an author who had actually had a book published, *Adventures in Arabia.* We both thought him charming. He had a peculiar way of looking at people, sideways, and he looked at me frequently during the game, making me play worse than ever.

The next day a florist's boy delivered a long box to my apartment. There were a dozen American Beauty roses in it and a card that read: "If these are indiscreet, press them against you and throw them away." I arranged them in a glass vase and kept them. I was a little uneasy, but the roses were beautiful.

A few days later, on a Saturday, Willie phoned to ask if I would go for a walk with him along the East River. I asked Lyman if he minded and he said to go ahead, he had something else he wanted to do. I found Willie waiting for me on the curb across the street from the apartment house. He was wearing brown corduroys and a dark blue beret *basque,* and carried a thick heavy walking stick. On his thumb was the wide silver ring with a black stone that Ibn Saud had given him in the Arabian Desert, to keep him safe from attack. I walked at his side along the East River, which had not yet been turned into a Drive, and along South Street, and then we took a cab back to the Village. In the cab he held my hand, and he kissed it as we said good-bye. We hadn't said more than a few words to each other, but we were in love, inevitably and incurably. And before long everyone knew it, and Katie knew it, and Lyman knew it, because I told him.

But nobody expected it to last. When the Seabrooks left for France, I wept and Lyman tried to console me. He was, and is, a very fine person, and much wiser than I. When he agreed to my going off to Paris in April, I think it was because he believed I was caught up in something that time could cure, and that, no matter what he said or did, he couldn't help me except by letting the fever run its course. I am sure Katie felt the same way, and so they waited for us, and were very good for each other.

That first night of our return, at the Brevoort, in the room I shared with Natasha, I walked the floor until daybreak. I told myself I should be back with Lyman, as long as he wanted me back and expected me back. I was very fond of him, I suppose I loved him, really, and I was unhappy about Natasha and a lot of other things. When it started to get light I put through a phone call to Willie's room. I said I had to talk to him and he told me to meet him downstairs. I dressed quickly and met him in the lobby, and we walked to Washington Square and sat down on a bench.

I told him how I felt, and that I had decided to go back to Lyman, and Willie asked me not to leave him. He said he loved me and needed me, and I belonged to him. I agreed to stay, and as we got up to walk away from the Square, I watched my bridges burn, and left the ashes under the Arch, without turning my head again.

Absorbed as we were in our tangled personal affairs, Willie with his forthcoming book and I with seeing Lyman and Katie again, and my family, it was a few days before I recognized the

61

fact that somehow, and in a very big way, our own country was wearing a different look. It came as a tremendous shock when I noticed the men who were selling apples on street corners, and the preponderance of beggars, and heard the whine, "Sister, can you spare a dime?" Suddenly the whole force of the Depression, then a year old, struck me.

In our dream life in the South of France we hardly ever read the newspapers. If we did, it was to read what the critics said about this or that book or play in which we were interested, or what the *Petit Var* printed about the latest *"crime passionnel."* And yet for twelve months, more or less, our wonderful, prosperous, self-confident country had been writhing in an economic anguish whose only effect on us had been the increase of royalty checks as people read to forget.

All that winter in New York, as I passed from one fantasy to another, I would catch glimpses of a national crisis; but, as far as I could tell, Willie ignored most of it. He gave money away when he was asked, but if he was aware of the millions of men who were out of work he didn't mention it. He had a deep-rooted fear of failure, he worshiped success, and he was an intense individualist. I believe he honestly felt that each beggar he met on the street was there through some personal failure, and that "the time to kick a man was when he was down," because when he touched bottom, there would be no place to go but up. His fear and hatred of poverty, of failure, may very well have sprung from those early years as the child of a small-town preacher who had left a prosperous law practice because of a "call," and of a mother who followed her husband from one poor parish to another and never forgave him for the genteel poverty he had forced on her and his children.

We lived that winter in an apartment, or rather a collection of rooms, that Willie found in a building on lower Fifth Avenue with the Dauber & Pine bookshop and an avant-garde movie house on the ground floor. He took it because of the one vast room that had a stage at one end of it, left behind by some little theater group. There was a bedroom in the rear of the apartment, a couple of smaller inside rooms, and a kitchen-ette.

Willie bought some Oriental rugs, a couple of couches, a few chairs, and a bedroom suite for the back room. He hired a piano for the stage and occasionally I played on it. But mostly the stage was used for his fantasies. I thought it was the ugliest room I had ever seen in my life, but Willie loved it.

On the day *Jungle Ways* was published, he stayed in bed. He was actually sick with apprehension, expectation, and pure blue funk. There is an old wives' tale that among primitive people in Africa when a woman is about to give birth to a baby it is the husband who stays in bed and suffers labor pains. Willie's performance each time a book of his came out, while not exactly analogous, at least contained the syndrome of psychosomatic labor pains.

At that time there were many more daily newspapers in New York than there are today, and I went out and bought all I could find, even including the tabloids that occasionally ran book reviews. With my arms full, I returned to the apartment and dumped them all on the bed, and then Willie and I began a feverish hunt for the literary columns. *Jungle Ways* had the lead or sole review in all of them—and they were all enthusiastically good! William B. Seabrook had another best seller.

The phone began ringing and kept ringing all day, and people came to see us to offer congratulations. Willie received them in bed, and I kept bringing chairs and drinks, and nobody questioned the chapter on cannibals. Willie's relief was tremendous.

In spite of, or perhaps because of, the Depression, people gave a great many parties that winter in New York. There were speakeasies and night clubs, and there was Harlem. After dining at a speakeasy we would pile into cabs and rush up to Harlem to catch the floor show at Small's or the Savoy or the Cotton Club. One night we went up there with Carl Van Vechten and a party of his friends that included Noel Coward. It was Coward's first visit to Harlem, I believe, and he was entranced by the dancing. It may have been the Lindy Hop that year, but whatever it was called the movements were original, frenetic, and utterly unself-conscious. He withdrew himself from our talkative party and, leaning against a pillar at the edge of the dance floor, absorbed everything, wide-eyed and unsmiling but with total and concentrated enjoyment. Watching Noel Coward getting his first impressions of Negro Harlem was like observing Keats first looking into Chapman's Homer.

We went several times that winter to Madame Allelia Walker's Thursday "at-homes" on a beautiful street in Harlem known as "Sugar Hill." Madame Walker was a handsome brown-skinned woman who had made a fortune out of a product that would straighten hair. Her lavishly furnished house was a gathering place not only for artists and authors and theatrical stars of her own race, but for celebrities from all over the world. Drinks and food were served, and there was always music, generously performed and enthusiastically received.

Willie decided to give a dinner party for Allelia, and consulted his friend the headwaiter in the Brevoort's basement dining room. To Willie's indignation, the Brevoort regretted it could not serve a dinner in its restaurant to Negroes, celebrated or not. However, they did compromise. They sent waiters and bus boys, together with tables, cloths, napkins, silver, and dishes —and wonderful hot food—across Fifth Avenue to our apartment. It turned out to be such a successful party that it lasted well into the following afternoon.

Natasha stayed with us for about a month. She had made friends of her own, Carl Van Doren (with whom Willie, in spite of a warm friendship with Irita Van Doren, was not on good terms) and Maxwell Anderson.

It may have been such an unsettled and problem-filled time in history that writers found it hard to dig into their souls for the timeless stuff of which great plays and novels are made. Those men on the street corners, with frayed collars and the faces of college professors or dispossessed angels—they weren't just Bowery bums that one accepted in passing and threw a coin to, against one's principles. They were, some of them, people you might have grown up with. They could have been you, but for the grace of God. In fact, if you were a very sensitive writer who had escaped, you felt a deep sense of shame and an obligation to do something. But what?

One writer we knew well who was writing a book that winter which was never published was Sinclair Lewis. I had long admired his books, but in spite of the fact that he and Willie were good friends, I had never met him. When I did, it was in the most peculiar circumstances.

The Saturday before Easter, Willie decided to invite a few friends in to tea. I had made other plans, and left the apartment late in the afternoon and didn't return until around midnight. I let myself into the apartment with my key, and found everything quiet and no lights on anywhere. I gathered that the party had ended early for parties in those days, and that Willie had gone to bed. I lit a light in the small foyer and went into our bedroom, and started to undress in the dark so as not to disturb Willie.

I don't know what made me first sense that something was wrong. Suddenly, I reached for the switch and turned on the light. There, sitting up in my bed with a wide grin and a topknot of red hair, was someone I'd never met before in my life.

"You're Red Lewis!" I gasped.

"And you're Marjorie," he said.

It didn't take long to gather what had happened. Red had passed out at Willie's tea party and had been put to bed in the best, if not the only, bedroom.

I put on a kimono and gave Sinclair Lewis one of Willie's dressing gowns, and we went in search of Willie. We found him fast asleep on one of the big couches in the so-called living room. Ordinarily he was a very light sleeper, alert in a moment to a decibel of sound, like a cat. But this night he refused to be aroused. The most we could get from him was a mumbled, "Get the hell out of here!" So we did.

I made toast and a pot of coffee and scrambled some eggs,

and we ate in the little middle room. Red got his briefcase and took out a thick manuscript, the first draft of his novel about labor. He read me parts of it. Even at two in the morning I could tell that he was having trouble.

Thus began the strangest and busiest weekend in my whole life. At the beginning, the next morning, all seemed to be fine. Willie had awakened early and made coffee and for a while he and Sinclair Lewis talked and I listened. Then Red asked me if I would telephone across the street to the Grosvenor Hotel, where he sometimes stopped, and order a limousine and chauffeur to drive him to Connecticut. I did as requested, and by the time I returned from the phone Red had poured himself a stiff drink and so had Willie.

They were still talking. I seem to remember the subject of that conversation: it had to do with the Glory of God and the True Religion. They were both excited by now, and the words and phrases they used were magnificent. I believe they were expressing what they deeply felt, but they were also trying to impress each other.

The doorbell rang and I went to answer it. The elevator operator was there to announce that a limousine was waiting downstairs at the entrance for Mr. Lewis.

When I returned with the information, daring to interrupt the dialogue, Red dismissed me with a wave of his bony arm. "Send it away!" he roared, and returned to the discussion after pouring himself another drink. I went back to the door and gave the elevator man the message.

Just after he had asked me to order the limousine, Red had telephoned Dorothy to tell her where he was and to say he was driving home immediately, and I could gather by Red's apologetic tones that she was very angry. But at this point, with the bottle almost empty, Red had no thought for Dorothy or anybody living. He and Willie were reciting Scripture, mostly from the Epistles of St. Paul. For an atheist, Sinclair Lewis knew a lot about the Bible.

When I returned from clearing away the breakfast things and making up the bed in our room, Red had passed out on the stage in the front room, and Willie was asleep again on the couch.

The rest of that long weekend resembled a few reels of an old-fashioned silent movie, turned by a prankish operator who speeded up or slowed down the film at eccentric intervals. Except at the very beginning, when they started their dialogue on the nature and glory of God from the viewpoints of a Lutheran minister's son, who had joined the Church of Rome when he was a young man on a walking tour of Italy, and a Nobel Prize winner who insisted he was an atheist, they were rarely awake at the same time thereafter.

At some point the rhythm had become syncopated: now, when Red had passed out, Willie woke up, and vice versa.

I made coffee, scrambled eggs, sent out for sandwiches, answered the phone, and kept on ordering the limousine and chauffeur from across the street. At least three times Red told me to order it, and three times when it drew up to the door of 66 Fifth Avenue, he ordered me to send it away! And all the time Dorothy Thompson kept calling up from Connecticut to know when he was coming home. If he was able to talk, he went to the phone and, using endearments in German that might have moved a heart of stone but did not move his wife's, he swore he would leave at once.

I forget whether it was Monday or Tuesday when Sinclair Lewis, dressed smartly and with his briefcase under his arm, finally left in the Grosvenor Hotel limousine. I only know I went to bed, exhausted.

There was one more little incident that I might describe because I believe it may shed further light, although I'm not sure what kind, on a very complex person. At one point during Red's visit we ran out of liquor and Willie ordered a case of Scotch from his own mysterious source. It was delivered by a sinister-looking type with lacquered black hair and a sallow complexion and wearing a black Homburg, exactly like a top gangster in the movies. He presented his bill, and I went to wake up Willie, who was the one who was asleep at that moment. I couldn't rouse him.

67

I had some cash but not enough, so I started to write out a check; but the man with the Homburg wouldn't accept it. Red was roaming around the apartment at that point, looking for a drink. I explained the situation and asked him if he would cash my check for twenty-five dollars, which, added to what I had in bills, would have paid for the new case of Scotch. Red counted out two tens and a five from a roll of bills and I handed him my check, and that was that. Or almost.

We were leaving New York a few weeks after Easter, and Willie told me to close out our account at the bank the day before we left. Which I did by simply withdrawing all the money that was left in it.

A few months later, when we were in France again, Willie received a letter from Red Lewis demanding to know where I was. He had just tried to cash my check and been told by the bank that the account was closed. He wanted his twenty-five dollars back! Willie sent it to him, along with a couple of his choicest invectives, advising Red to learn to cash checks promptly instead of letting them lie around until they were moldy.

Our winter in New York drew to a close. From the crowded weeks that remained, I recall one incident that I think is interesting as a side light on Willie's character. Although he really loved his friend Sinclair Lewis and was overjoyed when he was awarded the Nobel Prize for Literature, Willie was one of a great number of people who thought the award should have gone to Theodore Dreiser, who had expected it. I remember a remark that was going the rounds and that Willie repeated as if he had invented it, as perhaps he had: "Dreiser will be granite when Sinclair Lewis is dust."

Knowing how Willie admired Dreiser, our friends the painter Jerome Blum and his wife, Frances, took us along with them to an "afternoon at-home" at the Dreisers. There were about a dozen or more people milling around in a great Gothic room, and the center of attention, naturally, was Dreiser, a big man with grizzled gray hair, a heavy face, and a surly expression.

When Willie was taken over to be introduced as the author

of *The Magic Island* and *Jungle Ways,* Dreiser glanced at him, looked away, and made some cruelly cutting remark about "yellow journalism." The gracious speech of adulation that I knew Willie must have prepared was left dry and unsaid on his tongue. I felt terribly sorry for him, and so did everyone else who witnessed the slap. It was as if a devout believer had brought flowers to lay at the feet of a saint, and had been kicked in the face by one of the sainted sandals.

I expected that Willie, who was never one to turn the other cheek, would thereafter blast his idol with all the strength of his vocabulary. But I was wrong. Not long after this bitter incident I overheard Willie repeating to a group of people at a literary tea, that Dreiser would be granite when Sinclair Lewis was dust.

We sailed back to France on one of the big English ships, in separate staterooms on opposite sides of a corridor. A great many people came to see us off, many of them bringing bottles of bootleg Scotch and rye. Alfred Harcourt brought me an enormous bouquet of yellow roses.

I sat alone in my stateroom while bedlam was going on at the other side of the corridor, and I tried to be glad I had decided to return to France. But I could smell in my nostrils the smoking embers of the bridge I had long since irrevocably burned behind me. And as the party in the other room was getting wilder and wilder, I wept. Funny thing—I have always hated parties.

Chapter Eight

We were in Paris the next winter, planning to stay in the South of France for the two months that were cold and rainy. We had a little *pied-à-terre* that Stella Bowen furnished for us with things she picked up at the Flea Market. The apartment was over a small café opposite the Hôtel Place de l'Odéon—the café where we had met the journalist with the grisly package.

Willie was making notes, desultorily, for the book he planned to write about his brother Charlie, and I was revising, with the help of Mr. Bradley, the last chapters of my novel *Mrs. Taylor*. Willie was also awaiting word from his American and English publishers regarding an advance of a substantial amount for another journey to Africa.

Because the apartment wasn't large enough for two type-writers going at the same time, Willie took a room around the corner and I rented one on the top floor of the Hôtel Place de l'Odéon, in which to write.

One morning as I was hard at work, the *valet de chambre* knocked on my door to say that Monsieur Seabrook was down-stairs and wanted to see me. Since we rarely interrupted each other at work, I knew it must be something important. Willie was standing at the foot of the stairs in the lobby with a wide smile on his face.

"How would you like to go with me to Timbuctoo?" he asked.

If he had asked me to go to the moon with him, I suppose I would have said yes, and, for one who has never been there, Timbuctoo does seem as far out as the moon. However, since I had been trying to prepare myself for a long separation if the new contract was to be signed, the invitation to share in the

African adventure came as an intense and wonderful surprise.

"How soon do we leave?" I asked.

"A week from tomorrow," Willie said. "Come along and we'll buy a couple of cork helmets."

In *Jungle Ways,* Willie had written about a white monk called Père Yakouba. Because that chapter had aroused a great deal of interest, the publishers thought that a whole book might be written about the eccentric old priest who had gone far down into the Sahara Desert to spread the Gospel, and had fallen in love with a native woman of Timbuctoo, Salama, begotten many children by her, and been defrocked.

While he was waiting for final word on a contract and advance, Willie had pulled a lot of wires, with the help of Paul Morand and the Bradleys. Arrangements were quickly made for the chartering of a private plane, and a pilot who had desert experience. By good luck, as well as the fact that Willie usually managed to get whatever he wanted hard enough, we acquired the services of Captain Wauthier, late of the French Desert Air Corps, who knew the Sahara as well as the palm of his hand. Willie had a theory that most aviators resembled birds, sometimes even eagles. Although Captain Wauthier had no beak, his features came to a point; he was smooth, compactly formed, bright-eyed, silent for a Frenchman, and he inspired complete confidence. His plane was a four-seater Farman, with the name "General Lapperine" inscribed upon it. Before the voyage was over, both Wauthier and the plane became inextricably bound up in our lives, like tried and old friends.

One cold early morning we drove out to the airfield, Willie and I and Captain Wauthier. It was the Orly field, which then consisted of two or three large hangars and a couple of runways and bore little resemblance to the big international airport travelers know today.

On the way, as we drove along the Seine embankment, I prayed because I was frightened. I had flown only once before, and that was on the big commercial plane between Paris and London, and here I was embarking on a flight to Timbuctoo!

71

This was like being thrown into the middle of the Atlantic Ocean before one has learned to swim at the beach. But that was a silly way of looking at it, I told myself. One can drown in a bathtub as well as in the sea.

It was still dark when we arrived before dawn. While Captain Wauthier and the Orly mechanics checked the plane's engine, we stood by, shivering in a cold black wind. Suddenly there appeared on the horizon a faint ribbon of light. We climbed into the small cabin, Captain Wauthier into the cockpit, and a few seconds later he put his head out of a window and cried: *"Personne!"* There was an answering cry of *"Personne!"* from the mechanics on the ground as they stepped aside. The engine warmed up, and we taxied away noisily for a while and began rising slowly and easily into the morning.

The Farman plane of our trip to Timbuctoo was a far cry from today's streamlined jets, but then it was the latest model. For one thing, it was enclosed. We sat in wicker chairs that were fastened to the floor of the plane. In front of us, where our knees touched it, was the fuel tank, filled with high explosive, so that we could not smoke for the whole eight hours our average daily flight lasted.

And was it noisy! Closely as we were seated, neither of us could hear a word the other spoke. We had to communicate by writing notes. I still have the two French paperback books we brought along to read. They were *Bidon 5*, by Martha Oulie, and *Vent de Sable,* by Joseph Kessel. When an idea struck us, Willie or I would pick up one of the books and write on the flyleaf or margin.

On the flyleaf of *Vent de Sable* I read in Willie's handwriting, "We must have a nice favorable wind behind us. Calm." That must have been when we were flying over Africa, because the first stage of our trip over central France was anything but calm. Nobody had warned me of air pockets, and when we hit one and started to drop, I was sure we were about to crash, and felt sick with disappointment that our adventure would be over before it began.

Our first landing was in the open field of a farm in Poitiers, where we were greeted warmly by a peasant and his wife. We left our parachutes with them, to be picked up on our return. One of the very few regulations insisted upon by the French government was that we could not fly on our mission unless we wore parachutes. They were heavy, cumbersome affairs, and not one of us had any confidence in them. I know I would rather have dropped through the air at my own speed than expect myself to count ten before I pulled a string.

I used the word "mission" since, in order to get permission from the French government for our flight, we had to show that it had some importance. With the help of friends at the Trocadero Museum (which was the equivalent of our Museum of Natural History) we convinced the government that we were on an ethnographic mission whose purpose was to accumulate new knowledge for and about the human race.

The next note in Willie's handwriting is on the back cover of *Vent de Sable:* "See if your window will open a good half way. He wants me to shoot next time from the left."

That was not as murderous as it sounds. What it meant was that Willie was to shoot a flare out of the window before we landed, in order for Captain Wauthier to know which way the wind was blowing. The flare came from an object that looked like a big toy pistol. It made Willie feel important and me a little doubtful. Suppose the wind decided to change its direction between the moment the flare shot out, and the moment of landing the plane?

The other notes are comments on the wonderful things we saw from the windows of the "General Lapperine." They range from the ecstatic to such a prosaic remark as Willie's "Could you lend me a big clean handkerchief?" The point is that we traveled over some of the most thrilling landscapes in the world, all of them new to us, and yet we couldn't discuss them as ordinary travelers would because of the deafening noise of the engines that lasted as long as we were in the air each day.

And we flew only by day, because night flying was still too hazardous for us, although Saint-Exupéry and his colleagues had already flown at night from Dakar to Buenos Aires, carrying mail. I became used to being awakened at four or five in the morning, swallowing some instant coffee, riding out to an airfield while the world was still asleep, and shivering in the cold, while we waited for dawn to appear in the sky. We would take off the minute of sunrise, toward the new day and the wonders it would unfold to us.

We spent the first night at Cartagena on the east coast of Spain. The next day we crossed the Mediterranean to Africa. The approach was impressive: a shore line punctuated with palms and sandy beaches, and behind them a mountain range. People who have approached it from the sea describe a perfume that sweeps toward them from the land mass, an unforgettable odor of Africa. From the air we missed that perfume, but the magic was inherent in the sight of its shores.

We landed at the airfield of Oran and were driven swiftly into the town, which looked like an extension of the South of France. The hotel where we registered was modern and very comfortable. In the bar, over *apéritifs* before dinner, Willie and I were introduced to a group of French pilots who talked to us about their *copain* Saint-Exupéry, and of those rugged days and nights when they had pioneered the establishment of a mail route across the South Atlantic. I had just finished reading *Vol de Nuit* and was entranced not only by the story itself, but by the poetry of its writing.

We stayed in Oran for a few days while Captain Wauthier had the plane checked and rechecked for desert flying; and then, one morning at dawn, we started off for Timbuctoo. There were the Atlas Mountains to be crossed, and at noon there was a stop in Colomb-Béchar for a quick lunch and another check-up and weather report. Then we were off again, this time over the Sahara itself, and what is called the *bled*.

Willie took photographs of the sand formations that looked from the air like abstract paintings. From time to time, together with the shadows our plane cast on the sand, we could see crowds of the graceful little antelopes the French call *biches*. Otherwise there were long stretches of nothingness when we read or passed notes to each other. Then, suddenly, the desert seemed to rise up, and the next moment we were looking at it sideways. The plane bounced and swayed and shivered and we held on to the arms of our wicker chairs and looked grim. Captain Wauthier handed us a note that said:

"Vent de sable. Nous atterrissons."

And so we made a forced landing in the midst of a sandstorm, in a gritty yellow world and a wind that tore at us as soon as we left the plane and made our job of securing it with sandbags a painful one. We dug holes for ourselves and lay in them, covering our eyes, noses, and ears as well as we could. I recalled seeing the wreck of a plane as we passed over it earlier that afternoon, and realized how lucky we were to have such a skilled pilot. In a few hours, the air became clear again, and we continued our flight.

The next stop was Reggan. From the air it looked no different from other oases: palm trees, irrigation canals, and a compound of low white houses surrounded by a bleached mud wall. But once we had stepped inside the hotel, owned by the Trans-Saharan Company, we were back in France, and a very modish, chic France it was, comparable to Eden Roc at Cap d'Antibes, with a flavor of fashionable Marrakech in the cane and rattan furnishings, and the bright orange, purple, and pink of the cushions and wall hangings.

Perhaps the most fashionable, chic, or "smart" thing about Reggan was the young man from Paris who ran it for the company. His name was Raymond Bauret, and according to Captain Wauthier, who was only repeating a rumor, he had "suffered a disappointment in love" from some woman in Paris. He had applied for the job of manager of this remote hotel to get away from the people he knew. His manner toward us was at first coldly polite, almost supercilious, as if he were determined never to give another human being a chance to hurt him.

He was tall and beautifully made, with Norse features rather than Latin, and light brown hair. He dressed for day in loose khaki trousers banded at the ankles, such as Willie and I later adopted because they were cool and allowed for a circulation of air. They originated, I believe, with the Tuaregs. With these he wore impeccably tailored shirts, linen by day and silk by night. His evening trousers were of thin black silk, cut on the same pattern. His sandals were of soft leather brightly dyed, such as the Arabs wore. He was a dream out of a 1930 version of *The Sheik*, and I don't know why I didn't pay more attention to him that first night except that I was rarely aware of any other male when Willie was present.

Dinner was superb, with vintage wines, and the conversation was witty and gay. Willie was in top form and told some of his funniest stories in French that was larded with the argot he had picked up here and there.

There were still stars in the sky when we got up the next morning. Captain Wauthier was glued to the small radio, to find out about the weather along our route, and then dawn was upon us and we flew southward.

Can anyone imagine a gasoline pump stuck out in the middle of a great desert, with no roads leading up to it but just a vast expanse of sand in every direction? That was our next stop— Bidon 5. It was actually a refueling station for the buses of the Trans-Saharan Company that made routine trips from Colomb-Béchar to Gao about once every two weeks. Pilots making long reconnaissance flights also used it when they ran out of gas.

A solitary Arab was in charge of the *étape,* and he was over-joyed to see us. He had learned how to help pilots or bus drivers to refuel, but he spoke no word of any language but his own, which was the Arabic of the Koran.

The arrangements made for sleeping were of the simplest. Two abandoned motorbuses were fitted with bunks after the seats had been removed. For our evening meal and breakfast we heated water and cans of food over a primus stove we had brought with us, and ate at a metal table outdoors, as if we were sitting at an outdoor café on one of the Grands Boulevards of Paris.

It was about four in the afternoon when we reached Bidon 5, and, having traveled since dawn without more than a sandwich for lunch, we were hungry. We had a cold roast chicken which

76

we offered to share with the Arab guardian, but it was the season of Ramadan and, although he eyed the food as if he were famished, he wouldn't touch it before sundown. When he did eat, his sharp teeth crunched the bones of the chicken as well as the meat.

Willie, who spoke a little Arabic, found out that the lonely soul had been plagued for some time with a frightful headache. There was aspirin in our medical kit and I offered it to him. But the sun had not set and, suffering though he was, he refused. I left the whole tin with him, asking Willie to tell him to take only two at a time, after dark. I hoped he wouldn't crunch the tin container along with the pills.

Before we went to bed, Willie and I took a walk in the desert; not far, of course, because it was too easy to become lost. We went far enough, however, to lose sight of the gasoline pump and the converted motorbuses. We stood together for a while under the stars and Willie pointed out to me the Southern Cross. The night was cold and clear, and this was as beautiful a moment as I have known in my life.

It was as if we stood alone at the edge of the world, the only two people alive in it. Willie took my hand and held it firmly. Neither of us spoke. After a while, after a glimpse of eternity that we had shared with each other, we went back to the world —an ugly little encampment in the middle of the Sahara Desert.

In the years that followed our last separation, the one made final by Willie's death, I had a recurrent dream. I would be starting down a long corridor at the end of which stood Willie, with his hand outstretched, waiting for me to join him on another long walk.

Chapter Nine

"Yes, Marjorie, there *is* a Timbuctoo!"

I said this to myself as we circled over the biggest oasis we had seen so far, and realized that I had actually reached the place considered so remote it had become a symbol.

I don't know what I had expected, but down there was only a scattering and a cluster of white clay houses such as we had seen when we passed over other oasis towns. Willie was even more excited than I. The last time he had visited Timbuctoo he had come, with Katie, by boat up along the Niger, and then by donkey from the river port, Kabara. Now he was dropping down upon it, as it were, from the air.

I saw no reason why we couldn't land in the city, since there was plenty of sand all around it, but there were regulations, and we came to earth at the military airport, several miles away. The young French pilots stationed there were so glad to have company that we lingered longer than necessary over *apéritifs* and lively conversation. We were to see a lot of those lonely men during our month's stay. Now we left our plane in their care and rode on horseback into Timbuctoo.

It was late in the afternoon, but the sun had not begun to set when we arrived, and I was struck with the grayness of everything: the low flat buildings, the mosques, the sand where streets should have been. This was no city, I thought, but a mausoleum. And that was not surprising, because Timbuctoo is probably one of the oldest cities still in existence. Nineveh, Tyre, Sodom and a dozen others came to mind. Why had Timbuctoo survived?

As a meeting place between the terminals of the salt trade, Timbuctoo had once been a rich and powerful city. In addition to its mosques it possessed a university and a library of ancient books and manuscripts. Because of its wealth it became the object of frequent raids by bands of Tuaregs and other warlike nomads, until the citizens of the town, fearing to make any display of their wealth, tore down many of the handsomely studded doors of which they were so proud and hung rags at the openings. Toward the end of the nineteenth century the French drove out the Tuaregs and established themselves as protectors of "Tombouctou." In accordance with their system of colonization, they did little to change the customs or religion —or welfare—of the inhabitants.

At certain times of the year the salt caravans with some three or four thousand camels converge on Timbuctoo and there is great drama and excitement. But this didn't happen while we were there, and the only excitement was the parties given for us by Wauthier's *copains* at the airfield, or by the French administrator and his wife, Monsieur and Madame Dubois.

The streets between the houses were of sand; there were no street lamps or signs and we were frequently lost, especially at night, when we traveled on foot, carrying lanterns. What concerned us more, however, was that there was no hotel. There was instead a big, low structure called the caravanserai. It consisted of many bare rooms for the convenience of travelers, and it was infested with bats.

The room given to us was enormous, and empty except for a big double brass bed and one wooden chair. Travelers were expected to provide their own bedding, kitchenware, and whatever else they needed, and because most of the visitors to Timbuctoo were nomads who traveled light, the arrangements had sufficed for a century or so.

Willie, who had traveled this way before, knew what was expected of us. He dumped his personal luggage in the middle of the big room and departed at once, with Captain Wauthier, first to pay his respects to the Governor of the region, and then to stop for supplies, including liquor and glasses, at the general store, which was run by one of the few Europeans not in uniform of some sort.

I was alone. I moved the one chair to the window and sat for a while looking out beyond a columned porch to a vast stretch of sand and sky. It was so inconceivable to me that I, a female who had been born near Mt. Morris Park, New York, of middle-class and more or less conventional parents, should be in Timbuctoo that I had to jump up, find a pad of paper and a pen, and write a letter to my sister, Debby, heading it *Timbuctoo, Africa,* to make it an actual fact.

Once I started the letter, my pen raced on. There was so much to say. . . . But suddenly I stopped writing. I had one of those uncanny feelings we get when we sense the presence of a stranger. I turned around quickly to face a rather tall, rather elderly bearded man wearing a djellaba and turban.

He smiled broadly and bowed, and I smiled back, and wondered who he was and what I was supposed to do. He just went on bowing and smiling. I stood up and offered him my chair, and he waited until I was seated on the edge of the bed. We sat facing each other, smiling. I tried a few words in French, but it didn't help. He didn't speak my French.

Then suddenly he reached into his flowing sleeve and brought out a beautifully filigreed silver cigarette holder and held it out to me. I took it, admired it, and started to hand it back. The smile was replaced by a frown, and I realized I had made a terrible mistake. I said, "Thank you," in English, and the smile returned.

"I know," I said to myself. "He met Katie when she was here with Willie. That's who he thinks I am. But how I must have changed!"

Just when I felt I was going to spend the rest of my life exchanging smiles with this generous but total stranger, Willie and the Captain returned and took over. There was a lot of bowing and *salaam aleikums,* and Willie then opened a box of supplies he had dumped on the floor and took out two jars of strawberry preserves. He presented these to our visitor, who looked relieved and happy and soon departed.

"In Africa," Willie said severely, as if I should have known all about it and had done something wrong, "you don't just take gifts—you exchange them! That was the Cadi, an old friend."

The first thing we did next morning was call upon Père Yakouba. He lived in a street of houses that seemed to have no windows. A curtain or sheet was hung over the doorway and that seemed to be the only source of ventilation except for a few curious slits in the clay walls; but just inside was a courtyard filled with sunshine, goats, chickens, and pigs, and café-au-lait babies running around and falling over things. An old woman sat stirring something in a pot over an open fire, and a younger man was sweeping up debris with a broom of twigs. He grinned when he saw us, and pointed upward. We saw a rickety flight of stairs and climbed to the second story.

Willie described Père Yakouba at great length and depth in *The White Monk of Timbuctoo,* a book which he himself preferred to all his others, perhaps because he put so much of his own philosophy into it. What I saw in that large, book-lined study on the second floor of the strange clay house was a stout, short old man with a full white beard and a shock of uncombed white hair, wearing a short-sleeved tricot sport shirt, a pair of loose Tuareg trousers, and floppy comfortable slippers.

He welcomed us with a shout of joy, embraced Willie, and beamed at me with approval and not a sign of surprise that it was I and not Katie. It was amazing how much he knew of what went on in the world—and what went on in Timbuctoo—without a telephone or even a wireless.

He offered us Pernod, which he poured for us, adding water but of course no ice, and then he plunged at once into a discussion of the book he had just finished reading, which was, if I remember correctly, *"Moby-Dick."*

I sat in a chair that was a little removed from them and began making notes, as Willie had asked me to do. I wish I had them before me now. After all these years I can only try to convey the general tone of those conversations. They talked, I know, of Jack London and Mark Twain, whose novels filled one of the bookshelves in that wonderfully untidy room, and they talked of Gide and Voltaire and Racine; Yakouba's tastes were

81

universal and he had no narrow prejudices so long as an author had something to say and that something was not only well written but proved him to be a man of good will.

And, under Willie's skillful prodding, the old man told his own story, beginning with his decision to enter the Order of the *Pères Blancs*.

"The bird of God," he said, "knows where to build its nest."

He was very earnest when he set out as a young man, with a mission as burning as the sands his bare feet walked over, to convert everyone he met in his path to what he believed to be the one, the true, religion. Slowly he made his converts and moved farther and farther into the Sahara. Others before him had fallen by the way, some were murdered, some perished from hunger or thirst or disease. Yakouba succeeded in reaching as far south as Timbuctoo, where he established a little mission and taught school. All was well.

But Père Yakouba was a young man still, filled with healthy appetites and zest for life. And among the people of many dark races whom he met and instructed there were the beautiful women of the Songhai. Among these was Salama, tall and dignified, with golden skin, dark eyes, and a clever tongue. They fell in love, and because Salama came from a very proud family, Yakouba married her and hoped that his sin would be hidden from the notice of his Order, whose headquarters were so far away, and whose Superiors might even have forgotten the eager young monk who had left them so long ago.

He spoke of the warfare within himself, of the nights when he felt he had betrayed not only his Order, the Church, and God, but his own soul. But his Superiors in France learned of his marriage. They sent other *Pères Blancs* to call on him, to persuade him to give up the *indigène* and return to his senses and his duty. By this time Salama had given him two sons and a daughter and he was more in love with her than ever. Besides, for the first time in his life Yakouba was happy. He refused to return to the fold and was expelled from the Order.

And now Salama was middle-aged and he was old, and they

had many grandchildren. Did he have any regrets? Willie asked him.

"Who has not, who has lived so long?" Yakouba answered sadly. "But I have come to terms with myself, with my conscience. I have helped populate the world," he added, with a sly smile. "And is that such a bad thing?"

We spent many mornings in that long room, so surprisingly filled with light, not only from the sun in the courtyard, but from a clear and generous mind. Very often Willie and Yakouba drank to excess, slipping from one to another of the five stages of drunkenness that someone has described as jocose, bellicose, morose, lachrymose, and comatose. Before the last stage, I had ceased to make notes and managed to get Willie back to the caravanserai for lunch and the long siesta.

I don't think Salama approved of any of it. She was an enormous woman now, still beautiful in her long white robes trimmed with embroidery and hung with amber beads and silver jewelry. She was much too busy to spend any time with us. She was, in fact, the head of the baking industry in Timbuctoo. Every day there would be gathered on her street men, women, and boys, to cart off trays of flat bread loaves baked in her ovens. We ate the same bread at the caravanserai, and it was always gritty because the ovens were in the open air and the sand flew everywhere, permeating the dough as it was pounded into the circular loaves.

The days passed quickly—mornings with Père Yakouba; sometimes a luncheon at the house of M. and Mme. Dubois that lasted three hours or more, French fashion; and sometimes a luncheon that lasted all afternoon at the airfield at Kabara with Wauthier's friends. There was a lot that went on that I think I missed, because my French at the time was not too fluent or because I was even then too engrossed with Willie and what he was doing and saying or might be thinking. However, vaguely, I gathered some impressions, and one of these was of Lallah and the youngest of the lonely young pilots.

I think she must have been Arabian. Her skin was so pale, and there were Arabs in Timbuctoo, along with Berbers, Songhai, Bambara, mixed Tuaregs, and other races. She was hardly more than a child, somewhere between twelve and fifteen. Madame Dubois had acquired her—how I don't know, except that her husband was the Civil Administrator of Timbuctoo, which was something like being a dictator of a small state—as a baby-sitter for her small children. She was kind to Lallah, giving her European clothes and showing her how to wear her thick dark hair, brushed and combed and hanging to her shoulders, like French school children of the time. But Madame Dubois was bored in Timbuctoo, and liked to give parties, and she gave a lot of them for the men from the airfield.

Lallah was very much of a flirt, I noticed, and apparently she had chosen the youngest of the aviators to tease and torment. One night, at a party in the Administrator's house, when the champagne had flowed freely, the young man, aroused to such a point that he was a little bit crazy, told Madame Dubois "good night," grasped Lallah around the waist, put her on his horse, and rode away with her to the airfield and his own barren quarters.

All this had happened just before we arrived, and by now Lallah was attached to the airfield. She wore native costume, her dark hair was braided and pinned up close to her head, her eyes were darkened with kohl, and around her neck, in addition to the little silver cross Madame Dubois had given her, she wore a leather *gris-gris*, or charm. Her arms and ankles were covered with bracelets, and she tinkled musically as she followed the young aviator around like a tame household animal.

At one of the all-day luncheons I observed the young man and thought he looked on the verge of a serious illness. There were deep circles under his eyes, and he was filled with some inner disease that was more of the soul than the body. I'm sure he was conscience-stricken and at the same time bewildered. His leave was soon coming up; one could take home a tamed cheetah or lion cub or gazelle to one's parents in Dijon—but not a tamed little Arab girl.

There was another girl at the airfield, small and slender, who I thought was about Lallah's age; but Willie told me she was a prostitute, aged about thirty, who had taken Lallah under her wing. I could understand why the young aviator looked worried and unhappy. He was an intelligent boy, fundamentally decent, as were all of Captain Wauthier's copilots.

The late afternoons in Timbuctoo were really wonderful. At sunset everyone mounted to the roofs of the flat houses. The Moslems served tea to each other, sometimes accompanied by music and gossip. We and the French served *apéritifs* or lemonade, with biscuits we bought at the general store. And sometimes we had no company, or the company was late, and that's when I came to understand Timbuctoo a little better.

The setting sun painted the houses pink and cast purple shadows on the streets of sand. Long-robed men and women passed between the houses or farther out toward the horizon, where the town gave way to the desert. They were like characters from the Old Testament: Jeremiah, Ezekiel, Habakkuk and Zechariah. The women, some of whom carried pottery jars on their heads, reminded me of the Biblical women: Sarah, Ruth, Esther, and the one who offered that cup of cold water to a Stranger.

When one was alone on the roof of the caravanserai in Timbuctoo at sundown, it was easier to think in terms of ancient history than it was to think of M. and Mme. Dubois and their Parisian customs, or of the isolated airfield and the gossip. Timbuctoo whispered then of centuries gone to dust or sand, of a civilization that had died but had not yet been completely buried. It seemed to be waiting, in silence and dignity, for its own funeral.

Once, however, when I was up on the roof, I saw our handsome turbaned young guide rolling over and over on the sand. I picked up Willie's binoculars and saw that he was not in pain, as I had thought at first; he was doubled up with laughter which he was unable to contain, over some tremendous joke. I had forgotten that there were young people in Timbuctoo—Yakouba's grandchildren, for instance—who might bring the city to life again. Perhaps they are doing just that, today.

Our mission was drawing to an end. Willie had enough material for his book and was satisfied that there was nothing more to be gained by lingering in Timbuctoo or getting drunk with Yakouba, who even now was beginning to regret that he had spoken so freely, because the book might embarrass his grandchildren. Willie reassured him by saying that it didn't matter a damn what his grandchildren or great-grandchildren thought, because the only thing that mattered was "the truth" —and "leaving one's mark on the wall."

There was one thing more we had to do before returning to Paris, and that was to buy presents for everybody back home. In this if in no other way we were like all tourists. M. Dubois arranged for us to meet the merchants of leather goods, jewelry, etc., at the general store, where he would preside and see that we were not cheated.

I mention this more or less ordinary transaction because of an incident that occurred which, for me at least, cast a cloud over our visit.

The general store was a low wooden structure that had a porch with a railing around it. By the time we arrived, the railing was crowded with men dressed in clean djellabas and in fine humor, not unlike a crowd at home waiting for the circus to start. A space was made for us in the center of the store, and the first merchants came before us, with finely made leather goods, then silver and amber jewelry, copper, and carved wood. Willie bought some ancient locks, and several Tuareg shields which were made of something like parchment and which as insigne bore the Maltese cross, a relic of the Crusaders who had passed through Tuareg territory centuries before.

M. Dubois did the bargaining that was expected, and totaled the sums that were to be paid, and Willie took out his wallet and paid for everything we had bought, which was a lot. Then we all thanked each other profusely, the merchants departed, the crowd dispersed, and we walked slowly back to the caravanserai, followed by our two guides, who carried our loot in sacks on their head.

We had gone most of the way when Willie discovered he had lost his wallet. There was still a lot of money in it, but that didn't worry him as much as the loss of some important papers, not the least of which were the little scraps of notes he made on match folders and whatever bits of paper were at hand. He began to swear in French and English, and when Willie swore he could make a longshoreman sound like a maiden aunt.

He began by swearing at the trousers made for him by Mamadou Machine, so called because he was the only tailor in Timbuctoo to own a Singer sewing machine. "These ―― ―― trousers were made for women, not men," he said. "Come on, we'll retrace our steps and see if I dropped it in the sand."

We went back the way we had come, but there was no sign of the wallet—not on the sand, or on the veranda of the store, or in the store itself. We reported the loss to the Civil Administrator, who told us not to worry; the wallet would be found and returned. I noticed a peculiar gleam in the eyes of our friend, Monsieur Dubois, as if his own honor were involved and as if he were very angry. I was annoyed, too, because I thought that if Willie hadn't had three big drinks of the store's best brandy while buying those souvenirs, he wouldn't have had trouble finding the pockets in his trousers.

That night, as we were having our late dinner of goat—which was evidently the only meat our cook knew how to prepare, and of which everything seemed to smell and taste, even the wine— there was an interruption.

We were seated at a crate that served as a dining table. On it was a guttering candle stuck in a bottle and shedding light only in its immediate vicinity. We suddenly heard footsteps, and then out of the massive shadows in the empty room stepped Monsieur Dubois, followed by a section of the native gendarmerie. In their midst were two tall, handsome citizens of

Timbuctoo, dressed in long robes, their heads turbaned, their necks hung with *gris-gris*. They also wore handcuffs.

Without preamble, the little Administrator held out a wallet. "Is this yours?" he asked Willie, who nodded.

Monsieur Dubois said something in Arabic, and the prisoners were shoved so that they almost stumbled. They were now standing where we could see them clearly.

"Where was it found?" Willie asked, breaking an unbearable silence.

Monsieur Dubois pointed to one of the tall, frightened men. "This one had it, but they were both spending money like fools in the market place. Count, and see how much is lacking." He threw the wallet on the wooden crate. Willie pushed it aside. "Thank you," he said, quietly. "I'm glad it was returned."

"Canaille!" said the Administrator, furiously. "They knew it was the property of a stranger in their midst. They should have returned it immediately. They have dishonored the traditions of hospitality, and that is a crime more serious than stealing."

I had been staring in embarrassment down at my plate. Now I felt the eyes of the two prisoners boring into me and I looked up. They were pleading with me, as the only woman present, to ask for mercy. I started to say something, but Willie put out his hand and stopped me. "We must not interfere," he said, in English. "Be quiet!"

And so we kept silent as the prisoners were led from the room. Monsieur Dubois nodded, apologized, and strode out.

"What will happen to them?" I asked.

"They will probably be whipped," Willie said. Then he added, "What puzzles me is why they kept the damn thing. They knew it belonged to me. They were, in a way, my hosts. I remember a story I heard when I was here last. A party of strangers came to Timbuctoo on a very cold night. The city was poor at the moment because it had just suffered a raid from the Tuaregs. There was no firewood to be had, so they took down the handsomely studded door of their finest house, chopped it up, and made a fire for the strangers within their gates."

"Our European civilization has had a demoralizing effect,

then," Captain Wauthier said. "There are some races who do not lend themselves to conquest. How they must hate us!"

I have often thought of those two proud men, and how they asked with their eyes for me to speak up in their behalf, and how, because Willie ordered me to say nothing, I kept quiet.

A few days later, our notes finished, we thanked Père Yakouba, promised to let him see the book when it was ready for publication, said farewell to the Duboises and our friends at the airfield, and left Timbuctoo. It had been a tremendous experience, this month in one of the world's oldest cities, but I was not sorry to leave. And neither, I think, was Willie.

Chapter Ten

Our next stop was Bamako, on the Niger River, not far from the coast. From there we expected to head north for Casablanca, Barcelona, Biarritz, and home. That is, Paris. We had a brief-case full of notes about Père Yakouba. Our Mission Ethnographique was completed.

Compared with Timbuctoo, Bamako was a teeming, modern, progressive city, with a large, well-run hotel that seemed the last word in comfort and luxury. We wallowed in hot showers and *apéritifs* with ice before dinner, and I took a walk by myself through the market place, until I was followed by so many laughing children it became embarrassing and I felt like the Pied Piper of Hamelin without his flute.

Captain Wauthier had a number of friends in Bamako, and we had planned to stay a few days. I remember we did a lot of sight-seeing by car, went swimming in a swimming pool called the Lido, and visited the local celebrity, a French artist named Francis Boeuf, who gave me a small painting of one of the mosques of Timbuctoo. (I have it here on the wall above my desk in Fort Lauderdale as I write, and I can feel the heat of the day easing a little as the sunset stained the ancient building purple and rose. I can feel the sand on my bare feet again, and smell the leather and the goatskin. And I can sense again the mystery that no writer or painter has ever really described, and the sadness.)

During dinner the second night of our stay in Bamako, Captain Wauthier was handed a message that was to change all our plans. A French flyer named Régenancy, on a reconnaissance flight over the Sahara, had failed to report at the scheduled time, and it was feared that he had come down *en panne*, as they called a mechanical failure, or had lost his way. He had not been heard from in nearly eight hours, and an order had gone out for every plane available in the area to join the search for him.

I remember that we were dining in the open courtyard of the hotel, with French spoken all around us and everything so patently European it looked like a deliberate attempt to hide the fact that Bamako was in Africa, that nine-tenths of its teeming population was African, and that we really didn't belong here at all.

Captain Wauthier, who had been gay and charming, suddenly turned gravely serious. "Seabrook," he said, "I must join the search. I hope you don't mind. Régenancy is an old *copain,* you understand."

"Of course you must go," Willie said. He patted Wauthier's shoulder, and I knew he was scenting excitement and preparing for it. He had been getting very bored with Bamako. "What is more, *mon vieux,*" he went on expansively, "I will go with you, as copilot."

I sat and looked at both of them. I was about to say, "When do we leave?" but they turned to me, and my heart sank.

"This will be a very dangerous mission," Captain Wauthier said. "We will, of necessity, have to fly without a chart. There is danger of running out of gas where there is no place to re-fuel. We must unload our plane and fly as light as possible."

"Sorry, Mink," Willie said. "You can't go along. We'll have to come back for you."

Mine not to reason why, mine but to do or—what? So I said, "Oh, please, not Bamako."

They talked it over and decided that since Gao was on the route to Fort-Lamy at Lake Chad, where the orders were to report before joining the search party, they would drop me at Gao and come back for me when and if Régenancy was found. We left at dawn the following morning.

Of all the towns in the Sahara that I visited, I liked Gao the best. I was tired, and the relief of being on my own for a while

91

was tremendous. Living with Willie was like living next to a dynamo, or maybe I should say a steam roller. It was exciting but exhausting. This was a chance to catch my breath. Pretty soon I started to worry about Willie—but at least for the first twenty-four hours I was alone in Gao, I enjoyed it.

Because this was a terminal of the Trans-Saharan Company, there was a comfortable hotel, but it made no pretense of being chic. It was run by a bourgeois French couple, and the bar was a meeting place of the handful of French soldiers stationed in Gao.

There was a moment of near panic when I saw our plane go off at dawn and I returned with the officer who had driven us out to the airfield. I suddenly realized that I was on my own in a little town in almost the center of Africa!

As I rearranged the baggage from the "General Lapperine" that had been dumped in my room the night before, I asked myself what I should do if something happened to our plane, and Willie and Captain Wauthier were lost. After all, *I* didn't have a contract for a book about Père Yakouba, and I couldn't expect anyone to send me all the money it would take to fly me back to the United States. Then I began worrying about Willie; and then I thought that if anything did happen to him I wouldn't care what happened to me, and I stopped worrying.

I left the cluttered room and went out for a walk. To walk about in any unknown city is always interesting. To walk about in Gao on the Niger was exciting and delightful. I found myself on the bank of the river, where women were washing clothes, children were wading, and blue herons, pink flamingos, pelicans, and birds I couldn't name hopped around or dove into the brown water with no more fear of human beings than pigeons in Central Park.

Along the embankment was a low stone wall on which young men and women were seated with their legs dangling. They wore brightly colored clothing, spotlessly clean, with jewelry hanging from their necks, ears, arms, and legs. They smiled to me and waved as I passed, and I smiled and waved back and loved them. Gao, I discovered, was a much happier place than

Timbuctoo. The people seemed to carry their history more lightly.

For the next few days, in spite of a natural anxiety, I found plenty to do. Walking through the open market was fascinating, as always, and I was particularly interested in watching a man being shaved by the local barber, who used a piece of sharpened glass for a razor. The local storyteller was standing in the midst of a group of interested men in djellabas and abas, conveying the news and padding it with bits of remembered legends. It brought home to me more than it had before, how the French, with their general stores, post offices, and comfortable hotels, had not changed local customs.

I was invited to lunch at the home of the Commandant, an event that consumed a whole afternoon, and then I walked back to the hotel because the Commandant had been summoned to the airfield and I insisted that I could find my way. I passed the native compound, composed of thatched-roofed, round huts. I heard angry voices, shouts, and then a blood-curdling scream, and hurried by, scared to death, with visions of being caught all alone in the midst of a one-village race riot! Later it was explained to me as the normal ill humor that existed toward the approach of sunset each day during the month of Ramadan. Fasting for twenty-four hours seemed to shorten tempers and there was often fighting and sometimes bloodshed.

The end of Ramadan is celebrated with a grand fête, and I was lucky enough to be in Gao when it took place. As the sun went down on the last day of the long fast, there was shouting and laughing and a great hubbub that continued all night, so nobody was able to sleep. The next day all the townspeople were dressed in their best finery, and there was dancing in a great open space near the compound.

The Commandant's wife, a charming, delicate little woman, very kindly asked me to join her group to watch the dancers. I had the feeling that I was back in Harlem again: the same or very similar movements of the handsome dark bodies, the same rhythms beaten out on ornamental drums. Here was the origin of *le jazz hot,* ragtime, rock 'n' roll, the heady syncopation that

93

we have thought of as America's cultural contribution to the world. I wished that Carl Van Vechten and Noel Coward were with me. The performers were gay, impudent, brash, and happy, drunk not on gin, as they were in Harlem, but on cola nuts which their enthusiastic audience tossed at them to show approval.

I wished, of course, for Willie to share this excitement with me. It seemed very strange to have such an experience without him, almost as if I were acting in part of a film, the part with Willie in it having been left on the cutting-room floor.

Twice a day there were radio contacts with the rest of the Sahara, early in the morning and at sundown. I waited anxiously at both these hours for a message from Willie or Captain Wauthier. I learned only that the search for Régenancy was still continuing.

On the third night I sensed some unusual excitement in the hotel. A French lieutenant of the *Méharistes,* the French Camel Corps, had arrived with his entourage of Tuaregs. I had heard that these once-feared bands of men, who blackened their eyes with kohl like women and wore blue veils that hid the lower part of their faces, were no longer enemies but friends of the French. This friendship had been brought about by the tactful expedient of making each Tuareg an officer in the French army.

As I went to the bathroom before going to bed, I passed the door of the room in which the French officer slept. On either side of the door, guarding it, sat a Tuareg, fully clothed in white robes, turban, and blue veil, with a spear firmly held in front of him.

The next morning I was aware, every time I moved about the hotel, of dark eyes above blue veils regarding me with interest; and although I thought their interest might be flattering, it made me uneasy. There had still been no message from the "General Lapperine," and I was feeling worried and depressed.

The manager of the hotel, perhaps sensing my restlessness, told me that a couple of jewelry and leather merchants would like to show me their wares. What woman on earth could resist the temptation to spend money, especially if she was alone in a little town like Gao, where it seemed impossible?

I was seated in the dining room, with a space cleared before me, as the merchants brought out their amber and silver and semiprecious or worthless stones strung into necklaces. I was interested, and then fascinated. In fact, I was even unaware, at first, that I was surrounded by the Méhariste lieutenant's entire force of Tuaregs. They stood in a circle around my chair watching every move that was made and listening to every word that was spoken.

It made me very self-conscious, and so when I saw something I liked, I would point to it, the merchant would name a price, and I would reach into my purse and pay him. Gradually, I became aware of disapproval. The dark eyes above the veils had been admiring and approving at first, but now they had become angry. There was an occasional headshake, but I didn't understand, and finally, one by one, my Tuaregs glided silently out of the room. I realized too late how much I had disappointed them. They had come to see the American lady bargain with the merchant thieves. What they had seen was a timid fool who actually paid the price that was asked, without a murmur.

That same evening the radio message announced that Régenancy had been found alive though his plane had crashed in the Ahaggar Mountains. There was also a personal message for me. Because Willie and Captain Wauthier were already so far north, they would wait for me at Reggan. I was to get a car and drive up through the Sahara with our baggage and meet them. We would then proceed to Paris.

That made sense—except for a couple of drawbacks. I didn't drive and there were no cars available. There had been two cars in Gao, but the week before they had met head on in a collision.

There was, however, a Trans-Saharan Company truck, and it was decided to send me on that. The only question was whom to send with me. The choice fell between the Commandant's personal chauffeur, a huge black Kabyle, or the *chef du garage,* who was an expert mechanic. It was decided that I would be safer with the mechanic: if the truck broke down in the desert, he would know how to repair it.

At this point I didn't care how it was arranged. Willie, Captain Wauthier, and the "General Lapperine" were safe, not to mention Régenancy, and I would be with them again. I even looked forward to the long drive because it would give me an opportunity to get to know the Sahara. Flying over it as we had done was hardly better than seeing it on a motion-picture screen or in a TV documentary. Now I was going to be living in it, feeling the sand, baking in its scorching days and freezing in its nights. I was too thrilled at the prospect to entertain the least vestige of fear, although everyone else looked terribly concerned, including the lieutenant of the Méharistes, who did his charming best to entertain me in my last few hours in Gao.

At last the back of the truck was loaded with all our stuff and with a cask of water, canned food, a camp stove, and some loaves of bread that became so hard after the first day they had to be broken with a hammer. I sat next to the driver. Behind us was another long seat to stretch out on when tired. I was sure everything was going to be fine.

We rode through scrub brush for some time, and then there was sand, nothing but sand, yellow, hot, and inexorable. The heat was intense; feeling the reflection of the sun in addition to its direct rays was like being exposed to a vast oven with the door open on its blistering hinges.

I was wearing the loose khaki trousers made for me by Mamadou Machine, a thin silk blouse, and sandals on my bare feet. My hair was concealed by one of the Toulon bandannas I always wore, and the part of my face below my eyes was covered by a veil the Commandant's wife had given me at the last moment to protect my complexion. It was a comfortable costume, if not exactly chic. For the cold nights I had the burnoose Willie had bought for me in Oran, and, of all things, a short *lapin* jacket, which somehow got into my luggage and which proved extremely useful.

The hotel had prepared a cold lunch for our first day, and we ate that during the fiercest heat, sitting in the truck for shade. We drank wine with it instead of water, having a vague idea of conserving our water supply. The driver let some air out of our tires, and we proceeded. The wine, the heat, and the monotony made me sleepy and I took a siesta on the back seat. My dreams of excitement were dying down. When I awoke, the dunes were beginning to change color and there was a magnificent sunset. The air turned clear and cold, and I came to life again.

Our first scheduled stop for the night was an oasis called Tabankor, where there was a French military post. As we approached it in the dark, the eyes of wild animals reflected our headlights and gleamed at us in anger or surprise, through the grasses and the scrub brush, and I felt a little shiver creeping up my spine. Much as I love animals, I would have hated at that point to have made my first acquaintance with a lion or a jackal. I was too tired to cope.

All that mercilessly hot day we had traveled without seeing another car or another human being. I rather looked forward to being with people, if only to reassure myself that I was still part of the world as I remembered it. But Tabankor was not part of that world.

We arrived at night, and there was almost nothing to relieve the darkness but a campfire around which were standing or sitting men and officers of the French Desert Corps. With them were a few girls who might have been sisters of Lallah and the little prostitute of the Timbuctoo airfield. We were invited to join them; I accepted a cup of coffee, passed around my cigarettes, and tried to feel one of the party, but by this time I was like a sleepwalker. It was hard to keep my eyes open, and my body was full of aches and pains from the long, jolting ride.

At some point in the charade an officer in charge of the post arrived with many apologies. His radio had not been working that day, and he had received no notice of our plans to spend the night at Tabankor. He regretted that it was only a crude army post and that it was out of the question to offer me a bed in the barracks. Would I mind sleeping in one of the thatched huts in the native compound? I would at least have privacy.

I had that, but I also had a few nameless fears, and was ill in the bargain. I must have fallen asleep, because I found an extra blanket over me in the morning, placed there by my solicitous driver when the night became very cold. In the dawn I was sure I had contracted dysentery and would never reach Reggan alive.

We started off, and I began to feel better, which was a good thing, because it was to prove one of the most adventurous days in my life. It began by my noticing a significant change in the terrain around us. Instead of the monotonous stretch of sand, broken by an occasional series of sand dunes, the landscape had become black. Rock formations that rose on both sides of us were black. The ground under our tires was black. It was as if we had been suddenly set down upon another planet. It was a landscape painted by the Surrealist Magritte. It was a preview of hell!

"We are now passing through the Tanezruft," my driver explained. "A region that caravans avoid, because there is no water to be found anywhere, not for days. You can speak of this passage to your friends with pride, Madame. I do not think any other woman has driven over it before."

I tried to work up a feeling of pride, but I failed. However impressed I was, it was a relief to see the dunes again and to roll along the yellow sand—forever and ever and ever, it seemed, each hour an eternity.

That afternoon I saw my first mirage. I was sure we were approaching an oasis, with palm trees refreshingly green against the pale hot sky. It was only when we reached and passed the spot I had been watching that I realized it was an illusion, like so many earthly hopes and desires.

That was also the afternoon we got lost. I had been dozing in the front seat when I opened my eyes and noticed a skull lying on the right side of our path. Beside it was a rusty tin can. I mentioned it to my driver, who craned his neck and said, "A camel. *Pauvre bête*. Left behind by a caravan." I shut my eyes again, wondering about the fate of the camel and also about how long it took for man or beast to die of thirst under that damned sun.

I kept my eyes open now, and after we had been rolling along for some time I saw the skeleton of another camel—or so I thought, until I noticed a rusty tin can beside the skull.

"Look," I said, pointing to it, "isn't that the same camel we passed before?"

My driver peered to the right with bloodshot eyes; then he looked at me, raised his hands, and let them drop back on the wheel.

"We've been going around in a circle," I said. "We're lost!"

He nodded, and looked miserable. *"Oui, Madame,"* he said, "I have known it for some time. We are off the route, and I have been trying to find it again."

"Haven't you a compass—or something?" I asked.

No. He had no compass, and no radio. We were just supposed to follow a trail left by the enormous motorbuses that crossed the desert at intervals. What had happened was that a severe sandstorm had covered the tracks of the heavy bus wheels, and although there were posts set up for guidance farther north, at this point in the Sahara there was nothing to help us but the setting sun, which at least would indicate where the west was. Aside from that, we would have to rely upon luck.

Robert Monot, my driver, was a conscientious man and an expert mechanic, but he had never driven in the desert before. Nor did he have that sixth sense developed by those who knew the Sahara well, the sense that Captain Wauthier had to a degree and that Bauret, I learned later, had to the point of the miraculous.

We drove on for a while until darkness forced us to stop. Then we made camp at the base of a huge sand dune. At least we had got away from the ubiquitous camel and his rusty can! We prepared a dinner of *cassoulet* from one tin and cream of chestnuts from another, and we recklessly boiled a pot of coffee, using some of our dwindling water supply.

Then we sat on the sand and watched the stars come out,

and tried to reassure each other by guessing what they would do at Reggan and Gao if we didn't show up on schedule. What we didn't take into consideration was the fact that we had been expected to arrive that night at Bidon 5, where there was nobody to know if we arrived on schedule or not except the solitary Arab guardian of the gas pump, who wouldn't even be expecting us. And by the time they became aware, in Reggan, that we were off schedule, we could have traveled so far off the trail that we might never have been found.

I don't remember that I was really frightened. The desert night was indescribably beautiful, and I was too thrilled to the depths of my romantic soul to have room for any emotion as ignoble as fear. Except for a few moments when I wished that Willie were sharing the experience with me, I forgot who and what I was, egregious young sinner, aspiring writer, lost traveler in the desert—none of that was of any importance. I lay wrapped in my burnoose under a blanket of stars, and for a fragment of human time I sensed God's eternity.

The next day, after circling around most of the time, we got back on the route by accident and arrived at Bidon 5 in the night. We slept in the converted trailers and left early the following morning for what was the last lap of our journey. We must have been rather bedraggled by this time. I had been bathing myself with Elizabeth Arden's skin lotion instead of water, using a box of green tissues for towels. Willie had told me how people in the desert kept themselves immaculate by rubbing their bodies with sand, and perhaps that is what my driver did. I preferred Elizabeth Arden and was glad I had brought along a big bottle.

By this time my driver and I, although we were not calling each other by our first names, had come to know each other a little better. He had told me about his wife in France, and of his hopes now that he had come so far north of being allowed to take his vacation and continue to France, where he would join his wife. I found it a little harder to tell him about myself

100

and Willie, because it was too complicated to explain. We did talk of the comforts we would find at Reggan, of the hot, well-cooked meals, the iced drinks, and the long, cool showers.

After lunch that last day I stretched out on the back seat for a siesta. The heat was as intense as ever, and the sand as uncertain, so that my poor driver had to get out innumerable times to deflate the tires and then pump them up again. He sat hunched over the wheel, trying to follow an almost nonexistent trail with bloodshot eyes.

Suddenly I was awakened by a shout, and then more shouts, and I was sure we were being surrounded by a warlike tribe of Bedouins. I sat up and looked behind us. I saw a sleek station wagon pursuing us, and heard a voice cry, *"Arrêtez!"* I called out to my driver and he stopped the car. We heard the blast of the horn now, and then the station wagon drew up alongside us and stopped, and, to my astonishment, Raymond Bauret jumped out.

"Where do you think you are going?" he demanded of my driver. "If you had kept on in the direction you are taking, you would have ended in the Ahaggars." Then he turned to me, and snapped, "Get out, Mademoiselle."

I got out, but not without saying a few words myself. "If we were lost," I said, "it's nobody's fault but the Trans-Saharan Company's. And Willie's," I added, suddenly realizing that he could and should have come back after me in our plane instead of enjoying himself in a luxurious hotel at Reggan.

I was so indignant that I ran out of words, and I don't think I made any impression on Bauret. He left me abruptly after he had helped me get into the front seat of the station wagon. He had more things to say to my driver.

Bauret had brought another man with him, and the three of them made short work of transferring all our stuff from the back of the truck to the rear of Bauret's new station wagon. Then, before I realized what was happening, the truck turned around, driven by the other man, with M. Monot sitting beside him.

I turned, furious, to Bauret, who was driving his car swiftly and silently in a direction opposite to the one we had been taking. "Did you send M. Monot back through that hell again without giving him a chance to rest for a day or two?"

"It won't kill him," Bauret said sternly. "There is no excuse for him to have let himself get lost while he had you as a passenger. He knew that you and Monsieur Seabrook were distinguished guests of the Trans-Saharan Company. Suppose you had never been found? We should never have forgiven ourselves."

The tone of his voice had changed. He was actually looking at me for the first time, and smiling. "Look," he said, "I have a bottle of Napoleon brandy in the back of the car. I think we could both use a little drink, don't you? I am glad that we have found you."

I asked him then a purely feminine question. "Was Willie worried when it was known that I was lost?"

"Oh, yes," Bauret said. "He was beside himself with anxiety."

I knew this was an exaggeration, but I managed to find some consolation from it, and joined Bauret in a much-needed drink.

The drive to Reggan was a long one. Evidently we had gone way off the trail this last day, and it was lucky for us that so experienced a Saharan should have set out to find us. In a favorite book of my childhood, *The Crock of Gold,* I remember a dialogue between the two philosophers that went something like this:

"She does not want to be found, but we will find her."

"She does not want to be found, *therefore* we will find her!"

At one sublime moment under the stars, when I thought of being lost I was not sure I ever wanted to be found, to return to all the problems of my life with Willie. I had even quoted to myself from one of my beloved poets, "To be lost, if it must be so!" But now, driving along beside Bauret, one of the most beautiful young men I have ever met, and romantic, I was glad that I was found. I accepted another drink of twenty-year-old brandy, and did what any normal young woman would do

102

under the circumstances. I fell promptly and unashamedly in love.

It had nothing to do with the way I loved Willie. That was something so intricately bound up with the breath I breathed and the blood that channeled its way in and out of my heart that only death could have put an end to it. My death—not his. As different as we were in so many ways, we had become one. I was never to be free of Willie, and I don't think, to the very end, he was ever free of me.

But this was different. This was another kind of love, graceful, tender, romantic, superficial, soothing, and altogether lovely! He kept his arm protectively over my shoulder as we drove along, and there was time to tell each other the stories of our lives, somewhat dramatized for the occasion. I think I made myself out to be someone rather like Brett in *The Sun Also Rises*, and he reaffirmed the gossip image of himself as a man once betrayed by a beautiful woman and hence suspicious of all others to the point of avoiding any attachment as he would the plague. This was an irresistible challenge to any woman, just as my implied promiscuity was a challenge. It was what we intended, perhaps, subconsciously.

We stopped the car eventually, and walked in the desert, and came to rest at the foot of an enormous sand dune. Above us were the stars, around us was the soft, cool desert air, and the nearest eyes, ears, and voices were hundreds of kilometers away. He was like someone out of Greek mythology and I thought of myself, if I thought at all, as a dryad or nymph. We were too exalted to belong to the common breed of earthlings. We were, in fact, a young man and woman in the most romantic and perfect setting for making love.

Love-making, for Willie, was a complicated process, all mixed up with his complexes, fetishes, and compulsions. Some psychiatrists, among them the eminent Dr. Brill, had related his sexual fantasies to his desire to punish his mother, Myra, for some childish hurt. I had almost forgotten this other kind of love-making, and I responded to it normally.

103

I shall never understand why we didn't carry the whole lovely thing through to its ultimate conclusion. I think it's quite possible that we both, at an inconvenient moment, thought about Willie. I was his property, in a manner of speaking, and Bauret was his host! We talked of telling Willie that we were in love and that I must leave him. We built for ourselves a wonderful future which involved traveling all over the world and at the same time never leaving the Sahara, where we had met and to which we were now subtly and inevitably bound. It was all very mad and ecstatically, miraculously wonderful.

At about ten o'clock that night, we drove into the hotel compound at Reggan. They had waited dinner for us, and it was to be a gala feast. Most important to me was the look of pride in Willie's eyes, as if I had done something special by getting lost and found again. The hot shower and the thick Turkish towel felt marvelous, and I put on the one evening dress I had brought along. I was the only woman at a table filled with attractive and admiring men, and it was hard not to feel like the Queen of Sheba at a royal feast. It was harder still to remember a skull lying in the sand with a rusty tin beside it.

The next morning, as our plane was being rolled out to the front of the hotel, I told Willie that I was not going back to Paris with him in the "General Lapperine."

"What are you going to do?" Willie asked gravely.

"Stay in the Sahara for the rest of my life," I said.

Willie was silent for a moment or two. Then he said, "You will get fat, like Salama, and you'll grow too lazy to ever write another line. Besides," he added, "aren't you anxious to see whether Mr. Bradley succeeded in selling your novel to Alfred Knopf?"

Maybe that did it. Or it may have been the glimpse I had of Bauret in the light of the desert dawn, as he gave orders, that made me suddenly shy and doubtful. I could always return to him and our Sahara at a later time, I thought. In the meantime, I had better return to Paris with Willie, and help him sort out the notes on Père Yakouba.

Besides, Willie was standing at the door of my room with his hand stretched out to me. I took it and we walked to the plane together.

Chapter Eleven

The newspapers in the United States and France had evidently followed our "ethnographic expedition" with interest. We had our first inkling of this when we stopped to refuel at Biarritz and were met at the airfield by the Mayor and his committee. They made speeches and presented me with an enormous bouquet of red roses.

At Orly the field swarmed with reporters and cameramen. Among them I recognized our friend Man Ray, who was an avant-garde photographer as well as an artist. I waved to him, but he was busy shooting and then he ran away. I had come to expect a certain amount of public interest in whatever Willie did, but I didn't think flying over the Sahara on a purely literary errand deserved so much excitement. Willie, however, took it all for granted. Having been a newspaperman himself, he had all the right answers and gave the press something to write about, for which they were, as usual, grateful.

William Aspenwall Bradley and Mrs. Bradley were on hand to drive us back to Paris in style. We were escorted into the limousine of a wealthy American widow, who made a great to-do over Captain Wauthier; a few months later she married him.

My memory of that ride and the reception that followed is hazy, because on the way from Orly to Paris Mr. Bradley told me that Alfred Knopf had accepted *Mrs. Taylor*. I was immediately transported into my own private paradise, and everything else that was happening shrank into insignificance.

There were, however, so many parties planned for us, and so many important people to see, that Willie decided we had to change our mode of life somewhat and move into more elegant quarters. And so we moved from the Hôtel Place de l'Odéon, where there were no suites or even private baths, into a duplex apartment at the Studio Delambre, where such affluent celebrities as Bob Chanler stayed when they were in Paris. It was on the Left Bank, though, and just around the corner from the Dôme, where at any hour of the day and night we could run into our old friends as well as new, and where it was easy for everyone to drop in to see us.

I think Willie was at the very peak of everything that winter —health, creativeness, finances, fame, and success. It made me very happy, because just before we left for Timbuctoo he had gone through a period of deep depression. Worried, as he was periodically, about his drinking, and even afraid he was losing his mind, with Bradley's help he had gone to the sanatorium of a French doctor who put him through a course of calisthenics and kept him sober for a few weeks. At the end of that time he had recovered and seemed in good health and spirits. Then came the contract for the Père Yakouba book, and our trip.

Now he was in full possession of himself, bursting with energy, good humor, wit, and charm. Everything, as the song goes, was coming up roses for him, and he loved it. The spirit of deviltry was back in his eyes and made me a little uneasy. But in the eyes of the world he could do no wrong as long as he gave people something to talk about. And he did just that.

Our "mission" to Timbuctoo having received the seal of approval of the Trocadero Museum, Willie decided that it was only proper for him to give them a report of his findings. And so, with the help of our good friend Michel Leiris, one of the youngest members of the Trocadero, Willie invited a distinguished group of stuffed shirts, as he called them, to a luncheon at Foyot's. It was one of the best restaurants in Paris, located near the Senate and patronized by that august body. Before going to lunch, Willie's guests were asked to meet at the Studio Delambre for *apéritifs*.

I was busy about clothes at that time, Willie having for once given me carte blanche to dress like other women and not like

107

a Toulon market girl. A good friend, Suzanne Fabre, had sent me to one of those "little dressmakers" smart French women use, and I was having suits and dresses made that would have pleased my own fashion-conscious mother. I hated to spend time on fittings, but reveled in the results.

Suzanne's dressmaker was way over on the Right Bank, and I took a taxi across Paris when I was finished. Never had the city seemed more beautiful to me. It had rained earlier, the pavements were glistening, and everything looked as fresh and beautiful as the flowers in the stalls behind the Madeleine. I had known what it was to be miserably unhappy in Paris, broke, sick, lonesome; but this morning I knew what it meant to feel well, prosperous, successful, and on top of the world. There is no worse city than Paris in which to be miserable—and no better place in which to enjoy a state of euphoria.

The minute Willie opened the door of our apartment for me I began to be worried. He was wearing the beamish, cherubic expression I had come to know meant he was up to no good!

"I'm glad you've come, Mink," he said. "I want you to pour the drinks."

I hurried upstairs, took off my hat, powdered my nose, and came down to the studio. Willie had all the bottles, glasses, and siphons arranged on a coffee table and I took a seat behind it. Only when I was settled did I happen to glance across the room to the corner under the balcony.

There, hanging by her wrists from a chain, was Mimi, one of the call girls of Montparnasse, who would do almost anything for money and who had her *"homme d'affaires"* or business manager. She was wearing a leather skirt that Willie had brought from Africa, similar to one that Lallah wore. She was naked from the waist up, and her bare toes just touched the floor.

Before I had time to say anything, the first of Willie's distinguished guests arrived. He was typical of the others who followed soon after him, a dignified, elderly Frenchman in conventional formal day attire, with a rosette or ribbon in his buttonhole, either red for the Legion of Honor, green for the Mérite Agricole, etc.

They entered, smiling or bowing, murmuring polite phrases. They started walking across the room to where I was sitting, to bow again and kiss my hand. But on the way there was a double-take as their sharp brown eyes caught a glimpse of the half-nude girl suspended from the balcony. There would be an almost imperceptible gasp, then the eyes were quickly averted and the ceremony of being introduced continued as if nothing extraordinary had happened.

I poured Cinzano, Dubonnet, Amer Picon, or one of the other bittersweet *apéritifs* the French love. I added ice and soda or water, and smiled, and the smile felt as stiff as if I had painted it on with abrasive material. The talk was about Timbuctoo and the varieties of African races to be found there.

I was afraid that Michel Leiris, who was a little later than the others, would make some remark about Mimi when he finally arrived. But he was thoroughly French, too, and said nothing. When it was time for them all to leave for the luncheon at Foyot's, they made polite farewells to me and filed out of the studio, Willie trailing after them with a smile of his own that was like the Cheshire cat's.

I gave Mimi a stiff drink, cleaned up the mess of glasses, and went out to buy myself an elegant lunch at a nearby restaurant where I would be surrounded by normal people.

Because of the tremendous sale of Willie's books in their French translation, we naturally met a lot of French people. Among them was Fernand D'Ivoire, editor of *L'Intransigeant,* one of the most influential newspapers of the day. It was he who introduced us to Daniel Leperq, a tall Norman Frenchman who had been connected in some mysterious way with the Vatican and still bore the title of Monseigneur. We paid many visits to his Montmartre apartment, where he continued to receive a flock of distressed people whom he advised and helped although he wore no clerical garb and did not have a diocese. He was a superb cook, and I remember one night when we were invited to dinner along with the D'Ivoires and some other friends. The food was incredibly good and so were the wines, and so was the conversation. But before dinner he had received us in a small room with an altar and had held a service for all of us. Willie said he was a practitioner of White Magic. He was certainly a good man and an infinitely kind one and he became one of our dearest friends in France.

Besides the French literary world of publishers and writers, we came to know a great many of the fashionable Parisians, the set to which Princess Murat belonged. There was, for example, the Hon. Mrs. Reginald Fellowes ("Daisy"), one of the world's best-dressed women, and I suppose one of the wealthiest, and possibly one of the least satisfied. She had a genuine talent and might have been a literary success had she not had so many other interests. Her wealth came from a family connection with the American Singer Sewing Machine fortune. She was small and slender, and looked American except for her mouth, which had a French mobility—she spoke with an English accent crossed with French—and she had a directness and a kindness that were American. Most Parisiennes are hard and impatient with anything that does not come up to their standards.

I liked her very much, and while I suffered from galloping jealousy most of the time, I was pleased when Daisy Fellowes took a strong liking to Willie. Perhaps because I sensed that he was a little in awe of her—she had so much of everything! And yet, when I told her I had read her novel, *Les Filles du Diable,* she looked so astonished and pleased (just as I would have looked had someone read my own first book) that I suspected she would have given up her reputation as one of the world's best-dressed women to be considered a serious novelist.

Willie had told me that Daisy Fellowes thought she was being hexed by an English actress and had asked him for advice and help to counteract the spell that was ruining her health and making her unhappy. Willie, who had written and was to write a lot about witches and witchcraft, really believed in it. I'm afraid I didn't, although I tried never to show my own skepticism. There were many sides of Willie that I found hard to understand or to go along with, but they all added up to the person Willie was—and I loved him. Being in love means accepting a lot one doesn't like or understand. I did my best to follow along, and when I couldn't we were both miserable.

When we returned this time from Timbuctoo, Daisy Fellowes gave an elaborate dinner party in her house at Neuilly. I remember the white dining room with walls of mirrors and tables of mirrors and crystal chandeliers; everything sparkled, including the beautiful women and the brilliant men and the conversation. I was seated down the table somewhere, and my dinner partner was Sir Charles Mendl, the husband of Elsie de Wolfe. He was charming and kind and humorous and soon made me forget my natural shyness. Later there was entertainment in the ballroom. Finally I was reunited with Willie and we went away together.

I had felt like a spectator all evening, but Willie had been in the heart of the thing and I thought he had enjoyed it. On the way to the Studio Delambre, though, he slumped back on the seat of the cab and held my hand, like a child who has been through an ordeal and escaped alive.

There was a dinner I enjoyed much more that Willie gave for Violette, Daisy, and Douglas Fairbanks. It was at the Brasserie Schmidt, our usual hangout on the Place de l'Odéon. Douglas Fairbanks and Mary Pickford were divorced by then, and he had not yet married the English beauty who was his third wife. He was very good-looking, with a little gray in his hair, and utterly charming, but he seemed rather subdued and a little sad. He talked of his days as a swashbuckling movie star, and said that the time had come when he had to be his age and he didn't like it. He and Willie got along well, perhaps because Willie, too, dreaded getting old.

Willie decided we were getting soft and fat from too much wining and dining, and so he hired an Algerian ex-prize fighter

111

to give him a workout every afternoon in our studio. Since the time for this workout coincided with the *apéritif* or cocktail hour in Montparnasse, people would drop in and enjoy their drinks while watching Willie spar with the Algerian. After a rubdown Willie would rejoin his guests clad in a Turkish towel wrapped around his middle, while I was getting a massage upstairs in the bedroom. I suppose it did help to rub out some of the alcohol we were consuming in great quantities, but it amused our guests, especially our English friends, who thought it another quaint American custom.

Willie's books had been almost as successful in England as they were in the United States and France. His English publisher had been up to then our friend Jonathan Cape, who was also my publisher. For some reason which I never understood clearly, there had been a disagreement over contracts or the advance for our Timbuctoo trip, or something that caused a rift between Willie and Jonathan. It could have been straightened out, but it wasn't. I only know that when we returned to Paris from Africa, Willie was still angry and insisted that his agents, Ann Watkins in the United States and Mr. Bradley in Paris, find him another English publisher. They did so, and *The White Monk* was promised to George Harrap, of London.

This explains why, one evening during that season in Paris, we were entertaining George Harrap, who was a stocky, hard-boiled Londoner, given to wearing racy clothes and to speaking bluntly. He was the exact opposite of Jonathan, who had a military bearing and looked the part of a distinguished English publisher.

Willie invited Captain Wauthier to join us, and we started with an excellent dinner at one of the famous Paris restaurants. Then, I think, we sat through one or two acts at the Folies-Bergère. So far all went according to the rules for entertaining visiting VIP's. But Willie wanted to do something special for his new publisher, and so we went to the rue Blondel.

This was a street in some ways like Fifty-third Street west of

112

Fifth Avenue during the forties. Night clubs blazed side by side, music crashed out of the swinging doors. Every form of entertainment, almost, could be found there, to suit all tastes, from legitimate to depraved. But the rue Blondel, before the police acquired a chief who cleaned it up, was more of *everything* than any American *boîte* would dream of being.

The *boîte* to which Willie took his new, solidly British publisher was to all appearances just a café entered directly from the street. It was called "La Belle Poule" and was rather famous, although we had never visited it before. I was prepared for a more or less risqué floor show, but there was no stage, no dance floor, no orchestra, no master of ceremonies. Just a lot of marble-top tables close together and all occupied by more or less ordinary tourists and a lot of French people.

What distinguished La Belle Poule from other cafés was that the waitresses were stark naked. They took orders for drinks, sat down at the table with the patrons, or acted as if they wished someone would invite them upstairs—if there was an upstairs. They looked like a lot of undressed scullery maids, I thought, and I found them sickeningly embarrassing. So, I am sure, did Willie's guest. He sat stonily drinking champagne. It was hard to tell what Captain Wauthier thought. He was so polite and agreeable. And French.

Willie ordered bottle after bottle of champagne, which the girls he invited to the table drank up thirstily. I felt as if I were taking part in some avant-garde play. It was real enough, and at the same time sub-real. I could feel George Harrap's disapproval coming out in prickly thorns all over him, and most of it was directed at me. I stopped trying to appear amused and just sat looking as depressed as I felt. Why, I asked myself, did vice when it was presented for public consumption have to be so ugly and sordid? There was a spirit of camaraderie in the room that didn't touch us. We belonged, I guess, to a race that undresses in the dark.

At last, Willie asked if we were ready to leave, and we all jumped up. We took a cab to the Café de la Paix and drank coffee to kill the taste of bad champagne and when we said good night to George Harrap, I felt that all was forgiven.

The cafés of Montparnasse were filled with Americans. Some had come to study and to paint and write or compose music. Some had come to France in order to be able to drink as much as they liked openly, since those were the years of Prohibition in our own country. And some came because the franc at that time was worth four cents in American money, and a small income could be easily stretched, even in Paris, where one could get a good meal for thirty-two cents and a room in a Left Bank hotel for as little as or less than a dollar a night.

There were other reasons for the influx, of course. There was "freedom," for instance. Freedom to live as one liked and with whom one liked—and to read what one liked! Censorship was rigid at home, but here you could buy the most outrageously pornographic books right out on the street. However, some books were not on sale in the ordinary book stalls of Paris. These dealt with what the French called *mœurs spéciales*. France being a Catholic country, and also, since the casualties of the First World War, interested in the increase of its birth rate, was not as lenient toward the variations on the theme of love as many people supposed. But there were shady little shops within the enclosure of the Palais-Royal that catered exclusively to strange forms of eroticism, and I knew that from time to time Willie received some of these books by mail.

One day he took me with him to the bookstore with which he dealt most often. We walked along the arcade of the Palais-Royal, past windows displaying all sorts of merchandise, including African masks, shrunken heads, antique jewelry, and made-to-order shoes. We entered one of the shabbiest of the stores, where the bookseller was seated at a roll-top desk, filling orders.

When Willie introduced himself, he was greeted with enthusiasm. During the conversation that followed it was learned that another of the bookseller's customers had expressed a fervent wish to meet the famous author.

This other customer, he explained, was a woman "of a certain age" . . . *une femme du monde* . . . who had had a slight misfortune. Someone had thrown acid in her face, and she was badly scarred on one side. Therefore she was timid about showing herself, and went out rarely.

I could see Willie becoming interested, and I feared the worst when he agreed to meet his admirer at any time or place the bookseller would arrange with her. And on this promise, we left the store.

For the next week we were kept busy with parties, art exhibits, theater, concerts: whatever we busied ourselves with in Paris, aside from sitting on the terraces of the Dôme or the Select with friends, absorbing *fine à l'eau* along with gossip.

And then, one day, there came a *petit bleu,* one of those small blue envelopes that could be mysteriously shot through a tube all over Paris, to arrive faster than a telegram. It was from the Palais-Royal bookseller and it announced a rendezvous with the scar-faced woman at a certain time on a certain day. Willie took me with him.

We rode in a taxi to a crowded, unromantic section of Montmartre and climbed several flights of stairs and rang a bell. After an interval, the door was opened by a large-framed individual wearing a tailored suit, a frilly blouse, glacé kid gloves, a hat, and a veil. From behind the veil issued a staccato rush of words, and we were led down a narrow hall with closed doors on either side to a small room at the end.

There was a couch with a fancy pink silk cover and lots of fussy taffeta cushions, two gilt chairs, several small tables, and cheap carpeting. On the typically French wallpaper—purple trellises with red and pink cabbage roses climbing up them to the ceiling—were hung several sentimental chromos. The lace curtains were drawn and light was provided by several pink-shaded lamps. This was a *"petit salon."*

I wondered why our hostess kept on her coat, hat, and gloves, as if she had just come in or were just going out. Then I stopped wondering or caring. She had lifted her veil and there was the

115

livid scar, purple and angry-looking, covering the entire left side of the poor creature's face.

She talked to Willie and Willie talked to her, fast colloquial French, all about their mutual erotic fancies and fetishes. I couldn't understand half and didn't care much. I had cultivated an ability to be present with the body and absent with the spirit. It was very helpful. I just hoped they would go on talking and forget about me.

At one point I was asked to pour sweet wine from a heavy cut-glass carafe into tiny glasses. As I handed one of these to our hostess I spilled a few brownish drops on her horrible kid gloves, and I was rewarded with a look so cruel and unreasonably annoyed that I was frightened.

Shortly after this, to my great relief, Willie decided to end the visit. At the end of the hall I saw a colored servant standing at a door in the wall that had opened. Some money passed hands, and the three of us descended to the street together. The woman asked to be dropped at another address and when the cab reached it she started to get out. She said good-bye effusively to Willie, and then she leaned across him, pulled up her veil, and planted a kiss on my mouth! The next minute she was out of the cab and the door slammed.

I felt as if an icicle or a cold sword had touched me. I also had a moment of illumination. "Willie," I said, "that wasn't a woman. It was a man!"

He stared at me for a moment, in disbelief, and then he roared with laughter.

More parties. More people. More drinking. Too much drinking. And Willie was worried and unhappy again. Periodically he would worry about his drinking and stop for a while. Now he had not one book to write, but two. Alfred Harcourt seemed to think that because of the publicity and the general interest displayed in our trip to Timbuctoo, Willie should write up an account of our expedition, to be called *Air Adventure*. Everyone thought it could be done quickly and easily before he settled down to the serious job of writing *The White Monk of*

116

Timbuctoo. That was a major mistake on the part of his publishers and his agent, Ann Watkins. Willie had been spending the early mornings in Paris sorting out his notes, and he was beginning to get the feel of the book about Yakouba. It would not be easy, as we were to find out, to switch his mind to something else.

It was time to get down to work. We left Paris early one spring morning and drove to the South of France in the Citroën. We felt as if we were going home again.

Chapter Twelve

While we were away that winter, electricity and running water had been installed at 2 bis Quai du Parti, and although that made living there somewhat more comfortable, for some reason part of the charm was gone.

Willie decided it was time to change our way of living anyhow, and so we moved from the stone-floored, stone-walled studio on the Toulon waterfront to a twenty-room villa on the Mediterranean suitable for an exiled Russian Grand Duke.

The Villa Les Roseaux was of pale yellow stone with a red roof. Its imposing front entrance faced the sea and a private bathing beach that we shared with the Aldous Huxleys. An entrance from the road approached the rear of the house and was the one we used. Here there was a courtyard with a grove of plane trees at one side making an oasis of shade. And here, when the moon was right, a nightingale sang to us.

There was a large and incredibly unattractive living room that we almost never used, and a small salon fitted out with gilded petit point chairs that we never found a use for, either, because we did all our entertaining in the paved courtyard. The dining room was crowded with heavy dark furniture and outfitted with enough Wedgwood china and heavily embossed flat silver for a banquet.

The kitchen, reached by a flight of stairs from the courtyard, had an old-fashioned charcoal stove with an enormous hood over it. There was a wine cellar in the basement, where, in the coldest, dampest, darkest corner someone had installed a bathtub, the only one in the whole villa.

The bedrooms, however, were large, beautifully furnished, and very comfortable. Ours had long windows and a balcony overlooking the blue sea, and a wood-burning fireplace to take the chill away from the tiled floor on cold days. There were dressing rooms between the bedrooms, and they had porcelain washstands and running water. Up on the third floor there were so many servants' rooms that we used them for guests when we had an overflow.

In the courtyard, at right angles to the villa, was a narrow two-story house which Willie took for his own use. He furnished the downstairs room with his Arabian hangings, African masks, a large couch, and his typewriter and table. In winter this is where we entertained and sat, because it was warmer and cozier than the big living room in the main house. One of our guests called it "Hell's Kitchen."

At the left of the entrance gates was a two-car garage with an apartment over it that I used for my workroom. Here, in the few hours a day I could have to myself, I wrote, or gathered the pieces of my own personality together. It was a haven of retreat at times when I badly needed one.

The Villa Les Roseaux was situated on a neck of land called La Gorguette. It was between the fishing villages of Bandol and Sanary, about an hour from Marseilles on the west, and a half hour from Toulon on the east, along a strip of coast that was not yet considered part of the French Riviera. There were almost no other Americans besides ourselves, and the Huxleys were the only English. It was, for the most part, a vacation land for the French.

Willie and I seemed to have embarked on a good way of life. He had contracts for two books, and I, encouraged by the enthusiasm of the Knopfs and Mr. Bradley, was starting another novel. We wrote in the morning, stopping a little before noon, when we would walk to either Sanary or Bandol before lunch for *apéritifs* at one of the waterfront cafés. Sanary still had the atmosphere of a fishing village. Nets were spread and mended on the shore, and in the central market fishwives offered whatever their husbands had caught that morning, silvery sardines, *rougets, rascasses,* and sometimes eels—all the best ingredients for a *bouillabaisse.* There was an open bakeshop where we could

119

watch the loaves of bread being shoved into brick ovens and pulled out again, brown and fragrant. All of us did our marketing in Sanary. Bandol, on the other hand, was beginning to get sophisticated. There were several cafés and there was even a fashionable *boîte* for dancing at night. We usually had our noon drinks at a café run by a couple from Paris, who would join us and our friends in rounds of drinks and gossip.

We ate lunch in our courtyard, at a long wooden table covered with oilcloth. At the beginning we had only two to help: Wioland, the gardener, who was tremendously helpful about a lot of things but who never did anything much about a garden; and Anna, the little *femme de chambre,* who came from a farm back of Sanary. She was small and stocky and had one squinting eye. She spoke no English. She couldn't cook very well, either. In fact, there was only one dish we could always depend upon, *polenta.* This was a sort of glorified cornmeal mush, left to harden and then cut with a string on a board. Over it was poured a spaghetti sauce. With a salad, crisp French bread and our good local wine, it made a fairly decent meal. Only, *polenta* was supposed to be strictly for the peasants, and we gave it to our gourmet friends such as Ford Madox Ford and William Aspenwall Bradley.

After Willie's nap, which followed lunch no matter where he was or whom we were entertaining, we would take a walk or go for a swim. On these walks we would pass the Huxley house, which was very modern for those days and had a garden with rose trees exactly like those in Tenniel's illustration for *Alice.* Everything about the place was very neat and English.

One day when I was alone in the courtyard of the villa, feeding my cats, Maria Huxley came to call. She was a small, slender woman with cameo-cut features in a long oval face. She wore a large straw hat and white gloves, and her linen dress was beautifully made. She was Belgian, and spoke with a slight and charming accent.

She addressed me as Madame Seabrook. I hesitated, and then told her I called myself Marjorie Worthington. She accepted

120

that with a grave smile, and invited us to dinner the following Tuesday evening at eight o'clock.

Because of those early novels, *Chrome Yellow, Antic Hay,* and the rest, which I had admired tremendously, I expected the company that evening would be devastatingly clever. Willie also was an admirer of Huxley's books, especially *Brave New World* with its prophecy of thought control and drugs that changed people's beliefs and made slaves of them.

I was a little nervous as we walked up the hill, both of us dressed as formally as possible. We were supposed to be ultra sophisticates, but we really weren't. Willie always remained seven-tenths small boy and I was often as shy and self-conscious as if I had never left home. In spite of all this we had a very good time.

Aldous rose to greet us as we entered the house, towering over everybody and everything. He was like a tall poplar tree that sways at the top, his head thrust forward in order to see better. An attack of keratoritis had almost blinded him while he was a student at Eton, and since then he had worn thick glasses that made his eyes seem enormous. (Later in his life, when he abandoned glasses, he reminded me, oddly enough, of Abraham Lincoln.) Maria, in contrast, was almost birdlike, exquisitely dainty, and that night beautiful in a white crepe pajama dress by Molyneux. In World War I she had been a Belgian refugee who fled to London, where Virginia Woolf befriended her and introduced her to the Bloomsbury set of writers and painters, and where she and Aldous met and were married.

That evening, in addition to their son, Matthew, and his little cousin, Sophie, there was another guest, a young German girl, very blonde and red-cheeked, wearing a dinner jacket and a monocle. She was introduced to us as La Baronne something or other, a long German name I've forgotten. She was a protégée of the Huxleys, and much later, as Sybille Bedford, was the author of several brilliantly written books published in England and the United States. With her mother and sister she had fled from Hitler, and was living in sudden poverty on the outskirts of Sanary.

The conversation after dinner turned to Germany and the sudden rise of the Nazi regime. Sybille told us that a number of writers had already arrived in southern France and had found houses in our little sheltered corner of La Gorguette. She named Lion Feuchtwanger, Arnold and Stephan Zweig, and a few others. Thomas Mann and his family were the latest arrivals, she said. And they, like the rest, seemed bewildered at what was happening and beset with fears for their beloved country and the people they had left behind.

Willie offered to give a party for the Germans in our courtyard, and Sybille promised to do the inviting. A day was set, and to our surprise, they all came: the Zweigs, the Feuchtwangers, the Meiergraefes, the Schickeles, and the Manns. Although they all knew each other by reputation, it was the first time some of them had actually met. Feuchtwanger and Meiergraefe were loquacious and amusing, but the others were heavy with the private sorrows they had brought with them. Thomas Mann, who knew very little English and hardly more French, said nothing, but let his wife talk for him.

Madame Mann was a small, brisk woman with light hair and a rather pretty face. It was she and not her husband who had Jewish blood, although with his intellectual honesty it would have been impossible for Thomas Mann to have remained silent in a Nazi Germany.

The party got off to a slow and heavy start. We had drinks set up on the long wooden table, and the sort of things that went with brandy and whiskey and gin, and the minor *apéritifs*. But most of the Germans didn't drink alcohol, and so I had to change course in midstream and rush into the kitchen to help Anna make coffee and tea, with bread and butter and cake.

Madame Mann told me her husband would eat only German cooking, and so they had brought their old cook along with them, and now, with their six children, the house they had rented on La Gorguette was much too small.

I looked at the twenty-room villa in which there were many rooms we never used at all, and I spoke to Willie about it. He told Madame Mann that if she cared to send any of the over-flow to us we would be glad to give them a bed to sleep in, if they would leave the house in the morning and not return until night. She was delighted, and eventually we acquired Golo, the second-eldest son. He was an unobtrusive house guest, with whom we exchanged hardly more than a daily *"Bon jour"* and *"Bon soir."* Anna told us that he slept with a loaded revolver under his pillow.

Once he brought an invitation from his mother to dine with them that evening. Willie promised to go, but when Golo came for us Willie had drunk too much cognac and was reluctant to move from his chair. He murmured his regrets, and we could both see that Golo was terribly disappointed. He described the *gâteau à la crême* his mother had baked especially for us, and at the mention of it I expected Willie, who never ate sweets, would be sick. Instead he rose unsteadily to his feet and said in that case we could not disappoint her and must go. I remember the overcrowded little dining room and the groaning table at which Thomas Mann, long-faced and solemn with pince-nez glasses, said nothing. His brother Heinrich was there, however, and he helped brighten the evening with funny stories that mostly fell flat. Sybille had told us that in Germany Heinrich was much more popular than his illustrious brother. He was a journalist whom we, in America, came to know for the *Blue Angel* in which Marlene Dietrich and Emil Jannings starred. I was grateful to him that evening for the way he covered up for Willie, who was making a valiant effort not to fall asleep or be sick!

It was, on the whole, a fairly happy summer, that first one at the Villa Les Roseaux. We had a lot of company, from Paris and from the United States. Some were old friends, such as Ward Greene and Max Eastman. Greene had written a novel about Willie called *Ride the Nightmare,* which I resented, but it did nothing to impair a friendship that went back to their days together on the Atlanta *Journal.* Max Eastman came with his

Russian wife, Ilyana, and stayed a few days. He and Willie had been poor boys together at Mercersberg Academy, both sons of ministers. Willie showed me a scar on his right hand and told me he and Max had cut themselves and mixed drops of their blood together to make them brothers. Philosophically they had grown as far apart as two men can grow, but there was still a bond between them, a sort of mellow tolerance.

Publishers and journalists came down from Paris to see Willie. And occasionally total strangers came, too, accepting our hospitality easily because they had read and admired—or disagreed with—one of Willie's books.

One day a telegram came from Paris announcing that So-and-so was arriving at the Bandol station at such-and-such a time, and would we please meet him. I'll never know why, but we did. We waited until all the passengers had alighted, and then a hand waved to us from one of the baggage cars. Two trainmen placed a flat box with wheels on the station platform, and then they lifted down, as if it were a sack of mail, a man without any legs. He was heavily built and extremely vituperative. When we got him to the villa he challenged Willie on certain statements on witchcraft with which he disagreed. He stayed two nights and days, until the point was cleared up to his satisfaction. We had a cook by this time, a big, dark gypsy woman named Madeleine. She and I had to help our uninvited guest to bed in Willie's little house, take him his breakfast, and perform other chores for him, without any thanks but a baleful glare from his fierce and angry eyes. Even Willie, who had a fondness for "characters," was relieved when we put him on a freight train for the return trip to Paris.

But while life on the surface seemed pleasant enough, I knew Willie was suffering. He was making no progress with *Air Adventure*. I would hear him get up at five A.M., his usual time, and I would rise later and go off to my own studio. But sometimes I would pause in the courtyard, expecting to hear the rapid fire of his typewriter, and there would be silence. Later, when I left my own typewriter to attend to something or other in the garden or the villa, I would see Willie sitting outside in the courtyard, with a bottle and a glass beside him, staring into space.

Sometimes I would sit beside him and ask if I could help. I went over incidents of our trip with him, some of them amusing, and I offered my notes about the time I was lost and rescued. But the spark that has to come from within was lacking, and it took more than my encouragement to get Willie away from the bottle and back to his typewriter.

Aldous Huxley was painting instead of writing that summer, and he and Willie had formed a theory that the warm south was not conducive to work for blond Nordic writers, that their bodies became lazy and their minds torpid. I don't know about that, not being a blonde Nordic writer myself, but somehow I managed to write another novel, this time about a librarian in New England. I had so little time to myself, with trying to run a big house and feed a lot of guests and keep Willie from drowning in despair and alcohol, that when I could get away to that quiet room above the garage my fingers raced like mad to get as much written as possible in the time that was mine.

All that spring and summer Raymond Bauret and I had been writing to each other. He was planning to take a holiday in France and to see us at La Gorguette. As the summer deepened, our letters became radiograms that he would tap out on the radio at the end of a brutally hot day in Reggan and that I would answer from the little post office in Sanary.

I looked forward to his coming, and yet, as our letters and radiograms increased in warmth, I grew frightened. I had been very unhappy at the time that we met in the Sahara, and so had Bauret. We were both lost, in a way, and we found something in each other that seemed to light our path. I knew from his beautiful letters that Bauret was returning to the France he had renounced in order to take me back with him; and whatever I had told myself, or told him, I knew I would never leave Willie.

He should have arrived in June, but at that time he was ordered to Gao on Trans-Saharan Company business. Then, in August, when all was set for him to come, I developed a sudden pain on my right side which the local doctor diagnosed as an appendix that had to be removed immediately.

Maria Huxley offered to drive us to the hospital in Toulon, and waited outside the post office with Willie, while I ran in and sent a wire to Bauret explaining that I was ill and that our meeting would have to be postponed again.

I'll never be sure just how psychosomatic the need for that appendectomy was. I know that during the long night after the operation, when I lay thirsty and untended until the dawn, I suffered more from having possibly hurt someone who had already been hurt than I did from any actual physical discomfort. Whatever common sense I had, which was never very much, made me realize that both Bauret and I, in our different kinds of loneliness, had been reaching toward each other for comfort, but that Bauret was really in love with the desert and I with Willie, and that therein lay our true destinies.

I had one final letter from Bauret, expressing regret that I had been ill. It was rather stilted and a little skeptical. In it he expressed his *"amitiés"* to Willie. He sounded like the cynical young Frenchman I had met the first night in Reggan. I let it go unanswered, and I never heard from him again.

Summer was over and we had our last picnics with the Huxleys and the Mann children on the little peninsula of La Gorguette. By the end of October the sun of the Midi had lost its warmth. The Huxleys, who always seemed to be following the sun, went off for a stay in Italy, and most of the Germans left Sanary, the Manns to make a home in Zurich, the others in South America or wherever they could stretch their diminished incomes.

The houses of the South of France, with their tiled floors, were almost impossible to heat. We made the most of the few hours a day of sunlight in our courtyard or on the terrace of the Bandol café. We bought complete sets of Dumas and Balzac in French paperbacks, along with the latest Gide or Simenon, and after dinner we would burn coal in a little stove in Willie's small house and read until it was time to go to bed. We drank a lot for warmth, or from boredom, or because Willie wasn't working and that wretched little book about our air adventure was long overdue.

Chapter Thirteen

The back of that short, cold winter in the South of France was broken by a visit at Christmas time from our friend Daniel Leperq.

Willie loved Daniel, but was also a little afraid of him. He put him in the category of "do-gooders" and thought that Daniel was determined not only to reform him but to bring him back into the fold. Willie had been converted to Catholicism when he was a young man spending a year in Italy, but as far as I knew he never went to confession or observed any of the rites of the Church of Rome. I remember once he told me he expected to be buried in holy ground when he died, and that he might even get special permission for me to be buried beside him, but I took this for one of Willie's enthusiastic exaggerations.

At one time, and that was before we went to Timbuctoo, Willie had the idea of writing a book about Lourdes. He believed, or was told, that in order to do this he would have to obtain permission from the Vatican, or at least from those in authority in France. His idea was to go to Lourdes as a *brancardier,* a stretcher bearer, and I was to have a booth and sell souvenirs. Thus disguised, he thought, we could see what was going on better than if he went as a writer-observer.

We were thrilled at the prospect. Willie believed in miracles, and to a lesser extent so did I. I am sure he would have written an exciting book about that shrine in the Pyrenees, but although he pulled every string possible, permission was not forthcoming, either from the Catholic Church or from the French government. Daniel Leperq would never tell us why he had been unable to help, but there may have been a reluctance to have the shrine of Bernadette treated with the sensationalism apparent in *The Magic Island* and *Jungle Ways*. It was a great disappointment at the time, but then came the Timbuctoo assignment, and we got over it.

I have often wondered whether, if Willie had been engrossed in gathering material for the Lourdes book and writing it that damp, cold winter at La Gorguette, he might have drunk less. It was, as he used to say, up his alley, something that really interested him and lent itself to his peculiar genius. The subject on which he is working becomes part of a writer's bloodstream. It can revitalize him or it can be a kind of poison. I know of two assignments, at least, that Willie should never have undertaken and that only succeeded in throwing him into the depths of despondency and alcoholism.

If we were ever homesick, it was, naturally enough, at Christmas time. Daniel was with us, and a friend of his to whom we had lent the Toulon studio. We held a religious observance at midnight in my work room, which Daniel first purified in some mysterious way with prayers and incense. When that was over we went directly to the dining room in the villa for a feast of wild boar that Daniel had spent the day cooking. We sang carols in French and English and went to bed happy.

When the rain stopped and the weather permitted, we took a number of trips either on foot or by car. Once we drove to Nice and hired an open fiacre, in which we rode very stylishly to Monte Carlo along the lower Corniche. We felt like characters in an Edwardian novel. But the trip I remember best is the one we took on the first of May, to a little town on the edge of the sea, west of Marseilles, called Les Stes.-Maries-de-la-Mer.

Long ago, according to legend, the three Marys of the New Testament got into a boat together and sailed away from the Holy Land. With them was their young servant, Sarah. They landed on a point that reaches into the Mediterranean, and that has been named the "Three St. Marys," after them.

For some obscure reason the gypsies of Europe selected the

little handmaiden, Sarah, as their patron saint. And on the first of May, from all over the continent, they convened at this spot to celebrate their feast day with appropriate religious ceremonies.

We arrived just in time to join a procession led by a priest carrying an enormous cross. There was a brief ceremony at the water's edge, and then the procession wound its way back to the church, which was soon filled to overflowing with the gypsies. At a certain moment a black box said to contain the relics of Sarah was lowered on a pulley and hung, swaying dangerously, over the heads of the crowd. A murmur rose until it became a full cry from the throats of ecstatic men and women. Gypsy mothers raised their children as far as their arms would stretch, so that tiny hands might touch the box and bring healing or good luck.

We came out into the fresh air and wandered around among the gypsies' wagons, donkeys, and horses. We ate our picnic lunch next to one of the gypsy families, with whom we exchanged cigarettes and wine, and afterwards Willie lay on the trampled grass and took his afternoon nap while I sat and watched the people as they moved about. The men were handsome in their pink or violet or green satin shirts and gold earrings, and some of the girls were beautiful; but as a whole, seen close up, they were a bedraggled, dirty, unromantic lot of people. Just the same, it struck me as really wonderful that on one day of the year they should be drawn to this one remote spot from Hungary, Rumania, and parts of Russia as well as England, Germany, Spain, and France, to pay their respects to the servant, Sarah, of whom nobody else ever heard.

There were other odd legends in Provence, where people took as much liberty with New Testament history as did the converts of Africa and Haiti. Willie was very much interested in them, of course, although he never used the material in his books on magic and witchcraft.

There was, for instance, a town in the hills behind Marseilles called St.-Maximin, where Mary Magdalene is supposed to have gone from Les Stes.-Maries-de-la-Mer to a secret rendezvous with St. Anthony. After paying a small fee to the custodian of the church in St.-Maximin, we were taken down to the crypt to see the skull of Mary Magdalene. It was enclosed in a gold metal cast of a beautiful head, with burnished bronze to represent red hair. The cast swung open on a hinge, to reveal a human skull! The effect on a lay spectator was one of awe mixed with horror. It was a long time before I could look at any beautiful woman without visualizing the grinning skull inside the lovely head.

Another town with a legend was Moustiers Ste.-Marie, situated in a little gorge between two hills back of Toulon. Once, at the time of the Crusades, the lord of Moustiers left to join a holy pilgrimage and fight the Saracens. On the eve of his departure he knelt in the village church and made a vow to the Virgin. If she permitted him to return safe and sound from the Crusade, he promised to put a new star in heaven to honor her.

After many years had gone by, the lord of Moustiers returned home unharmed. Remembering his vow, he caused a heavy chain to be hung from one side of the ravine to the other. From the middle of this chain was suspended a star of shining metal for all who passed through the village to see. There it has hung for centuries, as a memorial and as a thank offering to the Virgin Mary.

These excursions with Willie, who was the most wonderful of traveling companions, made up for a lot of other things. In fact, we might have led a very pleasant life in the Villa Les Roseaux on the Mediterranean shore if we had just been a couple of ordinary Americans enjoying themselves in the South of France. But, as Willie sometimes remarked, we weren't people, we were writers. We were obliged to spend part of each day tearing bits and pieces out of ourselves and putting them on paper in order to live at all. When our writing didn't go well, nothing went well. Paradise became Inferno and we could find no peace.

Here is an account of a day, taken at random from the journal I kept. It was one of the good days.

May 3, 1932. Robert Lemercier, a painter who lives in La Cadière, was here to dinner last night with his beautiful friend, whom we all call "Choute." They brought us Gide's *Le Retour de l'Infant Prodigue.* Lemercier read it aloud to us after dinner, and it was so good it made us cry.

Then Robert read from a book by Maurice Barrès, an author who was greatly admired at the beginning of the century. Willie, who was lying on the floor of the little house, where we had taken our guests after dinner, said that he couldn't stomach writers like Barrès. They were too precious for his taste. But Robert went on reading all about a poor sensitive intellectual who was threatening to commit suicide because of a materialistic bourgeois world. Then he read what Renan, the French scholar, told the young man: to go out and get drunk and sleep with whores, and be tactful to people who could help him. And Willie sat up at that and roared with laughter, and said Renan was right.

After Robert and Choute left, at 1:30 A.M., we shut the gates and listened for a while to a nightingale in the grove of plane trees. There was a moon and stars and all was clear and bright after the great storm that had lasted three days. Willie put his arm around me and said he thought he could get down to work the next day, and we went to bed happy.

Although he usually worked until noon, the next day at eleven I found him brooding in the courtyard, with a glass in his hand and I knew he was miserable again. I suggested we go for a swim, and for the next hour we loafed in the warm blue water or sat on the sand in the sun. But before lunch he opened another bottle of Courvoisier and drank half of it.

Not long after this we were invited to La Cadière for lunch. We walked in the fields with Robert and Choute and picked wild flowers for Robert to paint. We had several *apéritifs* before lunch, the local absinthe called *pastis.* Then there was wine with our meal, and afterwards a white *eau de vie* called *marc.* Willie, characteristically, drank more than anybody else. When we got up to leave I suggested he take his siesta there instead of waiting till we got home, but he insisted on leaving. So I got into the seat beside him, and we started off.

La Cadière was situated on top of a hill, a typical Provençal village with terraced gardens and houses clustered around a church. The road leading down from it was very steep. I don't know just how it happened, but Willie suddenly slumped over the wheel, his foot pressing down on the gas, and before my horrified eyes the road became a ribbon winding so rapidly up on a spool that I could scarcely see it.

When the Citroën hit the bottom of the hill, it threw me out into a vineyard on one side, and turned over with Willie underneath it, the wheels still spinning in the air. There is no telling what might have happened if Choute had not insisted that Robert and she follow us in their car, because she was worried about us. Together with two men who were working in the vineyard at some distance away, they righted the car and pulled Willie to safety before it caught fire.

They drove us to the Clinique Mallartique in Toulon. They told me I sat beside Willie, stunned and almost incoherent, murmuring over and over again, "Où est Willie? Il est mort."

But, miraculously, he wasn't dead. We were allowed to leave the hospital after they had strapped Willie's two broken ribs and given us both tetanus shots, with the advice that we spend a few days in bed. As for the Citroën, the garage report was no more serious: a broken steering wheel that could be easily repaired.

They were right about the car, which continued to run, and I was fine except for a swollen kneecap and a trauma that throws me into a panic whenever a car I am riding in goes more than fifty miles an hour. But I believe Willie must have had a concussion that the Toulon doctors ignored. For the rest of that summer he had double vision in his right eye, which was hellishly annoying when he tried to read, and it meant that he couldn't drive a car and he couldn't use his typewriter.

We hired a chauffeur, the young husband of Maria Huxley's

maid, Giulia, and bought him a uniform. Now we drove to the café in Bandol in the Citroën truck with a liveried chauffeur, who waited for us in the sun until we were ready to go home. And Willie hired someone else, too. Another writer, to finish *Air Adventure*.

Joe was a young, going-on-to-middle-age liberal and intellectual whom we had met several times in Paris, at the Dôme or the Select, or on varnishing day at the art galleries on the rue des St.-Pères. He had literary aspirations, but he also had a wife and child to support. Even with the franc at twenty to the dollar he had a hard time making ends meet, especially since, like most Americans in Paris, he preferred Scotch to cognac, which was cheaper.

I don't know how Willie approached him, but whatever the inducement it was tempting enough to make that decent, high-minded intellectual consider the needs of his pallid child and grim wife, and accept. I think I was more sympathetic to Joe than Willie was, because Willie was used to success, both financial and critical, and I was more or less on the same side of the fence as Joe, where it was quieter and possibly more virtuous— a reward rarely known to ease anything but a conscience.

At any rate, Joe arrived one day at the Villa Les Roseaux, lean and cadaverous and stayed a few weeks. He tackled Willie's notes and set to work on what he couldn't help regarding as a hack job, so that's what he made it read like. It was obvious from the very start that this bright idea of Willie's, to get one book out of the way so he could start the one he really wanted to write, wasn't going to succeed.

In the mornings Joe would write in the big, ugly room facing the sea and Willie would sit in the sun in the courtyard and drink. After consulting Madeleine about meals for the day, I would go off to my studio over the garage and work on my novel. At noon we met for *apéritifs* and lunch, after which Willie took his nap and I went back to my novel, and poor Joe walked or swam or just wallowed in feeling lonesome for his family and disgusted with himself. At night, after dinner, he

134

went off alone to the café in Bandol, or to the little *boîte* called "Suzy's," from which he returned to the villa around midnight, drunk, either under his own steam or brought home by a stranger.

Willie read over what Joe had done with his notes, and tore the manuscript up. He thanked Joe, paid him, and said good-bye, to the great relief of us all. Then, every morning for a month, he dictated to me until the book was finished and sent off to Harcourt, Brace. It was published and didn't do too badly.

Now all should have gone well. No longer stymied, Willie should have begun writing the book about Père Yakouba. But he couldn't. For one thing, there was still the double vision to plague him. For another, there was Courvoisier brandy.

He was now drinking almost a whole bottle before lunch, and another bottle between the time he awoke from his siesta and nine o'clock at night, when Madeleine and I put him to bed.

It was a kind of living hell for both of us. With dread and an utter sense of inadequacy, I would watch the man whose intelligence and strength I loved turn into a babbling child or idiot. I had seen Willie set out deliberately to get drunk, to celebrate a job of work finished. But this was different. This was to deaden some inner anguish that lay so deep a whole ocean of brandy couldn't touch it.

The sun of the Midi shone down on the Villa Les Roseaux. The fury of the Mistral, lasting three days at a time, blew over our courtyard, sweeping bottles and glasses from the oilcloth-topped table. Cats from all over La Gorguette came to join our miscellaneous assortment in search of food or kindness.

Our little maid, Anna, who loved us, and our old dog, Coco, whom Willie designated a *chien de sanglier* or boar hound and decorated with a green rosette on his collar for the Mérite Agricole, watched us and were silently sad. Our chauffeur, Emile, sat around whittling or doing nothing, and our gypsy cook, Madeleine, stole our linen sheets and everything else she could get away with. And the nightingales no longer sang to us in the plane trees at night.

135

Maria and Aldous Huxley, Robert Lemercier and his wife, and all our other good friends invited us to dinner and tried to shake us out of the spell that had fallen over us, but at the last minute I would send regrets, because at sundown Willie was too drunk to be led anywhere but to his bed.

He got up at dawn one morning, went to his study, and wrote a long letter to Alfred Harcourt, and then he came and read it to me.

It was a very beautiful letter. In it he told Alfred what had been happening to him and why he had been unable to write. He wanted to be saved. He thought he still had his best book to write. He knew he must stop drinking and he needed help. If Alfred could have him met at the dock in New York, he would like to return to America and be shut up someplace "behind bars," where he couldn't get a drink for love or money.

He added in his heavy black penciled scrawl: S O S, and signed the letter, "Willie."

I dressed and we walked together to the post office in Sanary. It wasn't open yet and we sat hand in hand on the steps until the postmistress arrived at eight-thirty. We could see the fishermen walk toward their boats, dragging their carefully mended nets. We watched the shopkeepers open up for the day's business in wine, cheese, picture postcards. We breathed in the fragrant aromas from the bakers' ovens where the town's *croissants* and *brioches* were being baked for their *petits dejeuners*.

We took to our hearts the whole *mise en scène* that we had come to know as well as we knew the Washington Square Arch and its vicinity at home. This we had made our own, and now we were giving it back to the French, who would know how to live in it better than we did.

I knew that the letter could mean my giving up Willie, and his giving me up. My heart was sick because I realized I had failed, and in spite of Alfred Harcourt's assurance to me once that I was helping Willie, I could not help him stop drinking. But in the letter that Willie still had in the pocket of his denim slacks there was hope for him, a desperate but positive hope, and this was the only important thing to us both that morning.

We mailed the letter and sat down at a café on the waterfront and had our *café au lait*. And Willie ordered a double brandy to go with it.

Chapter Fourteen

A cablegram and then a long letter came from Alfred Harcourt, who assured Willie that he would be at the pier to meet him in New York, and with him would be someone to carry out Willie's plans. He wrote that he had been deeply touched by Willie's appeal to him, and that he agreed something drastic was necessary if he was to return to work.

Once his mind was relieved, Willie got busy. In spite of the fact that he kept on drinking even more than before, and that he was really sick, he took care of most of the details of the move. He got in touch with the agent from whom we had rented the villa, and paid off the remainder of the lease. He arranged about moving the African masks, the Arabian wall hangings, the swords from Damascus, and our books to the studio in the Toulon warehouse, where they would be safe until Willie had an address in New York to which our friend Tony Fayet promised to forward them.

Everything was happening so swiftly that I was too bewildered to be of much help. My first concern was with all the cats who had attached themselves to us, and with Coco, our big old dog, and with Anna, the *femme de ménage*, who had learned so much from us, both good and bad, that it was cruel to send her back to her family's farm, where she would become a drudge again.

And then I kept thinking of the separation from Willie, not only for a few months as we had been separated before, but possibly for the rest of our lives. The thought was so annihilating that I moved about as if I were one of the zombies Willie introduced to the world in *The Magic Island*.

I approached the subject only once, when we were seated on the terrace of the courtyard in the morning sun. We knew that we loved each other deeply. I was even ready to admit, in spite of Willie's own publisher and friend telling me I was good for him and for his writing, that in the last months when he had been completely stymied I had been no help at all.

We were physically drawn to each other, and yet I was totally unsympathetic to all the business of chains and leather masks and the rest of the fantasies that were so important to him. That was one reason I had put up with a series of Mimis and others, for whom I had a generic name, "Lizzie in Chains," after a character in one of the books that came from the *librairie* in the Palais-Royal. I knew I was on dangerous ground there, and now that the ground was crumbling under my feet I couldn't do anything about it. I was no longer any help in that department of Willie's life, either. I had to admit it when he mentioned it.

I was not even very practical, in the way that Katie Seabrook had been. It was not enough just that I loved him more than anything or anybody in the world, or that I had cut myself off from wherever I had belonged in order to be with him. That was nothing to be dragged in now, when the important problem was Willie and how to stop his drinking and restore his ability to write.

"You agree, don't you, Mink?" he said. "That I've got to save myself?"

"I know you do," I said, in a whisper, because the words were hard to bring out. "I want you to . . . only . . ."

"There's no *only*," Willie said, reaching for his drink. "This is the only way out. Christ, if you think it's going to be easy for me, handing myself over to a jailer, getting myself locked up behind bars! Come on, Mink, show some guts. It'll only be for a little while—maybe."

"But suppose it is forever," I said. "I don't want to go on living without you, Willie. I don't think I could. If I can't be with you, I want to die."

139

But Willie wasn't listening any longer. A vacant, opaque look had come into his eyes and his head drooped to one side. The last drink had done its work, and there was, or would be, no sign of his mind working at all until he had slept it off.

I found what homes I could for the cats, and the rest we had to leave, to fend for themselves among the tall reeds between the villa and the sea. Willie drove Coco to the farm with Anna, who promised to look after the old *chien de sanglier* as if he were her brother, she said. We wept and clung to each other, and then she was gone in a flood of tears, and with a bundle of Paris clothes I had given her and that she would never wear.

We said good-bye to our friends in Sanary and Bandol, and the doctor, the baker, the wine merchant, the Algerian book-seller who had invited us to a dinner of couscous behind his shop, the café owners. We gave the key to the studio at 2 bis Quai du Parti to Daniel Leperq, for his own use.

And at last the evening of our departure was upon us. Shutting the door of the house at La Gorguette was saying good-bye not so much to what had happened to us there as to what might have happened; not to the life we had led there but to the life we might have led there together. It was a villa for anyone to dream of living in some day, in the beautiful South of France. Our dream had become a nightmare. And there would be no going back for another chance.

The Huxleys drove us to the Toulon railroad station in Maria's red Bugatti. Because she drove so fast, we reached the *gare* ahead of time and had to wait what seemed like ages on the dark platform for the Blue Train which would come roaring in from Ventimiglia at nine o'clock. I remember Aldous walking up and down, up and down the platform, talking a blue streak. Maria sat on a bench with Willie, consoling him, listening to him, mothering him. He often poured out his heart to lovely ladies, and this night there was a heavy load to unburden. I sat a little distance from them, hugging my own misery, glad that I didn't have to say anything to anybody.

Behind us were the buildings on the Boulevard Strasbourg: the Grand Hotel where we had so often visited Violette Murat; the cinemas where we had passed so many winter evenings, eating *pralines* and *sorbets,* and watching our *"Charlot"* with French subtitles; the low houses and crooked streets behind the Boulevard that we had walked over so often in our espadrilles; the room on one of the narrow streets where Sunlit had introduced us to the poetry of Rimbaud; Charley's restaurant, where we had dined superbly with so many friends and visiting Americans. And down beyond all that, the quays, Cronstadt and du Parti. How deeply this city of Toulon had cut into my heart! For almost seven years it had been my home, spiritually as well as actually. And now, on this dark autumn evening, I was bidding it good-bye forever.

Each time Aldous passed me on the platform I caught snatches of his monologue. I had no idea what he was talking about, but I knew it dealt with an abstruse subject that he would tear apart until he found some bone of truth in it. I had listened to him often, and was to listen again, always in so much awe of his brilliance that I failed to gather what he was talking about. Aldous never talked down to anyone, he remained serenely on his own intellectual plane. And that's where he was this night at the railroad station, seeing two friends off on a train, feeling very sorry for them but not as able to cope with emotions as he was with abstract truth.

The rails began to hum, and out of the black night the train rushed into the station, swooped us up, and proceeded on its way. At the last moment, as I was mounting the steps, Maria thrust a little package in my hand. It was a bottle of perfume— her special scent, she said, to remember her by. To remember Maria, and La Gorguette, the Villa Les Roseaux, Coco, Anna, and the nightingale. To remember for a lifetime, and even after the gracious, lovely Maria was gone.

"We last," Santayana said, "as a strain of music lasts. And

141

we go where it goes." And as a scent of some precious perfume, I might add, or the cindery smoke of a French train rushing through the night.

We arrived in Paris early the next morning. I have always loved it at that hour, when the sidewalks have been freshly washed down for the day and the city looks as if it had been drenched by a light, clean shower. The smell of freshly ground coffee, chicory, and bitter-sweet chocolate came through the cab window, mingling with the smell of the damp pavements. Early workers were grouped at the *zinc* bars for their morning drink of white wine or rum, and on the terraces of the cafés chairs were still piled, bottoms up, on the marble-topped tables.

Traffic was light, and we arrived without the usual snarls at the Place Vendôme and drew up at the Ritz. It was part of Willie's pattern of life to decide to stop at the Ritz for this terminal stay. Just as he had engaged first-class passage for this last crossing on one of the biggest and fastest ships. When he was on top, he could afford to go to third-class hotels and travel tourist class. Now that he was admitting defeat in one department of his life, he had to live as if he were on top.

The bathroom of our suite was as big as the room we usually had at the Hôtel Place de l'Odéon, and the other rooms seemed enormous in proportion. Everything suggested graceful pleasant living for gracious happy people. But as soon as our luggage was deposited, Willie phoned down for a case of Courvoisier and a case of Scotch, and then got undressed and went to bed. There he stayed, more or less, until the day of his departure.

He gave me a list of people to telephone and ask if they would come to see him. They came, all of them, not at one time, fortunately, but in a stream that filled the days. There was, I remember, Bernard Grasset, one of Willie's French publishers, a brilliant, strange little man whom I disliked as thoroughly as he disliked me. And Michel Leiris, the young man of the Trocadero who was also an avant-garde poet, and whom we both loved. He was fascinated by Willie at that time, as

142

were most of the Surrealists because Willie fitted in so well with their strangely distorted view of life.

In addition to editors and publishers who came to present their respects and farewells to Willie—who received them in bed, like a king holding a levee—there were personal friends, and William Aspenwall Bradley, impeccably dressed, with his pince-nez and little mustache and dry New England wit. I was quite sure he thoroughly disapproved of Willie, but he never showed it. After all, he must have been used to eccentric authors, having handled most of the French geniuses as well as the Americans. I think he even enjoyed his contacts with a Bohemian world, while he and his French wife, Jenny, lived mostly in circles radiating from the Faubourg St.-Germain. One indication of the esteem in which he was held by most of us was that we never called him by his first name; he was usually referred to as "Mr. Bradley." But he had always been most helpful to us, and I was very fond of him; when he came to see us in our rooms at the Ritz, and seemed to approve of the step Willie was taking, I felt better.

There were many errands Willie asked me to do for him that kept me dashing in and out of the hotel at all hours. Sometimes as I passed through the lobby I would catch glimpses of beautifully dressed women and attractive men, meeting each other for lunch or dinner or cocktails. I would hear, sometimes, even up in our darkened rooms, sounds of light music from the Japanese Gardens. A whole gay, seemingly carefree world was enjoying all that the Ritz had to offer, but we took our meals upstairs and had no part in any of it.

Among other things I had to do for Willie that week was to buy him clothes, since he had nothing but the Breton slacks of sailcloth and short-sleeved tricot shirts he had worn in the Midi. Several suits were on order for him at Lloyds of London, in Paris, where they had his measurements. These were of Irish homespun, a rough tweedy material that looked very well on him. Like the brown corduroys, they would become a part of

143

Willie; he would wear them and wear them until they could hold no more patches. They never looked new.

Once Willie decided to get a letter off to Alfred Harcourt, with a few new instructions. It was very late at night, and at the desk in the lobby they told me the letter would have to wait until morning to be mailed. I went back upstairs to give Willie the message, but he insisted it could not wait. He was drunk and growing angrier with every glass of cognac he swallowed. By telephoning I found that there was an all-night Poste Restante near the Bourse, the French stock exchange.

I took the letter and rode with it in a taxi across Paris to an almost deserted post office, and demanded stamps for air mail, special delivery, and whatever the French equivalent was for registered mail. The sleepy clerk took ages to fill out slips and pound his rubber stamp, and then he woke up sufficiently to give me a lecture to the effect that even if I was American, it was not necessary, *tout de même*, to squander all that money.

I drove back in the same cab, across a Paris in which the theaters were just letting out. I thought of the fun it had been going to plays with Willie, except, perhaps, the winter when we had gone to see Offenbach's *La Belle Hélène* six times, to the neglect of other plays. When Willie enjoyed anything, he had to have lots of it, like a child.

Most of that week was like the passages of a dream, and this midnight ride was one sequence of it that remained in my memory when a lot that was more important had vanished. The cafés were filling up as my taxi honked its way through traffic. The arc lights shone on the siphons and glasses and the faces of men and women eagerly beginning the little duels that would end up in bed. I didn't envy them, exactly—as long as I had Willie. But tomorrow I would not have him. I would be alone, with another future to begin. Tomorrow I would be free, and I would not know what to do with my freedom.

The morning of Willie's departure came at last. There was an early knock at the door, and when I opened it a tall, muscular young man entered. He was the bodyguard Willie had

144

hired to travel with him and deliver him into the hands of whoever was to put him behind bars.

I have often wondered whether Willie would have been ultimately better off if someone had recognized this seemingly desperate request to be locked up for what it was: the almost inevitable and predictable course for sadism to run—the point at which it becomes inverted and turns into masochism.

Willie's image, not only to the public but to his intimate friends, was one of strength and aggressiveness. No one heard the voice inside him crying out for help, *real* help. Not even those of us who loved him the most. He had bossed and bullied and beguiled and charmed us for so long that the image was fixed, and it would take more than even he knew how to convey to change it.

That last morning, before noon, Willie managed to consume one full bottle of cognac and part of another. By the time we were ready to leave the hotel for the boat train, his head was lolling and his blue eyes were glazed. He had become, as no doubt he wished and had intended to become, a helpless child.

Madame Mirenda—"Choute"—who had saved us once when she insisted on following us down the steep road from La Cadière, appeared at the Ritz just as we were leaving, ostensibly to see Willie off but also to stand by me at a time when I needed a friend.

We got Willie on the train along with his young bodyguard, who wasn't exactly sure what he was supposed to do, and we stood outside the window until the train pulled away. There was so much I wanted to say to Willie, but he wouldn't have heard me.

Choute took me by the hand and went back with me to the Ritz. Then she held out her arms and let me cry until there were no tears left, only a bottomless void in my heart. When the paroxysm was over and I went to the bathroom to bathe my eyes, I heard Madame Mirenda at the telephone speaking to the Ritz valet, giving him hell because I had been charged the equivalent of $4.00 for pressing the skirt of my suit. It was outrageous, even for the Ritz, she said. I had been wondering how I could still be alive without Willie. Now I knew I would go on being alive in a world without heroics, a world full of little overcharges for *repassage* and laundry! I wouldn't like it, but it was there and I had to live in it. The French have made an art of it. I should have learned a lot during the years I lived among them. I decided to go on living, and try.

My own ship, the *Berengaria*, was to sail two days later. I spent the time shopping for family presents, and possibly a few clothes. I saw some friends; the Bradleys had me for dinner at their beautiful apartment on the Île St. Louis; I spent a morning sitting in the Luxembourg gardens, in my favorite corner, the Medici Fountain, and watched the yellow October leaves drop into the pool. I said my good-byes. And I also remembered Emily Dickinson's poem:

> My life closed twice before its close;
> It yet remains to see
> If Immortality unveil
> A third event to me,
>
> So huge, so hopeless to conceive,
> As these that twice befell.
> Parting is all we know of heaven,
> And all we need of hell.

Chapter Fifteen

The day I left Paris it rained. In fact, the entire transatlantic crossing on the *Berengaria* was wet, dark, and rough. I don't remember that I talked very much to anyone but my room steward, who brought drinks and occasional meals to my stateroom. He was a sympathetic Cockney, who told me on an occasion when I must have spilled out my troubles that "a brandy drunk was the worst of 'em all to cure."

It was different with Willie, I told myself. What he had to be cured of was something deep within himself—how deep I didn't know, except that it was connected in a subterranean, Freudian way with his mother, Myra, and his brother, Charlie, and a father who felt a call to preach. Love, hate, jealousies, genteel poverty, the complexities of family life that some children pass through without harm and that warp others: what could the doctors bring to light that Willie himself didn't know about and acknowledge freely? Still, there must be a cure, and if it was deep enough he would stop drinking.

During the damp cold days in a deck chair, all I could do was hope that there was some doctor wise enough and tough enough to find the answer Willie was seeking. As for myself, I felt like a ghost moving among shadows.

I had told no one the date of my arrival or what ship I was sailing on. Willie and Alfred Harcourt seemed to think it best to keep this new adventure a secret, and because of their decision, I had not even told my sister when I was arriving in New York. I couldn't explain my traveling alone, and I didn't know where I was going to stay. Besides, I was in no mood or condition to try to explain anything to anybody. Even to myself.

I was sitting in my deck chair about the third day out, looking over the ship's newspaper. Among the advertisements I saw the Hotel Gotham's. I remembered calling there upon some relatives of my first husband, and being impressed by the dignified quiet atmosphere. Quietude and dignity were two things I craved at that moment, and so, on an impulse, I sent a radiogram to the Gotham, reserving a single room and giving the date of my arrival. Now I had a place to go when I reached New York. It made me feel a little less disembodied.

We reached the Cunard Line pier early in the afternoon of the sixth day. On voyages with Willie across the Atlantic, either way, we had always been met by press photographers and reporters who came aboard with the pilot. There was picture-taking on the sun deck, and interviews. Now I was alone, and there was no one. It was going to be as hard to get used to anonymity, I thought, as it had been to the Seabrook brand of publicity!

Just as I was about to walk down the gangplank, I heard myself being paged. The Hotel Gotham had sent someone to help me through the customs and to be of any other service I might require. I was extremely grateful for the courtesy, and for the help of the young man who drove with me in the taxi and was very polite. During my stay at the Gotham I would ask for him whenever I needed anything. It was like having a friend in the enemies' camp, which was a strange way to feel about my own native city.

Although I believed I had accepted the fact of Willie's "cure" as something he would go through without me, my first telephone call was to Alfred Harcourt. And my first question was: "Where is Willie?"

Alfred answered readily, "He's in Doctors Hospital. Why don't you go right up to see him."

"Doctors Hospital?" I repeated. "But I thought . . ."

Alfred laughed. "Oh, well," he said, "we all know Willie's propensity for exaggeration. I met him at the pier, as he requested, with the best doctor in the whole United States. Lambert. He decided Willie needed rest and building up, that's about all. And to cut down on his drinking, of course. They've got him down to three drinks a day now, then they'll cut to two, and so on."

"But," I said, "what about . . ."

"That business of being put behind bars? Just more of Willie's little fantasies. Lambert thinks he's as sane as you or I. As I've always told Willie, he's crazy as a fox."

We exchanged a few pleasantries. I really loved Alfred and knew he had done what he thought best for one of his prized authors. But I had seen Willie's letter and I knew this wasn't enough—not nearly enough—and not what Willie had asked for at all.

After I'd hung up the phone, I walked around the small hotel room, wondering what to do. On the one hand was the decision, made in Sanary though never put into so many exact words, that Willie and I weren't good for each other. That I was the last one to help him stop drinking, that I was drinking too much myself, and together we'd made a fine mess of our lives.

On the other hand, here was Alfred, who was a good friend, urging me to go to see Willie. How easy it is to persuade ourselves to do what we want to do more than anything in the world! I put on a hat, picked up gloves and my handbag, and took a taxi to Doctors Hospital.

I've never seen a more cheerful place. Everyone smiled. There were none of the signs that distinguish a hospital from any other place: the marks of fear on people's faces, the life-and-death questions in the eyes of the doctors and nurses and relatives of patients, the occasional groans, the smells of disinfectant and ether and hothouse flowers, the rules and regulations. This hospital on fashionable East End Avenue was like a great hotel in which, if people had problems, they had the good manners to conceal them from view.

Willie, I was told by a nurse on his floor, was not in his room. I would find him on the terrace overlooking the East River. Iron bars, indeed!

I walked out on an enormous terrace, and there was Willie, in his red silk pajamas and yellow Timbuctoo slippers, seated

149

in a comfortable wicker chair in the sun, holding a glass of whiskey in his hand. He was talking to his friend Ward Greene, and to another friend, a pretty red-haired woman. They were joking and laughing and when I appeared they all greeted me as if I were someone come late to a cocktail party.

"How are you, Mink?" Willie asked, pleasantly. "Sit over here where you can see the view." I sat down. There was a sudden and awkward silence. These were old friends of Willie's, part of his life before I knew him. They shared old jokes, old secrets, adventures. For one moment I had a sense of relief, as if Willie could slide back in time and be well again—that is, merely eccentric, and not as sick as I knew he was. But the mood had been broken. None of us would be the same as we were a minute or years ago.

Then Willie looked down at the drink in his hand, and as if he were apologizing to me, he said sheepishly, "They've got me down to three a day. This is my last until six o'clock. Pretty good, eh?"

Ward Greene, whom everyone called Jimmy, said something funny and I didn't have to answer. I asked Willie how long he intended to stay, and he said he thought perhaps a couple of weeks would do the trick. He asked me where I was staying, and to write down my phone number, and he would call me in the morning. I wrote it down and handed it to him.

I looked at the view again, and after a little while I rose to leave. Willie looked at me and smiled, and I smiled back. But our smiles were a little sick. Although we were to learn more about stopgaps later, we both knew then that this was no way to cure anyone of drinking. And above all we knew that this was not why Willie had crossed the ocean. Somewhere, somehow, the answer was still to be found.

I found a room for myself in one of those lovely English basement houses in the East Seventies that were still holding on for dear life, in spite of encroaching apartment houses and shops. It was a large room, well furnished, with a fireplace and bath and a view of a city garden. Paul Morand once told Willie that it was important (to whom or what?) to have a good address and I had found one, all right, but there was something peculiar about that house, and for the most part I was too preoccupied to discover what it was.

There was an English butler, but no other servant as far as I could see. There was a young, gay wife and an older husband. And, besides myself, there was one other tenant whom I don't think I ever saw. I knew it was only a temporary foothold and didn't matter. But the foothold was slippery, and like one on a distant planet. Whatever roots I had now were still in France, entwined with Willie's and those of the friends I had made there. But at least, I had an address of my own.

Willie stayed only a few weeks at Doctors Hospital, and then he sublet a furnished penthouse in a new apartment building on East Twenty-second Street. He was going to get down to work on the Père Yakouba book. He felt fine, he said.

My second novel for the Knopfs, *Scarlet Josephine,* written in the Villa Les Roseaux, had come out and received good reviews. Blanche Knopf gave a cocktail party for me and I stayed as long as I had to and then left. I hate cocktail parties. There were book luncheons and book dinners and radio interviews, and more parties. I get them rather confused now, trying to remember. It all seems like one crazy party thrown together, in which only a few people stand out: Alfred and Blanche Knopf; Carl and Fania Van Vechten; William Faulkner wandering alone in a crowded room, asking for a drink of water and explaining, "The wet stuff that flows under bridges." And so many people, well known then, and now forgotten. When I think how impressed we all were with the few who were talked about and written about, and how absolutely they have vanished in the rush of years and a flood of new names, I get a strange feeling that most of us are made of blotting paper over which a glass of water has been spilled, or a bottle of ink.

The strangest of all the parties was the one that was held in the house where I was living by the gay young woman who owned the place. Somehow she seemed to gather every writer within phoning distance, with a few odd celebrities thrown in for good measure. And, what was even stranger, they all came.

I bought a new dress, and the butler, who seemed very much impressed by me since he heard me talk on radio, presented me with a white gardenia made into a corsage. The party got bigger and bigger and spread all over the house, including my room. Willie came and stayed only a little while. I saw a few people I recognized, but mostly there were strangers to whom I was introduced over and over again by my hostess. I don't remember what was served, only I do seem to recall seeing a bald grapefruit on a silver tray. I suppose it had begun by being stuck with toothpicks and little sausages; that seemed to be the favorite cocktail snack of the year. Aside from that depleted and bald grapefruit, I remember no other sign of food offered to the milling guests.

Somehow, and I'll never know why, Dashiell Hammett was at the party. He was in the full fame of his *Maltese Falcon* and *The Thin Man*, which Willie and I, avid readers of Georges Simenon, had read and enjoyed, although I don't much care for the hardboiled school of detective fiction.

Dashiell seemed as mystified by the house and its people as I was, although even more fascinated. He lingered after most of the guests were gone, and he was invited, with me, to join a family dinner party downstairs in the dining room, where real food was actually being served. We refused, but hovered, and then Dashiell Hammett asked me to go along with him to see what was happening around town.

We dropped in and out of places, including one that was to become the ultra-respectable "21" after repeal. And I believe we went to Leon and Eddie's, where I lost Hammett for a while and found myself seated at a round table facing William Faulkner. We nodded and looked at each other, both too shy to make conversation. And then Dashiell took me home. As the taxi stopped before the house in the East Seventies I said politely, "Would you care to come up for a nightcap?"

He drew himself up and asked, in a shocked voice, "Are you the kind of girl who would ask a man in at this hour?"

I thought about that for a second or two, and wondered. I

152

didn't know *what* time it was, so that answered, in a way, the first part of his question. As for the rest—I decided not to answer, but said good-bye, and thank you for a pleasant evening, and let myself into the darkened house with my key.

In the light of what followed, it was too bad the creator of *The Thin Man* didn't come up with me after all. It was much more his cup of tea than mine. When I reached my room, which was on the second floor, rear, the door was wide open and several lamps were lighted. It seemed to me that I had turned them off, but then I thought that perhaps the butler had come in to clean up the mess from the party. I walked in.

As I did so, a man suddenly rose from the depths of a cretonne-covered wing chair by the fireplace where he had been waiting—a tall, sleek individual with black hair and dark eyes and a gleaming-toothed smile.

"Mrs. Worthington?" he asked.

He looked vaguely familiar, not somebody I knew, but someone in a dream, or a movie. That was it, a movie. He looked like George Raft in one of the roles for which he was typecast.

"What do you want?" I started edging back to the door.

"Don't be alarmed," he said, holding out a slip of paper. "I've been waiting for you, to present this little bill."

"A bill? For what?" I asked. "Who are you?" Fond as I was of George Raft, this counterpart had me scared to death.

"For the party," he said, with a smile that never reached his eyes. "For your nice little cocktail party. We don't send bills, so I just thought I'd hang around until you got back and collect."

"But it wasn't my party," I protested. "I was, well, just the guest of honor. Why don't you present your bill to the people who ordered your stuff?"

"They're asleep," he said simply. "I have to collect from somebody. Here." He tossed a slip of paper in my direction and I caught it. He sat down, crossed his legs, lit a cigarette and waited.

I walked over to the desk, took out my checkbook, and wrote

153

a check for some fabulous amount—*good* bootleg liquor came high, and this must have been the best, judging by the amount due for it. There was a telephone on the desk and I could have called the police, or Willie, or my sleeping hostess. But I didn't. George Raft is probably a very nice person, but this counterpart of his wasn't. He was a real bootlegger and he meant business—and I had read accounts of what they did to people who refused to pay up!

I handed him my check without a word; he took it, looked around, and said, "Nice room you've got here," and left. I locked my door after him.

Not long afterwards, even without Blanche Knopf's advice, I moved out of that house. However, my reasons for moving had more to do with Willie than anything else.

We saw each other frequently, and talked to each other on the phone at least once a day. But I felt curiously out of his life. I knew he was seeing his friends of the Katie-and-Willie days, as well as new ones I had never met, and the good part of me was glad because I felt he was returning to a more natural and in a way a healthier kind of life than our last year in France had been. I wanted him restored to the old Willie I had first met—amusing, strong, self-protective, and creative. At least, I hoped he was being restored.

For my part, I was seeing a lot of old friends, too, and also my family. But the life I was leading seemed oddly superficial, as though someone else was using my name, wearing my clothes, and living in a style that might have suited her, but not me at all.

And then I began worrying about Willie again. I knew he was drinking, and I knew he was having sessions of his sadistic games in the penthouse. I knew, because he told me about it himself, and how he had protected himself by having a trained nurse present to see that no one got really hurt. Somehow that clinical addition troubled me enormously. Willie had always been in control and had never got himself or anybody else in trouble. Now, apparently, he was less sure of himself; he was afraid. It didn't sound like Willie at all.

I decided to move. Not into the penthouse, but to a small one-room apartment in Willie's building, where I could be near enough to go to him immediately if he needed me. That's what I told myself, but I guess I moved because I wanted to be near him, and because there was nothing in all that exciting big city to interest me as much as I was interested in Willie Seabrook and what happened to him.

Chapter Sixteen

Early one morning Willie asked me to come up to the penthouse. He had been awake since five, trying to work on the Père Yakouba book. There was a blank page of the rough yellow copy paper he used stuck in the typewriter. He had been drinking. The bottle of bootleg rum with a fake Bacardi label was half empty on a table beside the chair where he was now sitting.

"I've got to have help," he said. "You can't help me. Alfred can't help me. But I think there's one person who has the guts to do it. She's angry at me now because of Katie, but we used to be good friends. I want you to get in touch with Dr. Helen Montague and ask her to come to see me."

He gave me her address: 27 West Ninth Street. "It won't be easy," he said. "She's a busy woman. Besides, she'll think I have a hell of a nerve. But I want you to get her here, by hook or by crook. I don't care if it takes you from now to midnight or if you have to shanghai her to do it. But start now and don't give up. And don't come back here without her!"

That day was one of the longest and strangest I have ever lived. I began by calling at the brownstone house on Ninth Street, between Fifth and Sixth Avenues. It was old territory, in a way, since I had lived in the Village when I was married to Lyman. This was still one of the nicest blocks. The Montague house had not been given a new face, as had many of the others. There was still an areaway with a tradesmen's entrance and a flight of brownstone stairs up to the front door.

I rang the bell with a brass shingle over it: Helen Montague, M.D. After a long time the door was opened by an Irish housekeeper. When I said I wanted to see the doctor, her voice was regretful and kind. "You'd never find her home this time of day. She'll be at the Children's Court. Would you like to try there now? It's on Twenty-second Street and Fourth Avenue."

I thanked her and walked down the front steps. It had been raining since early morning and I was wearing a raincoat and carrying an umbrella. I decided to take a taxi to the Children's Court. It was next to the Charities Organization Society, which I had often visited when I was trying to be a social-service worker. That went back a great many years, to when I was very young and had just graduated from high school. There was a war going on and I volunteered my services to what was called "The Mayor's Committee of Women." They sent me to the medical-service department of the Post Graduate Hospital, where, during an acute shortage of nurses, I bathed all the babies who came into the children's ward, took their temperatures, and then carried them up from the cold, damp basement to the wards and handed them over to the nurses who put them to bed. But once I made a fatal mistake. I accepted a baby with what I should have known was a death temperature. I knew it was pretty sick and rushed upstairs with it, where it gave a little shiver and died in my arms. How was I to know that I had done the unpardonable—adding another figure to the carefully watched mortality rates of the Post Graduate Hospital? I joined the Red Cross after that, and wrote psychiatric histories. This needed less practical sense than I had shown I possessed.

The Children's Court, later to be called the Court of Domestic Relations, had a dreary entrance. I was directed to an elevator that took me to the second floor. This was the Psychiatric Department, over which Dr. Montague presided.

I approached a counter in the middle of the floor and asked the young woman there if I could talk to Dr. Montague for a moment. I gave her my name and said I had a message from William Seabrook. Word came back that the doctor was to make an appearance in court that morning, and was too busy

157

to see me. I found out that after court she would be at her afternoon job in Inwood House on West Fifteenth Street. I decided to try there, later in the day.

For the next few hours I walked around the East Side of New York. It was pouring hard now, and even under my umbrella and raincoat I could feel the wetness through to my skin, and deeper than that. I was like a character in a New Wave movie whom the camera follows through depressing streets for reel after reel. These were the streets I had canvassed as a Red Cross worker, invading the smells of poverty and sickness, asking personal questions—"Was anyone in your family ever insane?" "Did any of them ever have syphilis?"—of dull, discouraged people who answered the questions and made no move to throw me out.

I went in one entrance of the Post Graduate Hospital and out another, through the basement where the free clinics were and patients sat for hours on hard benches until a nurse called their names. I passed the dispensary, the admittance room of the children's ward, and the busy, bright Social Service office, once headed by a rosy-cheeked Miss Bolen, who had been kind to me and forgave my mistakes.

I had not thought of this chapter of my past for many years, and now I was back in it, on my rainy errand, like someone drowning who, supposedly, sees his whole past float by. How could anyone who started life so idealistically, and, I might say, sociologically, wind up being part of a crazy international scene, a member of the cast of moral lawbreakers? Maybe, I thought in a sudden panic, I should be seeking psychiatric help for myself instead of Willie. Surely the least of what I suffered from was a split personality—half bluestocking, half sinner! With that idealistic beginning, how was I here, in the rainy-day present, dedicated to the kind of man I would have once considered dangerously antisocial? To hell with that nearsighted little bluestocking, I said to myself. If she wants to disown me, I disown her.

At three o'clock, I took a cab to Inwood House and rang the bell. Dr. Montague had helped start it years before as a refuge

158

for unmarried expectant mothers. The entrance requirements were even more specialized than that—the unmarried expectant mother had to be afflicted with the additional misery of venereal disease. A quarter of a century before I rang the bell, a group of wealthy women, charitably inclined and with money at their disposal, inquired into the whole field of human misery to find where there was the greatest need. It was Helen Montague who told them that while there were havens for girls who got pregnant without husbands, none of them could be placed if they were diseased. And so Inwood House was established. What it did, quietly and efficiently, was to shelter a girl until her baby was born, cure her and it of venereal disease, and find an adoption home for the baby and a job for the mother. Dr. Montague had been in charge of this program since its beginning.

I waited in a pleasant living room with ash trays around, and a victrola and piano. A message came back that Dr. Montague was making her weekly physical check up and could not be disturbed. I asked what time she went home, and was told five-thirty or six. I left.

It was obvious by now that she didn't want to see me. She was angry with Willie, for no doubt very good reasons, and she was too busy to add any more troubles to her already heavy pack. I couldn't blame her. And I couldn't persist any longer. It was against everything in my nature to persist where I had been so obviously rebuffed. I found a drugstore on Sixth Avenue and phoned Willie from a booth.

"I've got to see her," he said. "She's the only one who can help me. Camp on her doorstep, Mink, but don't come back without her. Please—if you have any love for me left, do this thing for me."

So I did. I walked around Greenwich Village in the rain, with the ghosts of my other selves. There was the apartment house on Waverly Place where I had lived a pleasant normal life with Lyman Worthington, of whom I was very fond, and always would be. There was Washington Square South, where I used to come after school to imagine myself already an artist or a writer, living a Bohemian life that seemed so wonderful to me then. Grace Godwin's Garret had disappeared, but I could remember myself going upstairs and drinking tea at tables lighted even in the daytime by candles thick with their own drippings of wax. It was here I met the young boy from Vermont with the long name, Carlton Beecher Stetson, shortened to "Stet," who was a reporter on the *Morning Sun*. He played a guitar and sang wonderful songs about pirates and sailors and Christopher Columbus. I went along on some of his assignments, once to Chinatown where a detective showed me the bullet holes on a wall made during the last Tong War. Stet bought me a little piece of jade and asked me to marry him. We were secretly married in the Lady Chapel of St. Mary the Virgin. Then he got a job, to show his good faith, as a respectable advertising manager in a factory in an ugly New England village. How on earth did one get so mixed up with intentions and realities? He lost his job and we lived for a year on the proceeds of a pearl necklace willed to me by an aunt. We were divorced, and while I was in Paris with Willie I learned that Stet had died, and I cried out of sadness for the promises of youth, the laughter and the guitar.

It was half past five, no, almost six. Dr. Montague must have returned home. So I went back to the brownstone house on Ninth Street, climbed the front steps, and rang the bell under the brass shingle.

Mrs. Satchwell, the Irish housekeeper, opened the door at last. "Ah, 'tis you," she said, exuding sympathy along with an air of being dragon at the gate. "She's home, but just this minute, and I wouldn't want to disturb her until she's had time to rest and collect herself."

She held the door open, however, and I stepped into the dry hall that was filled with tempting odors from the kitchen down below. I had forgotten to eat lunch and felt tired and rather faint. "May I wait?" I asked.

As that moment someone came running down the carpeted stairs, a slight woman with an amazing mop of red-blond hair. "Can I be of any help?" she asked. "I'm Helen Parkhurst." Willie had told me about Miss Parkhurst, who was Professor

William Montague's assistant in the Philosophy Department of Barnard College. I knew she had her own apartment on the top floor of the Montague house, and that she was a good friend of theirs. So I told her about Willie and why he had sent me, and why I had to wait.

She took me upstairs to her apartment and went into another room to phone. When she returned she said, "Nell will see you after she's had dinner. Would you like a drink? I've got some Gordon's Gin, the real thing, so I've been told." She chatted and tried to put me at my ease and I loved her for it. I could sense that she was a little afraid of Dr. Montague, too, but would do her best to help Willie and me. I asked her permission and then reported to Willie over the phone. He sounded hopeful and pathetically relieved. "She'll come," he said. "I'll be waiting."

A couple of hours and two Martinis later, I was told that Dr. Montague would go with me to see Willie. She would be waiting for me downstairs.

Like many important people, Helen Montague was short of stature. She dressed well and looked younger than the age I later found she was. Her features were attractive, but not pretty. There was a slight resemblance to a well-groomed, alert young bulldog. She was tired after a full day, but gracious. In the cab to Twenty-second Street she asked only a few questions and encouraged me to talk, to bring her up to date about the situation in which she was being asked to help. I told her all I could.

We let ourselves into the penthouse with my key. Willie was asleep in an armchair in the living room. "Hello, William," Dr. Montague said briskly, and he opened his eyes.

"Miss Nellie!" He rose, held out his arms, and hugged her. I left them alone and went into the kitchen to find something to eat. I was tired, wet, and hungry, and I'd swallowed a lot of pride. But I had carried the message to Garcia—and now Willie would probably be taken away from me for good. I sat and stared into the future, and it looked blank.

Chapter Seventeen

The next morning, accompanied by Willie's lawyer, Melville Cane, we met both the Montagues, Dr. Helen and Professor William Pepperell, at the Payne Whitney Pavilion of the New York Hospital, where Willie voluntarily committed himself to Bloomingdale Asylum for the Insane, as it was formerly known, for a period of at least six months. "Miss Nellie" was quick, efficient, realistic, and hard-boiled. There was no nonsense about her, and I think Willie counted on that when he sent for her.

The preliminaries took a long time. Dr. Galbraith, the examining psychiatrist who had come down from White Plains, had read and admired some of Willie's books and was obviously reluctant to find the sort of damning diagnosis that would admit him to Bloomingdale. He was very kind in a cool, pale way. He explained that they did not like to take alcoholics as patients because they were not sure there was a cure for them outside of the patients' own desire to stop drinking.

But at last Willie, who was able to persuade anybody to do anything he wanted (even psychiatrists), won out, and the papers were signed by him, carefully looked over first by Melville Cane, and witnessed by the Montagues and me. Nobody else seemed to be as distressed as I by the whole business, and my hand shook so that it could hardly guide the pen along the dotted line.

Then Dr. Montague and Melville Cane left us, and Professor Montague, a round, cherubic-faced, and brilliant man, drove Willie and me to White Plains. It was a long ride. The day was beautiful, for December. Willie sat in front, and I sat in back with my fears, under seven layers of which was a tiny spark of hope. Maybe among all those psychiatrists at Bloomingdale they would be able to get to the root of Willie's tangled complexes and set him straight, to live like other, normal men for the rest of his life. Maybe that was what Willie wanted, and why he was so set on taking desperate measures. But as I sat in the back seat, trying to picture the new William Seabrook, healed and normal, I failed utterly. And at that point Willie asked Monty (as he called Professor Montague) to stop the car. He got out and was sick by the side of the road.

I wanted to say, "You don't have to go through with this, Willie. We can go off together somewhere and you can write your book, and I'll try to keep liquor away from you. . . ." But I didn't say it, mainly because I knew it wouldn't accomplish anything except to make him angry. "A mark," he had said so often, quoting his old friend Epictetus, "is not set up for the purpose of missing the aim!"

The entrance to the Asylum, now called The Westchester Division of New York Hospital, was a winding road leading to an ugly red brick building, with a number of so-called cottages staggered around it. We stopped before the brick house. As I remember, nobody helped us with Willie's luggage, which consisted of a typewriter, a steamer rug, neatly rolled and strapped, containing clothes and shoes and underwear, and a red Toulon handkerchief wrapped around a sterno and a can of instant coffee. It was the way Willie always traveled, across the ocean, through the African jungle, and now to Bloomingdale. But in this instance he was not to see any of it for a long time.

The preliminaries having been seen to during that lengthy interview at the Payne Whitney Pavilion, it didn't take long to hand Willie over to a house doctor and say good-bye. We watched him go down a long corridor accompanied by a trained nurse. I felt he was frightened, but that may have been only my own fear. He didn't look back.

Although we weren't aware of it then, the day Willie committed himself to Bloomingdale, December 5, 1933, was the day the Twenty-third Amendment, popularly called "Prohibition," was repealed. It would no longer be unlawful to buy liquor in the United States. It would no longer be "smart." It would be what it had always been for some people—stupid!

I kept a sort of journal of that dark winter. Close-ups are often as far from the truth as memories. I find, however, that Willie adjusted easily enough to the hospital environment. There were no actual bars, of course, except a kind of equivalent in the wards for disturbed patients. He was allowed a certain amount of freedom, though not much at first. And, above all, he was immediately cut off from any alcohol in any form. They gave him sedatives in the beginning, and then even these were stopped. Bloomingdale didn't believe in stopgaps. And Willie never asked me, as his one link with the outside world, to smuggle any whiskey or brandy in to him.

I visited the hospital twice a week at first. Willie seemed to like where he was and to have made friends with some of the other patients. He was as interested in his new surroundings as if he had just entered a new country.

But pretty soon the rules and regulations bothered him and he began protesting. He accepted the fact that none of the patients were allowed to own a razor or shave themselves, and he didn't mind having his cigarettes lighted for him by an orderly because matches were forbidden. But what he did mind was the fact that they would not give him his typewriter. I don't know what the reason was, because surely it wasn't dangerous as a weapon for suicide or murder. I tried to convince Dr. Galbraith that one of the things that was disturbing Willie most was that he hadn't fulfilled his contract with Harcourt, Brace for the Père Yakouba book, for which he had received a large advance. With all the faults he may have had, Willie was too good a newspaperman to fail to meet a deadline. The fact that he had done so must have been killing him.

I accused the doctors, including Galbraith, of acting foolishly. They were treating Willie as if he were a child in a nursery who must be shown that he could not always have his own way!

164

I told Alfred Harcourt about it, and he went up to White Plains to see what he could do. He announced to Dr. Galbraith that of all the patients they had up there it wouldn't matter in a hundred years whether they were saved or not, but in Seabrook's case, it would. (Even if, after thirty years, the world seems not to agree with Alfred, I know he was right. Perhaps we must wait a hundred years to see!)

Willie was given his typewriter, and on my next visit he gave me pages to read that I thought were fine. He was happy again and quiet. He always thought *The White Monk of Timbuctoo* was the best book he ever wrote—and I think it pleased him that it was written in an asylum for the insane. He felt in good company, with Blake and Dostoevsky, who he believed would have found the environment to their liking.

I should have moved up to the penthouse, because the rent had been paid for several months. But when I went there to collect the rest of Willie's clothes to send to him, I was afraid of the place, especially of the sooty terrace, and the nights filled with despair, and the easy drop to a courtyard below. I was in no mood, even in the daytime, to live all alone on top of a busy building.

Jerome Blum, the painter, and his wife, Frankie, had just come back from France and were looking for a place to live. I offered them Willie's penthouse, and they accepted. And I continued living in my one room, bath, and kitchenette. It made a perfect retreat from the world when I returned from my visits to the hospital. It was like returning to the security of the womb; once I had shut my fireproof door, I could feel safe in nothingness and silence.

Those visits to Bloomingdale never got easier, although after a while, on Dr. Galbraith's advice, I cut the visits from two a week to one. In those days there was a Second Avenue El that I got on at Twenty-third Street and rode to the end of the line. Then I took a shuttle to the New York Central suburban train that went to White Plains. On the way from the station to the hospital I often shared a taxi with mothers or wives of other

patients, and we talked to each other with that strange camaraderie of people who share a common ailment or sorrow. Before the visit we had our laps full of packages and talked a lot.
On the way back our arms were empty and for the most part
we each had too much to think about to make conversation.

Part of the visiting routine was that before I was allowed to
see Willie I had to stop by Dr. Galbraith's office and talk to
him. I would first of all ask about Willie and would be told
as little as possible. Then began a kind of literal brainwashing.
I was supposed to tell all that I had done during the week,
between visits. At first I would find it hard to dig up anything
I thought would interest him; later there were lots of things to
tell. I began almost to enjoy shocking the blond, pale doctor
who was, I felt sure, a puritan at heart. He expected things of
a shocking nature, and with my social desire to please I didn't
disappoint him. I drank too much that winter; I was taking
Willie's avenue of escape, even when I knew where it had led
him. There was a strong *nostalgie pour la boue* in my efforts to
escape hopelessness and loneliness. Willie would have understood. I don't think Dr. Galbraith did, though talking to him
helped a little.

After this preliminary interview, I was allowed to walk up
a flight of stairs, preceded by a nurse or an orderly who opened
a thick door for me with a key, let me go in, and then locked
the door behind me. I can't explain what it felt like to hear
the lock click. It was like handing over one's freedom, as if it
were a passport, at a foreign border. And a foreign border this
was, between the world of the so-called sane and the ones who
had been diagnosed as mentally ill.

At first Willie was given a bedroom opening on a corridor.
There was no lock in this room because there was no door. He
was under constant surveillance, as were all the patients on
that floor.

We met in the large gray recreation hall where other patients
were playing billiards or checkers or cards, or sitting around
doing nothing. They all wore slacks and shirts and jackets, not
hospital garb but their own clothes. The atmosphere—like that

in T. S. Eliot's "Portrait of a Lady"—was of "Juliet's tomb."

Willie and I sat in two stiff chairs and tried to talk to each other. There was a window out of which we could stare when it got too embarrassing to look into each other's eyes. We who had been side by side in so many different places—on the Quai Cronstadt in Toulon, at the Dôme in Paris, along the banks of the Rhone in Arles, under the stars in the Sahara at Bidon 5 . . . We had sat in heaven together, and now we were seated side by side in an Existentialist hell, like two characters in Sartre's *No Exit*.

Later, after Willie began writing again, he was always cheerful when I came to see him. In fact, I had a feeling he was enjoying himself so much he wouldn't want to leave when the time came. He introduced me to some of the patients with whom he had made friends. One was a young schizoid, a very good poet, who knew Willie's books and admired them. He talked incessantly, and his movements were jerky, involuntary. He scared me a little, but he was pathetic, too, and so I couldn't ask him to please go away and leave us alone for the precious little time we had to see each other.

Another friend and patient was an attractive man who came from an old and wealthy Boston family. Willie played tennis with him. He would join us when the weather grew warmer and we sat out on the grounds of the hospital. He was amusing and charming until he suddenly forgot what he was saying, leaped to his feet, and ran like a fawn into the surrounding woods, pursued by a couple of attendants.

The dangerous patients were in another part of the hospital. Willie's playmates were all more or less harmless. But I was afraid of them. In spite of my superficial training in psychiatry, I have always had some deep-rooted fear of insane people— really psychotic, I mean, not those who were simply "queer." I would smile and try to talk to them, and all the time I would have to reassure myself that the guards were watching and near enough just in case! Willie had no such fears. He was much more sociable than I under the best conditions. And at Bloomingdale he felt perfectly at ease, and at home.

His health had improved. He looked and felt fine. And his work was going well. Everything else seemed to slip into insignificance.

I was having trouble with my own writing. A novel I had started in France, and on which I tried to work, was turning out badly. My novel *Scarlet Josephine* had now come out in England and had received favorable reviews there, too. To my great joy, Rebecca West had given it a column, filled with praise. But it didn't help when I sat at my typewriter and tried to make a new group of characters come to life.

A nice thing happened to me that winter, however. George Davis, our young friend from Toulon, had joined the staff of *Vanity Fair* as fiction editor. He invited me to dinner at his apartment in the Village, and in the course of the evening he asked me to write a short story for his magazine.

I said I never wrote short stories and didn't think I could. I only wrote novels. He asked me to try and I said I would, just to prove I couldn't write stories.

I went home and wrote one, in a single sitting, and the next day sent it off to *Vanity Fair* by a Western Union messenger, and then went back to the novel that was giving me so much trouble and that never got published.

The following day George phoned to say they were taking my story and Mr. Crowninshield would like me to have luncheon with him at Voisin. That luncheon remains as the one sunny memory of a dark winter. Voisin, which was still at Fifty-third Street and Park Avenue, was one of the pleasantest restaurants in the world. It was light and cheerful, with canaries singing in cages above the diners. The food was the best outside of France, and the service was impeccable and at the same time as friendly as in a beautifully run home.

Frank Crowninshield, tall, slender, well-dressed, with white hair and a white mustache waxed at the ends, was one of the most delightful and gracious men one could meet, and the perfect host, of course. Besides George Davis and myself, his guests that day included the Cass Canfields and a beautiful woman whose name I didn't hear.

After lunch Mr. Crowninshield told me he liked my story very much and asked me to do more for them. But, he added, "Try to write about smarter people. Not that we, personally, are snobbish."

So I went home and wrote one about Natalie Barney's famous salon in Paris and called it "Mary Peabody's Salon." It was fun to do and Mr. Crowninshield said it was "very beautiful" and accepted it at once.

Willie was proud of me and I was pleased that I had some good news to give him. But underlying this bit of success were too many misgivings and worries to make me really enjoy it.

Here are some entries from my Journal that spring:

Friday, March 30th. Willie may stay where he is after June, through the summer. Maybe six months more. I try not to show him how I feel about it. It was one thing to keep going until June, when there was an end in sight. Now, who knows how long it will be?

William Aspenwall Bradley just arrived from Paris, asked if we could have a quiet lunch *chez moi* as he wasn't feeling up to a restaurant. I am sure he was surprised at the smallness of my apartment. But I cooked lamb chops and sent down to the drugstore for ice cream. We had a good talk. I showed him what I had done on my novel and he told me it was boring!

Friday, April 6, 1933. Up to White Plains to see Willie. We got permission to walk outside on the grounds together. We sat down on a bench. A light rain began to fall but we didn't go inside. We watched a robin and a squirrel . . . the grass is getting green.

We talked about the things in store for us. Maybe, Willie said, we would take a trip around the world when he gets out. He told me I must never leave him. He told me he loves me and needs me.

In the meantime, he seems quite happy at Bloomingdale, and that's what frightens me. . . .

. . . sometimes coming home from there I am so upset I don't know what to do, where to turn. Jerry and Frankie Blum, who are always entertaining up in the penthouse, invite me up to meet celebrities, but I don't give a damn about any of them. I shut my door and take a drink and wait for the telephone to ring . . . though when it does, and if it does, it is never anyone I want to see, or about anything I want to do. . . . I never knew before how terribly lonely so many women must be in New York. There must be thousands of them, nice ones, too. Nobody would suspect. One clings to straws. I at least have my writing . . . but the others, without that . . . how do they pull through?

Willie finished *The White Monk of Timbuctoo* and everyone was delighted with it. I felt it was much more about William B. Seabrook and his philosophy than it was about poor old Yakouba!

The doctors at Bloomingdale, consulting with Dr. Helen Montague, decided to let Willie out in her care. Willie told me about it when I went to see him. I was so sure of Helen Montague's disapproval of me that I felt she wouldn't let me see him. I went home and wrote a suicide note. But then Dr. Galbraith phoned to say that Willie was going to stay at the Montague farm in Rhinebeck, New York, and would I be willing to go up there and stay with him?

I asked if Dr. Montague had suggested it, and when he said it was her plan, I said, "Of course I will go. When is Willie getting out?"

When I hung up the phone, I stood at my window that opened on a dusty courtyard, and I watched a flight of pigeons someone kept on a nearby rooftop. They were better than a ballet I had just seen. They were like messengers from heaven. I stood there with tears streaming down my cheeks, and thanked God.

Chapter Eighteen

The Montague farm, Krumvallen, consisted of about two hundred acres just outside the town of Rhinebeck, in Dutchess County. There was a large Dutch colonial house, several barns, beautiful woodland, an icy natural swimming pool, and a little wooden bridge that Professor John Dewey had built with his own hands over several weekend visits.

Except for the hired couple who ran the place, we had Krumvallen to ourselves during the week. The Montagues came up Friday night and left early Monday morning, usually with guests.

Willie ate well and slept well and was in better condition physically and mentally than I had known him to be in a long time. He still had some of the hospital psychology to shake off; the too-easy compliance with little rules, the lowered voice, even a certain secretiveness when, for instance, he lit a cigarette with his own lighter. He recognized this in himself and laughed at it. But he never mentioned wanting a drink or asked me to buy a bottle for him. The six months of total abstinence seemed to have healed him of any craving for alcohol. Besides, he was writing again, and at the old pace.

With Dr. Montague's permission he made an office for himself in one of the unused barns. The Montagues kept chickens but no other livestock because Professor Montague was a zoophile and wouldn't permit any animal to be kept on the place that would have to be killed and eaten. (Chickens didn't count.) The house was filled with yapping Cairn terriers, and the barn was filled with cats. One of these cats, a beautiful gray-and-white tabby, was curious about Willie when he set up his typewriter in a stall originally intended for a cow. She

171

watched and listened to him for a few days, but soon adopted him outright. From then on she sat on his shoulder while he wrote. He named her Pistaloun, the Provençal name of a cat we owned in Sanary. She was Willie's cat, and we took her with us when we had a place of our own. After presenting us with two litters of kittens a year, she mysteriously died one cold winter night, much to our sorrow.

While Willie was writing the book that was to be called *Asylum,* I wrote a novel in our bedroom. The setting was La Gorguette and Sanary, and 2 bis Quai du Parti. It was the story of a priest (Daniel Leperq) and a woman who was in love with him. It was a true story, except for the details and changing the woman into an American. It was a story that had moved me deeply, and somehow, sitting upstairs in someone else's house, not feeling too sure of my position there, I found it comforting to write about close friends in another country. (The novel was given the title *Come, My Coach* by Louis Kronenberger at Knopf. I wanted to call it "Mrs. Benton" to follow "Mrs. Taylor." It was important to me, but nobody else cared.) In some ways, it was a better novel than my first. Writing it filled my days and saved my life.

We were both busy, and leading a healthier life than we ever had before. When Willie finished his morning's stint we had lunch, and after his nap we took long walks together without venturing outside the boundaries of Krumvallen. On weekends, the house was usually filled with guests. Willie played badminton, we swam in the icy pool, and we played Saturday and Sunday morning golf with Professor and Dr. Montague on the nine-hole course in Rhinebeck.

The Montagues' guests were usually Columbia colleagues of Monty's, and their wives. There was Arthur Livingston, nicknamed Pliny, and there was John Dewey, and there was also Professor Kasner, a homely, funny little man who gave the world of mathematics a name by which they could refer to a digit with an infinite number of zeros after it. He told us how he had been searching for a term that would go way beyond billions and trillions. He asked his six-year-old grandson to

172

suggest something, and the child came up with the word "googol." The term has stuck and turns up in the most serious discussions of mathematics. What amused us most about Dr. Kasner, the mathematical genius, was that he could never add up his chips correctly when we played poker, as we often did on Saturday nights.

It was a new world, for me at any rate, this professorial atmosphere and well-regulated country life. But Willie took it in his stride. He enjoyed the lengthy and heated discussions on academic subjects, and also the limericks they seemed to recite with so much relish. I just sat and listened and smiled. But I suppose, to paraphrase Walt Whitman, to have great limericks you must have some audiences for them.

It was easy to get to know and become very fond of William Pepperell Montague, a rotund, smiling, silvery-haired, friendly man, even if there was steel at times showing behind that benign front. But it was harder to know his wife, Doctor Helen. I admired her for her accomplishments and her good works, but it took me longer to feel at ease with her, and eventually to love her, as I did. Willie called her "Miss Nellie," from way back, and although they frequently came to swords' points in their differences, they were always friends in the deepest sense of the word.

In August of that year, and for many years to follow, we went up to Maine with the Montagues to the place where they spent their vacations. They owned a small frame house on Swan's Island, which was one of a group stretching out into the Atlantic off Mt. Desert. Pliny Livingston had a house there, too, and some other close friends of the Montagues, the Rodmans, of whom I became very fond.

The Rodmans had a boat and we often picnicked on the other islands, boiling lobsters in big pots and eating them with our fingers while we sat on hard rocks and talked or sang or looked at the friendly brown seals. Bayard Rodman was a teacher of physics, and the brother of the radical Henrietta Rodman. He and Loretta, his wife, were liberals, but mild ones. That is to say, like Monty, they were always taking the side of

173

what they considered the underdog. They were very fond of Willie, who disagreed with almost all their principles.

It seems to me we were always uncomfortable during those vacations at Swan's Island. The weather was usually damp and cold, and there was no heat in the house except what the miserable old cookstove in the kitchen gave out. The beds were lumpy and there wasn't a comfortable chair in the house to read in. But Willie was of the same hard-grained stuff as the Montagues and the Rodmans, and he loved the weeks we spent in Maine each year. Sometimes when it got very wet and cold and my bones ached and my spirits dropped to the insides of my soggy sneakers, I would think longingly of a drink of rye or Scotch. Of course, I said nothing. And Willie never once mentioned liquor. He seemed to have forgotten all about it. He was his old delightful self again, enjoying everything— swimming, walking, fishing, digging for clams, or taking notes for the book he was writing. He frequently expressed himself in language that should have shocked even the broad-minded company we were in, but they were used to Willie and shock-proof.

I had been corresponding fairly regularly with the friends we had left in Sanary, and because Professor Livingston had just finished a translation of the works of Pareto, the Italian economist who was said to be the father of Fascism, I wrote to Aldous Huxley about it. In the return mail, and while we were still on Swan's Island, I had the following reply from Aldous, which I preserved because it was so typical of him.

La Gorguette
Sanary, Var.
10. VIII. 34.

My dear Marjorie,

About old Pareto:—I have the greatest respect for him, feel he's one of the very few people who have approached sociology in a genuinely scientific spirit, without any metaphysical axe to grind, without any violent political prejudices (beyond that conservatism and that disbelief in progress which seems always to come to people who spend a lot of time studying the facts of human activity) and without, above all, any propagandist zeal for any one, all-explanatory hypothesis. This last is what makes most sociology such rubbish— the mania to explain everything in terms of one set of causes—economic, climatic, psychological, religious and so forth. Pareto is prepared to admit that there are a great many causal factors always at work and proceeds always on that assumption. His book is therefore extraordinarily well balanced. If it were a bit more readable, it would be a great masterpiece. Unfortunately, he repudiated any "didactic purpose" and wrote purely for his own satisfaction and for the satisfaction of other like-minded people. Which is a pity. Your friend must have had a weary job translating his two thousand thick pages.

I wonder, by the way, if this is the same translation as that about which T. S. Eliot wrote to me this spring. He is a director of Faber and Faber, the English publishers; and there was some question of their taking on the publication of a translation which was being (or had been?) published, I think, by Harcourt, Brace in America. Now, I think, Jonathan Cape is going to do the book, or thinks of doing it—for they are all a bit nervous from the business point of view. For I fear it's not a potential Best Seller. I hope this translation is the same as your friend's; for I should hate to think of his going through those two thousand pages only to discover that the book had been previously done by somebody else. [Note: It was Professor Livingston's translation.]

You seem to be having a grand time in the country, with none of those droughts and dust storms of which we read such appalling accounts in the papers. Here we are having a cool summer—lots of mistral and *vent du large,* which makes bathing rather painful. Your house is full of about a hundred squalid-looking children, camping in the empty rooms. What a pity that good works and charity should always result in such unpleasantness! At the sale of the furniture, I bought two large mirrors and was furious at missing, by some stupid oversight, the most ravishing picture by the old man [Note: The former owner, from whose heirs we had rented the Villa Les Roseaux, was an amateur painter, and my studio over the garage had stored in it a lot of his paintings and photographs; but Willie, with his peculiar code of ethics, refused to let me take anything away with me.]—an interior, in the most charming douanier Rousseau manner which I don't ever remember to have seen while you were there, and so presume must have been hidden in the cellars. How glad I am we stole those indecent photographs! I regret we didn't go around snooping some of the paintings.

I am glad to hear that your respective works are going well. I tinker away slowly at a novel, trying to get exactly what I want and not succeeding, which is a bore: but in matters of literary composition I am a convinced Micawber. Something ultimately always turns up. In the intervals I accumulate notes for a projected history of the religious and philosophical justifications for sexual indulgence invented by people who wanted to have a bit of fun but couldn't bring themselves to have it unless they first believed that the fun was in accord with the dictates of Pure Reason, or God, or the Categorical Imperative, or the Higher Thought. You've no idea what extraordinary things people have thought of to justify the most ordinary acts. And sometimes having invented amazing theologies to justify the fun, they found themselves compelled by the logic of these theologies to pass from ordinary to really very odd acts—as when a clergyman of the Church of England thought it his duty to have a girl in public on the drawing room sofa, because he was acting for God and God had decided to reconcile Himself with the flesh.

Matthew and Sophie are here, both grown very large; and Maria is kept pretty busy dealing with them. The German population has diminished and passing visitors have been scarce—which is, on the whole, all for the best.

Our love to you both,
Yours,
Aldous H.

When our month's vacation on Swan's Island was over, Willie and I drove back to Rhinebeck together. The Montagues had gone ahead, and Willie and I spent the first night at a hotel in Keene, New Hampshire. It was the first time we had been alone, without some kind of restraint, since Willie had left Bloomingdale Asylum.

I was a little uneasy, but I needn't have been. Just off the drab brown lobby was a bar, and we could smell the fumes of drinks past and present as we crossed to the elevator. But Willie showed no interest, even when he went downstairs later for a magazine to read before going to bed. I waited for him with some anxiety, but he returned as he left, without alcohol. I felt it was a sort of test and was reassured, although I remained awake all night listening to the sound of cards slapping and chips clinking in the room next door where some drummers were holding an all-night drinking and poker party. Willie slept through it all. I thought that night how protected we had been for a long time, almost as if we had been wrapped in cotton wool. Soon we would have to remove the protective covering and face the world.

Asylum was finished in record time, and Ann Watkins sold it before publication to the *Atlantic Monthly* for serialization. I don't know why we were so surprised that it was the *Atlantic* that bought it, because they had also run Gertrude Stein's "Autobiography of Alice B. Toklas." But ever since Willie learned that the *Saturday Evening Post* considered him "morally subversive," he believed the other "family magazines" felt the same way about him. We were delighted, of course, and what was more immediate, we felt rich again. The six months' stay at the hospital in White Plains had rather depleted Willie's bank account. Now it was flowing over.

We decided to buy a house of our own in Rhinebeck. We liked what little we had seen of the town and its environs. It would be a good place to live and work. What we found and bought was as far a cry from the Villa Les Roseaux, the Château d'Evenos, and a Toulon warehouse as possible. The cottage was small, although we added an extra room later. The original four walls had been built by Indians and then added to by the Dutch settlers. We exposed the original rafters and dug out a wonderful fireplace, which we needed for warmth until we got richer and put in an oil burner.

What interested Willie more than the house itself was a huge saltbox barn, where he installed himself and his typewriter after putting in a second story and a flight of stairs. Later we remodeled it so that there was a large living room downstairs, a kitchen, bath, and guest room, and we did most of our entertaining there. His work room was hung with the cloths from Arabia, the African masks, the brass ornaments from the jungle, and his other trappings. The place became much more like Willie than the cottage ever was. But I loved the little house and hated the barn.

177

We owned nine acres of land. There was a path running through a little wood and there was a knoll on it from which we could see the Hudson River. Next to our small property was the Langdon estate. Old Mrs. Langdon had a niece as companion, Daisy Suckley, who was also a favorite cousin of Franklin Delano Roosevelt. Often in late afternoon we would see a white sports car fly past our front gate, followed eventually by a car with Secret Service men in it. I was tempted to stand by our front wall and wave to the President as he whizzed by, just as, when I was a very little girl, I had stood at the back fence of my grandmother's summer home in Long Branch, and, with my sister, waved to President Theodore Roosevelt, who passed on a train. Of course, being much older and infinitely more ladylike when I reached Rhinebeck, I did no such thing. I just smiled as he drove by to have that afternoon cup of tea with his cousins. Willie, I suppose, scowled.

Miss Suckley and I became good friends. When she was training Fala, whom she gave to the President, she brought him to our cottage to show me his tricks. The Scottie I later owned came from the Langdon household, and had been taught all the smart things Fala had learned. I was very proud of this, and Willie thought it funny.

Rhinebeck, when we came to live there in the middle thirties, was still somewhat feudal. There were vast estates along the Hudson owned by what were known as "the River People." Most of the villagers depended on them for a living; not only the tradespeople but a great many who worked on the estates. To be even distantly related to a superintendent of one of the estates, such as Vincent Astor's, gave one social status in the town. And Willie's friend the jeweler, Chet Haen, obtained a sort of status because his father had for years a standing order to wind all the clocks in the River mansions. That was all he had to do, but there were many fine houses and many fine clocks and apparently it kept him busy.

There had once been a thriving industry in Rhinebeck, the culture of violets, but violets went out of fashion. A few of the greenhouses had survived, however, and it was a treat to visit them, to stand in the doorway and look upon row after row of violets, some pure white, and to drink in their moist fragrance. Scents, like music, stimulate memories, and I was reminded of the corsages my mother used to wear on her sealskin muff—intoxicating to a child whom she bent over to kiss good-bye. There was a song she used to sing, too: "Every morn I bring thee violets." But that was a long, long time ago, when violets were in fashion.

While I lived in Rhinebeck I used to send corsages of white or purple violets to my friends at Christmas and Easter, until Maria Huxley asked me if I understood what the gift had come to symbolize? And I remembered the play by Bourdet, *The Captive*, in which a Lesbian sends violets to the frail young woman she is bent on destroying. All too quickly the lovely little flowers with their perfume of earth and woods, once sold on nearly every street corner in New York to courting men, became to sophisticates the symbol of a sick love. I continued to send them to my friends, but I wondered if so small a thing could have helped to destroy a town's industry.

Whenever Willie found himself in new territory, whether in Africa, France, Spain, or the West Indies, he always explored the surrounding country. In time, he became friends with most of the River people, as well as the people who worked and lived in the town, plus a few miscellaneous people like ourselves. He enjoyed them all and made friends everywhere. The dowagers along the River loved him, and the younger women were attracted by a suggestion of danger, as usual. He often played poker—five-card stud—in the afternoon or morning with Jake Borowsky, in his Men's Furnishing Store on Main Street. He had long, interesting talks with Mrs. Travers, the Episcopal minister's wife. He went off on hunting or fishing trips with Irv Staley, the carpenter who had remodeled our house and barn. He made friends with the headmistress of the exclusive girls' boarding school on the old Tracy Dows estate and with the whole Dows family—mother, daughter, and son—who had built new homes for themselves along the River. And with old Mrs. Kilmer, who lived down the road from us and came in to

179

help me with the cleaning and cooking. Whatever his other genius may or may not have been, he had the rare talent of making friends, and keeping them.

My sister and her husband came for a weekend, and, later, brought my mother and father to visit us. I don't know whether they were more pleased or astonished to find us leading the lives of respectable human beings for a change. Willie, who objected to families on principle, was charming to them, and all was forgiven. They were loyal admirers and sympathetic friends from then on to the end.

On January 23, 1935, I wrote in my Journal:

Mrs. Kilmer in the kitchen washing up dishes. She brought me a pink carnation today, with two violet leaves, from the greenhouse where her man works. Willie is writing a story for *Vanity Fair* in my upstairs little study because his oil stove in the barn doesn't burn right. I hear him muttering as he writes.

We now own the house, but we feel poor, and will have to work hard at our jobs to earn bread, like other people. It will be fun. This is the beginning, I believe, of the best period in his life and mine. I hope our work goes as well as life promises to go for us. We shall see. "We do our best," as Willie says. The rewards, so far, are many.

In July, the first two copies of *Asylum* arrived. Willie spent the evening reading it from cover to cover. When he had finished he said it was a good book, almost as interesting as Dashiell Hammett. He also said it had less "bunk" in it than any of his others, and that in the *White Monk* he had tried too hard to be literary.

On August 8th *Asylum* came out, and all the leading critics gave it full columns of praise. John Chamberlain of the New York *Times* said: "Very few people could be as honest as Seabrook is here, and it is honesty, plus the talent that Seabrook already had, that makes a book of this sort first rate." And Harry Hansen capped a favorable review with the opinion: "it is a fine personal record . . . the last word in that form of experience which began when Stanley went to find Livingstone."

Willie, of course, was very happy at the reception of his book.

180

He had gone through all this before, however, with his other books. Now, I think, he was proudest of how impressed his Rhinebeck friends were—especially Irv Staley and Jake Borowsky—and the fact that he was invited to give the commencement address at the Rhinebeck High School!

And I was happy with his success. I was glad, too, that we were not living in New York City for all the fanfare. In Rhinebeck we just went on with quiet, beautiful days, with our walk in the afternoon, our golf with the Montagues on weekends, and our mornings at the typewriters.

There were hundreds of letters to answer, letters from people all over the United States, thanking Willie for the hope he had given them and asking for the name of the hospital that he had described. Rarely was the letter from an alcoholic himself, but from a mother, a wife, or a sister. Willie tried to answer each one of them, saying the same thing to all, which was that the only way a person could be cured was by *wanting* to be cured, himself, not because someone else wanted it. He also said what he had said in his book, and it was one of his most valuable contributions: that alcoholism was a disease, a sickness, and should be treated as such and not as a social offense. I won't say, of course, that he was the first to suggest this, but at least he helped people not to be ashamed of a sick husband, son, or brother—or sister, for that matter.

One lovely day, while Willie was taking his nap and I was finishing canning jars of string beans that John Lattin, our gardener, had grown in great profusion, I saw a car, driven by a liveried chauffeur, come slowly up our driveway. By the time I had awakened Willie there was a knock at our door, and my Scottie, Bobbie, instead of barking, began to wag her tail furiously with joy.

Our visitor was a beautiful, slender woman with white hair who introduced herself as Mrs. John Jay Chapman of Barrytown. Willie knew her immediately as the sister of his old friend Bob Chanler, and made her welcome. She admired the portrait that Chanler had painted of Willie and that hung in the cottage living room across from the portrait of me that John Koch had painted. The portrait made a conversational wedge, and then, graciously, she brought up the subject of *Asylum*, which she had just read.

She had come, she said, to thank Willie for writing it. She said that there was a member of her family who was going to be helped by it. The book had given them all a basis for hope, and for this she was very grateful.

Willie was at his most charming best, too. I served tea. We talked politely about Rhinebeck and how much we liked it, and of the writings of her husband. We talked of Bob Chanler and his notorious exploits as well as his genius as a portrait painter. She said we must come to visit her and see her collection of screens that Bob had painted, and then she rose to leave.

Turning to me, she said, "Good-bye, Mrs. Seabrook. I hope you will enjoy living among us." She held out her hand, and Willie bent over and kissed it. And then she left.

After the car had rolled majestically down our graveled road we both sat deep in thought for a while. Then Willie said, "I think that blessed dowager had a message for us, Mink. As long as we're living here, in a small American community, I suppose we should get married. What do you think?"

I had been very proud of the fact that I, a writer, should be living with another writer, just as George Sand and George Eliot had lived with the men they loved without feeling it necessary to go through a bourgeois ceremony. But, well—Willie and Katie were divorced now, and I had obtained a divorce from Lyman in Toulon, and they had married each other. There seemed no good reason not to, and every reason for us to marry.

And so, one afternoon of the following week, Professor Montague drove us over to Sharon, Connecticut, where we were married quietly by the justice of the peace.

Chapter Nineteen

This new kind of life was as interesting and thrilling to us both as if we had embarked on a voyage to another Timbuctoo. We woke up happy and found plenty to keep us busy until we went to bed at night, together, in the cottage. It was as if we had found each other again, and were closer than we had ever been before, in love and in understanding. With all our differences of personality and interests, we had become one, as people really in love become one. In spite of the apparently insurmountable differences—because sexual compatibility is supposed to be so important in marriage and we were never to find it—we found comfort and security in each other's arms, in the nights that were sometimes very dark.

After the success of *Asylum* Willie was given assignments by several of the top-paying magazines, and I think he enjoyed getting into harness again. However we both felt about his kinship with Blake, Dostoevsky, Jakob Boehme and the other mystics, Willie always said of himself that he was, above all else, "a damn good reporter."

He had been writing for the *American Magazine* when Sumner Blossom, its editor, suggested to Willie that he try entering a public institution for the insane, under an assumed name, and compare it with the way patients were treated in a private hospital such as he had described in his book. Only the superintendent in charge would know about it; to the rest of the staff he would be just another patient.

The idea delighted Willie and frightened me. Perhaps, knowing him as I did, I was afraid that if they discovered his deviations from the normal behind those thick walls they might not let him out again. But Willie gleefully set to work pulling wires, with the result that Dr. Galbraith, his psychiatrist at Bloomingdale, arranged for his admission to the New Hampshire State Asylum. And one morning Willie set out for New Hampshire in the car of a friend who was to sign the necessary papers. He was wearing the clothes he had worn in Toulon, blue denim trousers, a short-sleeved tricot shirt, a red bandanna handkerchief tied around his neck. His hair was uncombed and a little wild. The few belongings he took with him were tied up, hobo fashion, in another red bandanna. It was the way he usually traveled, even when we went to New York to stay at the Gotham.

Often, when Willie was bored or when he wanted to retreat from a difficult situation or a stupid conversation, he could make his face a complete blank and stare, with blue eyes become opaque, at a world that displeased him. This is the blank expression he assumed as he set out for the New Hampshire State Asylum for the Insane. I thought to myself that he could fool anybody. And then I realized he didn't need to fool them very much, after all.

He was a patient for only a few weeks before a nurse or an orderly remembered seeing his picture accompanying a review of *Asylum*. But before that happened he had managed to get himself passed along from observation ward through several others to the violent ward, after putting on a wild act. He gathered a lot of material and turned in several stunning articles. What he had found was that, except for the lack of certain luxuries and occasional pampering of patients in a private sanitarium, mentally sick people stood as good a chance of being healed in a public institution as they were in the hospital in White Plains. He spent as much time with psychiatrists and found them as interested and concerned and helpful as at Bloomingdale. He could then, in all fairness, assure people who could not afford the steep prices at private asylums that they should not hesitate to commit their relatives to a state hospital. He saw no brutality, no neglect. In fact, there was an intensity of treatment because the public hospitals were overcrowded and the sooner a patient was "cured" the sooner there would be room for another.

One of the more or less amusing results of the series of articles in the *American Magazine* was that some of the literary critics who reviewed *Asylum* had suggested that Seabrook committed himself to Bloomingdale as a stunt to get material for a book, the same motivation that had taken him into Haiti and the jungles of West Africa or the Arabian Desert. And now certain columnists hinted that Seabrook had had a relapse and had been sent to a state hospital for the insane.

Willie, who did more than most people to cause gossip and hearsay, often remarked that what was said was rarely true, and that often the truth, if the gossips only knew it, was much worse than anything they repeated.

The Reader's Digest, about this same time, gave Willie assignments for which he was paid handsomely and further rewarded by a bonus at Christmas. Apparently, even if the *Saturday Evening Post's* editor disapproved of William Seabrook's morals, DeWitt Wallace—the redoubtable publisher of the *Digest* and as much a guardian of the American people as George Horace Lorimer—thought that Willie had redeemed himself with *Asylum*. At any rate a friendship sprang up between DeWitt Wallace and Willie, as disparate a pair of men as could be imagined.

There were editorial conferences at the temporary offices in Pleasantville, and once Willie was invited to the Wallace house in Chappauqua to discuss something or other. Willie returned as much impressed by the magnificent modern palace as he had been by the black tents of Ibn Saud. Later, when I saw the new offices I was equally impressed. Perhaps the reason was that we had lived for so long in the South of France, where most of the architecture had remained the same for centuries. We were unprepared for the strides that had been made, in architecture as well as in a great many other things, here in America during our absence. The new offices and the new home of the Wallaces were the first of their kind we had seen.

185

DeWitt Wallace was a tall, slender man with a noble face. He looked like a minister of the gospel, which was why Willie, who distrusted what he called "do-gooders," never felt as close to him as he inevitably felt to his editors, although he greatly admired the Wallaces for the success they had made of a pocket-sized magazine.

Once, when we were in town for a few days at the Gotham, Mr. Wallace came to call on us. I remember him standing by the window, talking quietly. I felt there was an essential good-ness about him that success and the Madison Avenue rat race would not touch. I don't know what he expected to find in Willie, but I knew that he was puzzled and tried to draw him out.

That fall, when the Madison Square Garden Horse Show opened, the Wallaces asked Willie and me to be guests in their box. To my delight, another guest was John Gunther, whom I had not seen since Paris. I remember saying to Lila Belle Acheson Wallace how much I appreciated her inviting us, and her rather strange answer that it was DeWitt who had done the inviting. They had the box for the week, but she had been unable to invite any of her own friends because DeWitt had filled the seats with his favorite authors. I knew how she felt, and sympathized.

Things were going extremely well with us now. We loved Rhinebeck and our neighbors. We were working hard, Willie on his assignments and I at short stories that sold slowly but sweetly to *Mademoiselle, Harper's,* and the *American Mercury.* My checks were infinitesimal compared with Willie's, but I did pay for graveling the cottage driveway, an accomplishment Willie boasted about to everyone who came to see us.

And a great many people came to see us. For a while I did most of the cooking and housework, actually enjoying it for the first time in my life. But then the impromptu luncheons and dinners got too much for my small repertoire of recipes, and I appealed to a New York domestic agency for help. They sent us a maid who had once worked for other writers, "because she would understand us"; and she did.

Her name was Mae, and she was a lovely, pale-brown Southern girl with a soft voice and the ability to cook in the best Southern tradition. She was neat and clean about the house, and in every way what my mother used to call "a jewel." There were no other colored people in Rhinebeck that we knew of, and she was very lonely. She bought a guitar and taught herself to play, and every night, from her room over the living room in the cottage, we would hear the gentle ping of the strings as she plucked out a melody. It was, as Willie remarked, like the shy mating call of a dove.

After a weekend in Harlem, Mae came back with a tall, dark-skinned man and announced she had gotten married, and would we hire her husband as houseman and valet for Willie. To Willie's delight, Mae's husband had been a barber. We found a red plush antique barber chair somewhere in the village and installed it in the barn studio, where every day Willie received his friends while George shaved him or cut his hair. It was the height of luxury to Willie and made him feel as successful and important as if he owned a yacht to anchor in the Hudson beside Vincent Astor's.

George bought a flashy second-hand car and was soon spending his evenings at a bar in Red Hook, the next town, where he found some colored people of congenial tastes. Soon, at night, we began hearing the plaintive tunes on the guitar again from Mae's room. Then George described some of his friends who had a jazz combo, and Willie hired them to entertain at a Saturday luncheon we were giving for the Allan Ryans, in the barn. It was an unusual luncheon, as anyone might expect from Willie Seabrook, and I think our guests were enthusiastic, but that night we discovered a lot of loose cash and some jewelry was gone from the cottage, where George's friends had wandered between numbers. Reluctantly we notified the local police, and they arrested all of them, including George, who may have done nothing more serious than to fall into bad company. To my deep regret, Mae left soon afterward.

We kept on entertaining a lot, and went through all kinds of hired help, and most of the time I did all the work myself, in addition to acting as Willie's secretary and writing my own things. It wasn't easy, and yet I was happier than I had ever been in my life and Willie was as happy as I had ever known him to be. Nobody seemed to mind that we didn't offer cocktails or any hard liquor. People were very kind about understanding our problem. Or, if they didn't understand the whole problem, they knew that as the author of *Asylum* Willie couldn't let his public down!

One of the first things we bought, after the house and barn and nine acres, was a Capehart, the latest word in phonographs. Willie proceeded to buy all the Beethoven and Brahms symphonies, and then Mozart, Handel, Haydn, Bach, Stravinsky— and Verdi. In his early career as a reporter on the Atlanta *Journal,* Willie had taken over the job of music critic. That was when the opera first came to Atlanta. He told me he had never attended a live opera before, nor had he heard Verdi sung. The first was *Il Trovatore* and he was so emotionally stirred by the music, he said, that after the first act he went outside into a dark alley and threw up.

One of our new friends was the headmistress of an exclusive boarding school for girls. Because Willie was a literary celebrity we were invited to reception days at the school, and to attend their plays, including *As You Like It* on the broad lawns of the old Tracy Dows estate. In return, we used to invite the entire music class and their teacher to a concert on our Capehart in the barn. I would write the programs and illustrate them, and serve up cookies and cider. It was fun.

Incidentally, it was on the same estate that Thomas Wolfe, as a guest of Olin Dows, wrote a good part of his novel *Of Time and the River*. Once, as I was being shown around what was now the school, I paused before the huge refrigerator in the kitchen and remembered Wolfe's description of the contents, shelf by shelf.

What makes a writer feel impelled to release such a spate of

188

words upon so ordinary a subject as the contents of an electric icebox? Was Thomas Wolfe himself hungry at the time, and so impressed by the lavish supplies of food that the words poured out to increase or torment his great appetite, as a game he played on himself? Or did he have trouble with the action, the plot, of his novel, and by dwelling on detail after detail did he grasp a chance to put off the moment when his characters would have to be *doing* something instead of feeling something? Or did the words come tumbling out in sheer ecstasy at the sight of food to a man with such great appetites as Thomas Wolfe? Or, again, was it just a private love affair with words for their own sake?

Perhaps it was this same gigantic refrigerator, in the kitchen of what was no longer a private family house but a girls' school, that impelled me to write a short story called "Hunger." Or the idea may have been conceived at a tea we were invited to attend by the headmistress, given in honor of a shabby but brilliant Viennese woman with a title of some sort. Who knows where the idea for a story comes from, or how it comes? An impression, a spoken phrase, the nod of a head or another gesture—at any rate, I was in a receptive frame of mind. Willie was away on an assignment, and I was not only lonely but secretly worried. It was the first time he had been on his own since his departure from the hospital in White Plains.

I couldn't explain just why I was worried, because he had shown no interest in drinking or even in his sadistic games. But I felt that although we were safe together, out there in the world beyond our nine acres lurked all kinds of enemies. In fact, I quietly worked myself up into a psychosomatic "heart condition" which almost fooled Dr. Montague. She prescribed small doses of strychnine, I believe, and then she sent me to be examined by a cardiac specialist, who, on finishing the examination, looked me in the eyes and said, "Mrs. Seabrook, I am glad to be able to tell you that it would take nothing short of a dumdum bullet to stop your heart." Which was comforting since I never expected to get in the way of a bullet, but it did throw me back on another escape tack, which was writing. The story

189

of the headmistress, the school, the German teacher, and her friend the shabby little Countess, took hold of me and wrote itself.

The history of "Hunger" is a Cinderella story and should be encouraging to young writers. Willie liked it when I showed it to him, and I sent it to an agent I had at the time. She returned it, saying she was sorry but she just didn't believe in it, so I put it away in a desk drawer and forgot it. A long time after that, my friends John and Dora Koch came to see us and John asked what I had been writing. Willie had been going through a bad spell at that time, and the truth was that I hadn't written anything. But I didn't want to admit that to John and Dora; I remembered the story I had put away, and I showed it to them. They were enthusiastic and insisted I send it off again. So I sent it to Ann Watkins, and it was sold to *Harper's Bazaar*, the first magazine to see it. To my infinite surprise and joy, that story was selected by both the O'Brien and the O. Henry prize collections of short stories for the same year, and afterwards it appeared in numerous anthologies of short stories, including one called *New Highways in College Composition*. It is the sort of fairy tale that members of writing classes always bring up, and I have been very glad to be able to tell about my one story that might never have seen daylight except for a happy chance. Usually I have found that when a good agent isn't sold on a story, he is right.

Willie liked people, and he talked to people whether he had been introduced or not. And one day he came home and said that he had talked to a lovely lady who had read his books and was very nice to him. She was Mrs. Lyman Delano. Now, while all the River people were more or less related to each other, the Delanos were especially related through the President's mother, Sarah Delano Roosevelt, who lived in the neighboring town of Hyde Park.

The town of Rhinebeck was hotly Republican, and although they all loved and respected the President's mother and told wonderful stories about what a grand old girl she was, they did not like nor did they approve of F.D.R. One of those who disapproved of him the most was his mother's first cousin Lyman Delano.

A few days after Willie had told me of his meeting with Mrs. Delano, the phone rang in the cottage where we were having lunch together. I heard a few snatches of the conversation, and then Willie returned to the table, smiling. He said that Mrs. Delano had phoned to invite us to dinner the following Wednesday.

This was, I knew, being asked to visit the most impenetrable of the fortresses along the sacred river. None of the friends we had made, even those who were on intimate terms with the Astors, the Redmonds, the Ryans, and the Livingstons, had been received or entertained in the Delano house. I was sorry Willie had accepted so quickly. I was sure it would be a stuffy evening, but Willie thought it might be interesting.

When that Wednesday came, he put on his dinner jacket without a murmur and I wore my most conservative long dress. We drove to the river in the village taxi because Willie hated night driving. After we passed the Delano gate house, there were miles of curved road, as there were on all the River estates, and then we arrived at the brilliantly lighted house, where we got out and dismissed the taxi.

We rang the bell, and eventually a liveried butler came to the door. He seemed surprised and waited for us to say something. "Mr. and Mrs. Seabrook," I said grandly, and walked through the door which he held open. Willie followed me and began taking off his beret and top coat, which he handed to the butler. We were ushered into a small room at the side of the entrance hall and respectfully asked to wait. I began to sense that something was wrong.

The butler returned and led us into a drawing room that was swarming with young people in party clothes. A charming gray-haired woman came toward us and put out her hand. "How nice of you to call on us," she said, and started to introduce us, first to her husband, a tall, dignified man in dinner jacket.

I asked Mrs. Delano if I could talk to her for a moment, and

191

when we stepped aside I said, "I'm sure there's been some dread-
ful mistake. Willie understood that you had asked us for tonight
. . ." I told her about the telephone call, and her face broke
into a smile.

"How funny," she said. "The children are just home from
school and we are having a dinner party for them. We would
be simply delighted to have you join us, but I have an idea
what might have happened. Do you suppose it was Laura
Delano, our cousin, who phoned you the other day? Let's call
her and find out."

Willie, by this time, was perfectly at ease and talking ani-
matedly with some of the young people, and I was getting more
and more uncomfortable. Mrs. Delano came back, laughing.
Our invitation had indeed been from Laura Delano, the President's favorite cousin, and she was holding up her dinner party,
waiting for us. Would we get there as soon as possible?

Everyone thought it was a great joke, including Willie, who
was reluctant to leave all those pretty young girls. Someone
offered to drive us to Miss Delano's, and when we finally got
there we had a delightful time with a brilliant and witty hostess,
our good friends Olin Dows and his sister Deborah, and a few
other writers and painters.

We did a lot of entertaining, mostly of people who formed a
nucleus of what was then called café society. Willie was back at
the height of his fame, and could always be counted on to say
or do something original that people could talk about later to
their friends at other luncheons or dinner parties.

We worked, too, at our typewriters, Willie in the barn studio
and I in my little room upstairs in the cottage. And we made
occasional trips to New York, where the Gotham became a kind
of second home. We would take the manager and his wife
strawberries from our garden, and there were always flowers for
me in our room when we arrived at the hotel. They even let me
bring my dog, Bobbie, although it was breaking a house rule.

Once a year we had dinner at the Van Vechtens' to celebrate
the joint birthdays of Carl, Alfred Knopf, and James Weldon
Johnson. And when we had to be in town we managed to see a

few plays and art exhibits, and attend concerts. We were given a trip to Bermuda, all expenses paid, for a publicity stunt thought up by the Bermuda Chamber of Commerce. Phil Stong, who had just written *State Fair*, and his wife, Virginia Swain, had been offered the same trip for the same reasons. We met on the *Queen of Bermuda* and became lifelong friends. It was in February, and every day was cold and rainy. But we had to stand out of doors in summery clothes to be photographed for whatever were the purposes of the publicity. The governor's wife invited us to a cocktail party and she and Willie got along beautifully, but the rest of us were bored. We played poker, the four of us, most of the time on the boat and in the lounge of the Bermudiana Hotel. I don't know whether we were supposed to write about Bermuda on our return, but I was the only one who did. I used it for a scene in one of the chapters of a novel called *Manhattan Solo*, the last one I wrote for Knopf, and not a very good one.

Willie wasn't drinking at all, and life was beautiful and fun, except for the ups and downs of a writer's life, the encouragement and despondency, the hopes and the despairs. Willie always insisted that writing was agony for him and that he hated the actual putting down of words on paper. While I can't say actually I enjoyed the process, I have been happier when writing than at any other times. It was only when I didn't like what I had written, when the spark of life was absent from it, that I suffered, but that was mostly from frustration or disappointment. When we were both busy at our respective typewriters I came the nearest to enjoying a sense of peace. That was what I felt we were born to do. The rest of our living was incidental.

I believe it was about then that Willie decided to write a book called *Witchcraft*. One of the things that had interested him passionately all his life was what he called Black Magic. He read everything he could find on the subject, including all of Montague Summer's books, and his knowledge of werewolves, poltergeists, and such phenomena was extensive. In some way— and I believe it dated from his earlier association with Aleister

Crowley during the Greenwich Village period in both their lives —Willie's witchcraft and magic were tied in with his sexual sadism.

There is much talk today of something called psychedelics, which, loosely, means expansion of consciousness, or what Willie called "going through the door." It is a sharpening of perception, such as Aldous Huxley later described in a little book called *The Doors of Perception,* an account of his own experiment with the drug mescaline.

Willie's experiments in an effort to break down the wall of the senses into something indescribably wonderful—that is, into a state where one leaves the body and becomes aware of perceptions denied the ordinary senses—were through the medium of pain. How much this was tied up with his own sexual pattern, I have never been sure, but his interest in the higher perception, in the passage through "the door" to a keener awareness and sensitivity, was absolutely real and sincere. As he so often said, nothing is ever purely unmixed.

And so now, when he was starting to write a book about magic and witchcraft, he insisted he needed to make some experiments, and proceeded to hire a series of young women to help him with his research. I was deeply upset for several reasons, some of them obvious, of course; but since Willie had left Bloomingdale he had not only seemed to have lost any appetite for alcohol, he had also seemed to have lost interest in some of the games that had once taken up so much of his time. I always kept my fingers crossed, hoping they were over for good; now I knew they would be starting up again, and I found them harder to accept than I had when I was younger and more completely dominated by Willie and his ideas and desires.

I tried to keep things running smoothly, while knowing that in the barn studio some rather nice girl had been persuaded to let herself be hung by a chain from the ceiling until she was so tired she hardly knew what she was doing or saying, and might possibly "go through that wall" into a psychedelic state. Or she would be made to kneel on a bare floor for half a night or day, until the pain became so intense she might have visions, as the great Saint Teresa of Ávila had visions after a night of kneeling in a convent cell. There were new methods of inflicting pain or fatigue that Willie had read about or created in his queer mind and that he tried to tell me about if I let him. But the whole thing now made me ill, nervously and physically, especially when I had to receive friends or acquaintances who called while the sessions were going on elsewhere. I would use the excuse that Willie was working or taking a nap, and nobody suspected anything. But sometimes when I was alone with Willie I would lose my temper and we would quarrel. The girls were eventually sent away, each in turn, and life would become peaceful for a while, and no real harm had been done to anybody. But I lived in dread of the next time.

Among the letters and notes I have saved is a little one from Willie, probably written after one of our quarrels, in which he said he loved me and would try to do his best. He asked me to forgive him for that bad day, and hoped for some good future days for us both, and always together.

Aside from those nerve-racking sessions, we were leading what was for us an exemplary and incredibly normal life. We had put a badminton court next to the house, and Willie played a fast and furious game with me or with our guests; or he played tennis on the Billings' court or the Vincent Astors'. On weekends we played golf with the Montagues on the Rhinebeck nine-hole course. I gardened a little, but John Lattin did most of the work; between us we managed to win a prize in a contest sponsored by the *Herald Tribune*.

In Rhinebeck, as in all small towns, there was a great deal of gossip, and there was plenty of talk about Willie's "research girls," started by our friendly taxi driver, who picked them up at the railroad station in Rhinecliff and dropped them off there again after a few days. But people were very fond of Willie, perhaps because he showed that he liked them, and they were ready to forgive him his peculiarities.

It was at about this time that the Huxleys decided to come to America and to put up their Sanary house for sale. They stayed with us while they were getting their bearings. To my surprise they liked Rhinebeck, which was close enough to New York for Aldous to meet his publishers when necessary, and they decided to finish out the winter near us before going West.

With the help of Deborah Dows we managed to get them the dairy house on Foxhollow, the Dows estate, which by now had been sold to young John Jacob Astor. It may or may not have been the same little cottage that Olin Dows had lent to Thomas Wolfe, but I liked to think it was.

It was very exciting, having the Huxleys near us again. I loved them both. Maria had a knack of making any place they lived in, no matter how crude and uncomfortable (as the neglected dairy house surely must have been), seem as smart as an apartment in Mayfair. We sometimes took walks with them, for they were daily walkers, like most people except Americans, and we would have tea in the kitchen of their house, tea with something special that Maria had dug up in a prosaic market, gingerbread, or sweet cakes exactly like French Madeleines. I am sure they suffered from the cold that winter, but they didn't complain. Once their young son Matthew, whom they had sent off to school, came to stay with them for the Christmas vacation and caught a severe cold. I felt guilty and partially responsible because, knowing how frail they were or seemed to be, I thought I should have found them a warm, snug place in the village, whether or not it had literary or social ambience.

Sometimes when Maria had to go to New York to see to one of the numerous matters she was always taking care of—for Aldous or one of her sisters or Matthew or a friend—she would drive over with Aldous and leave him with us for the day. After lunch, Willie would go off to the cottage to take his nap and I would entertain Aldous, which meant listening as intelligently as I could while he discoursed upon a great variety of subjects in which he was interested.

Once I had gone with Professor Montague to the studio of an artist who had painted his portrait, which was to hang in one of the halls at Columbia University. In the studio was a photograph of a portrait the same artist had made of Albert Einstein, and under it was written a quotation from Einstein himself:

196

"One of the most beautiful things we can experience is the mysterious. It is the source of all true science and art. He who can no longer pause to wonder is as good as dead."

I believe this applied to Aldous Huxley, as I know it did to Willie Seabrook. Both men had an abounding interest in everything—except, perhaps, the banal and commonplace. It was what made them such fascinating people to be with, what made them so very much alive until the stroke of death put an end to —or answered—their curiosity about life.

Those were beautiful, happy, exciting and productive years, and I think we were happier than either of us had ever been in our lives before. Then a picture of Willie appeared in one of the newspapers, accompanying a review of his latest book, *These Foreigners,* a compilation of pieces he had written on assignment for a magazine. The critic wrote that Seabrook was getting tamed down, fat, smug, and prosperous. And Willie began to worry. It was the last kind of image he wanted the world to have of him.

One day he came home from the village with a brown paper bag. Out of it he drew several bottles of whiskey. He set them down on the table in the cottage and said, "I'm sick of being a cripple. From now on I'm going to prove that I can take a drink or leave it alone, like any other man." He poured himself a drink and swallowed it. It was the first time he had taken one since he left the hospital in White Plains. It was not to be the last.

Chapter Twenty

The winter of 1939 had overtones of foreboding both in our personal lives and in the world outside us.

Willie had signed up for a series of lectures, and was away a lot of the time. Before that he had been having difficulty writing, and now lecturing took him away from his typewriter for weeks at a stretch. And I was worried about him because he had taken that first drink and because he was out in the world without me. All the old feelings of insecurity came back, perhaps the more insidious because the past few years had been so beautiful, and for the first time in our lives we had been happy and at peace.

Most of the time when Willie was away I stayed alone with my Scottie and got some work done. But a lot of the time I carried on a busy social life as best I could without Willie, behind whose shining light I could always bask in comfortable obscurity.

I kept a journal sporadically and here are a few entries:

Friday, February 10, 1939. Willie left this morning, in a good mood and looking very well, to give a lecture in Buffalo. According to Colsten Leigh's brochure the subject is "magic," and I'm afraid that has led to misunderstanding. Once, when Willie was giving a lecture in Fairfield County, I drove over to hear him. The lecture was given in a private home, and the drawing room seemed to be filled with white-haired dowagers and a goodly sprinkling of scrubbed grandchildren. I am sure they expected to see the usual tricks of rabbits pulled out of hats and mysterious card tricks and were surprised to hear about Wamba, the friendly witch of the Côte d'Ivoire! Especially when Willie, carried away by his theme, used his strongest language and pulled no punches.

Saturday, February 11th. Jonathan Cape arrived for a short visit, which I think Willie was glad to escape as he and Jonathan are still harboring bad feelings over the Yakouba book, which Willie gave to Harrap instead because of a disagreement over the advance for the trip to Timbuctoo. But I am still fond of Jonathan, who published my first novel, written long before Knopf published *Mrs. Taylor.* It was the advance on that book, small as it was, that helped me get to Paris to join Willie in 1926, and perhaps, for good or bad, changed the course of our lives. Aside from a fairly lecherous approach to females, Jonathan could be a good friend and I like to think of him as one.

Monday, February 13th. Willie came back from the lecture trip feeling low in spirits and discouraged. I tried to tell him that he would still write good books and that this was just one of those barren intervals. I did my best to persuade him that he still had his best work to do. I am discouraged myself, but I dare not show it. I had written to Blanche Knopf for a copy of *Mrs. Taylor* to send to Lady Hastings, and Blanche wrote me that *Mrs. Taylor* has been out of print since 1934. There have been no demands for it.

Sunday, February 19th. Gloomy white fog, after beautiful winter weather with temperature at ten degrees. To lunch at the Montagues. Willie fought with Miss Nellie and I snarled at Monty.

I'm trying to get us to New York for a week or ten days during this interval while Willie waits to hear from DeWitt Wallace about a new project. How he needs one bright flash of good news! I can bear my own frustrations, but not Willie's!

We took a small apartment at the Shoreham, which was on the same street as the Gotham but a little less expensive. Willie didn't like it at first because the rooms were small and weren't ready for us when we arrived in the middle of the afternoon. We had been spoiled by our treatment at the Gotham, where everyone knew us. But we were in one of our economy periods —which usually meant that we made a great deal of fuss about saving a little with our right hand while we let twice as much flow through our left. Neither of us had any sense about money. Katie had taken care of it for Willie, and Lyman had paid the bills and kept a close eye on finances when I was married to him. Now, if we wanted anything and there was enough money in the bank to pay for it—or enough credit—we bought it. Apparently that is not the way to stay solvent.

The first night we had dinner with Melville Cane and his wife, Florence, and went to hear the D'Oyly Carte Company in *The Gondoliers*. Willie's birthday was the next day, February 22nd. Like a child, he always expected something wonderful for his birthday, and I had a hard time finding a present that would satisfy him. Most of the time, being nervous about it, I would get him precisely the wrong thing, like slippers that were too small. He never politely covered his disappointment.

I remember one Christmas that we spent in Paris. We were living in a *pied-à-terre* we had above a corner café on the Place de l'Odéon, on the same side as the theater. Our apartment was just one flight up above the street. For this Christmas Willie had expressed a wish for a new Waterman fountain pen. When I went shopping for it, at Brentano's, on the Right Bank, I allowed myself to be persuaded to buy a Parker pen, which was new on the market. I also, on an impulse, bought a plastic traveling inkwell, since ballpoint pens were then unheard of.

We exchanged presents on Christmas Eve, just before dressing to go to a party someone was giving in Montparnasse. I was wearing a black velvet gown, over the tightest of little black satin corsets. It had been made for me by a Paris dressmaker so that it buttoned down the back with dozens of velvet-covered buttons and hand-sewn buttonholes. I couldn't possibly get sealed up in it without help, and so I asked Willie to help. He began with the bottom button and started up. The buttons were tiny and Willie's hands were large and his finger tips blunt. He paused now and then to take a swallow of cognac and swear, and he kept getting angrier and angrier as the buttons fought his fingers.

Suddenly he stopped, halfway up, and said, "I asked for a Waterman, not that bitch of a thing you gave me," and he went to the table where we had placed our gifts. "To hell with it," he roared, and threw it out of the window. Then he picked up the inkwell and sent it sailing out after the pen. I burst into tears, and a few moments later there was a knock on our door.

I opened it, with my dress half-buttoned, upon two very annoyed Paris gendarmes, one of whom was holding the plastic inkwell. Apparently the object had just missed his head as the two were passing under our window, and he had come to arrest us for jeopardizing the lives of pedestrians. I was too frightened to understand exactly what he was saying, and so was Willie, who stood petrified. He always considered policemen, of any nationality, his natural enemies.

Then I had an inspiration. With the tears still streaming down my cheeks, I explained in French that I had given my husband a Christmas present and he hadn't liked it. French policemen, I think, are exceptionally gallant men. These two looked at each other and then at me, expressing infinite sympathy and pity. Then they shrugged their shoulders, and one of them said, "Poor Madame!"

Willie had recovered sufficiently to fill four little glasses with cognac, and we drank together with a wish for a Merry Christmas to us all, and the gendarmes left. Willie was angelic for the rest of that holiday season.

The night of his birthday in New York we walked over to Broadway and went to a newsreel and then to see *Hellzapoppin,* and for the first time in months I heard Willie laugh!

Here are a few entries in my Journal for that week—the week that was a conscious effort on our part to get out of a rut by filling ourselves full of pictures, music, theater, and stimulating companionship.

Thursday, February 23rd. In the morning Willie and I went to see Laurence Tompkins' water colors at the Carstair Galleries. Then to the Valentine Gallery to see a show of Utrillos that we were crazy about. Then to meet John Koch at the Kraushaar, to see his new paintings that are going on exhibition next week. Willie so enthusiastic he arranged to meet Harry Bull of *Town & Country* there at 2:30. Harry was so impressed that he plans to run a color reproduction and wants Willie to write an article to go with it.

In the afternoon I went shopping and bought velvet ribbon for my hair and stockings and gloves, but resisted temptation to buy any new clothes.

Marvelous dinner at Laurence Tompkins' . . . Betty Fields Finan, her husband, and some other charming people there. Laurence gave me the water color of red roses that Lady Hastings painted for me, beautifully framed.

Friday, February 24th. Lunched in the apartment, then we walked to Broadway to see a movie with W. C. Fields in it. Then cocktail party at Henry and Gladys Billings', mostly for painters and art critics we didn't know. Dinner at Ward ("Jimmy") Greene's. Talk and bridge afterwards. Seeing Jimmy and Hallie again after all these years was not the strain I expected it to be. We have all grown mellower and kinder, and perhaps a little tired! News of Lyman and Katie. They have bought a remodeled farmhouse in Bucks County and seem to be happy.

Saturday, February 25th. Wonderful round of exhibitions with Willie in the morning. Tintoretto at the Durlacher Gallery, Rembrandt's portrait of a lady ("Petronella Buys") with a ruff. "Like listening to Haydn," Willie said. Then to see early American paintings by James Peale and his family—watermelons, birds, fruit. I loved them. Willie excited by the Roualts at another gallery, but somehow they do not reach me. In afternoon to see Tallulah Bankhead in *The Little Foxes*. Then dinner with Alfred and Blanche Knopf, André Simon, and Logan Clendenning at the Passy.

Sunday, February 26th. Lunch at Harry Bull's narrow little house in the East 50's. Met Kay Blow and her husband. Dinner at "21" with Jonathan Cape, and to Radio City Music Hall after.

Monday, February 27th. John Koch here in the morning, to show Willie some other paintings of his for the *Town & Country* article. Then I had lunch with Elsie Arden and Willie went out to look over the World's Fair with Henry Billings, who is doing a mural out there. At 5:30 we went to call on Eddie Wasserman at the St. Regis. Maugham's secretary, Mr. Haxton, was there, also Aureole Lee, Mary Astor, and the Van Vechtens. Champagne and amusing talk. Then to Harlem with Carl and Fania, dinner at the Cotton Club. Either it or we have changed. Nothing seemed as amusing and lively as we had remembered it.

But it was we who were tired. After our rather quiet life in Rhinebeck we had been overstuffing ourselves with food, people, plays, pictures—with New York itself. We had another lunch with Jonathan, called on Mai Mai Sze, dined with the Montagues in their house on Twelfth Street, went again to hear the D'Oyly Cartes—this time *Cox and Box* and *Pinafore* —after which we walked back along Broadway to the Shoreham, admiring the neon lights like a pair of country bumpkins. "Let's go home," Willie said, holding my hand as we walked. "Let's," I answered.

The next day we returned to Rhinebeck. John Lattin had painted the floors and woodwork in the cottage; it looked beautiful. Willie was out of his depression and we both got back to our typewriters. But not for long.

Willie had expected to find some word from *The Reader's Digest* about an idea he had suggested for a piece on Hitler, but nothing had come from them during our absence. DeWitt Wallace was in Florida and had not yet returned. I suppose in all professions and in all kinds of businesses there has to be a loss of time waiting for a decision to come through the mail or over the telephone. But it seems to me that writers do more waiting than anyone else. Let's say you get a bright idea, either out of the blue or by hard thinking and wishing. You put it into shape and with the first fine flush of enthusiasm you send it off to an editor, a publisher, or your agent. You walk on clouds or in a fever of creative excitement. And then what happens? Nothing. For days, weeks, and sometimes months, nothing happens at all. The editor is taking a vacation. Or he is getting a divorce or a new baby—or, what is most likely, the various editors who have to okay your idea can't reach an agreement. All this is perfectly reasonable and legitimate from any point of view but the author's, who has to live out the suspense somehow, realizing that if he starts something else, it will be almost impossible to get back the first flush of en- thusiasm for the idea if the editors finally decide to accept it.

Some writers stay drunk during the waiting period, some just try to put it out of their minds and act like human beings. Willie played tennis—and hired a girl to play "Lizzie in Chains" up in the barn.

Fortunately a lecture date in Detroit cut the session short

and he was gone for a few days. When he returned, he had an idea for a book and dictated an outline to me, as he had no secretary just then. We took walks, and looked for signs of spring in the woods, and adopted a pet skunk and her family whom we found on our front porch. We fed them bread and milk, which they seemed to like, but my cats objected to them and they went away.

And we listened to the radio in the evenings. The news from Europe was frightening. Rumania, "placed in a difficult position by German seizures of her imports," was ready to be drawn into the Nazi orbit. Soviet Russia joined Great Britain and France in refusing "to recognize Hitler's absorption of Czecho-Slovakia and Britain seeks military alliance." The French ambassador left Germany for Paris. Premier Daladier began calling up reserve troops. War seemed inevitable. "We are both scared," I wrote in my Journal, March 20, 1939, "but so is everybody, I guess. Maybe Hitler is, too. Isn't it crazy!"

Golo Mann came to pay us a visit. During his stay some friends of his drove over from Wesleyan University to see him. One of them was a boy named Jaffey, exiled from Germany because, although his mother was a Von Richtofen, related to the famous German ace of World War I, his father was a Jew.

After Golo's visit we both tried to get back to work. But there was still no word from the *Digest* and Willie began drinking heavily. Over weekends we played golf with the Montagues and helped them entertain their company as they helped us with ours. It was a late spring. The weather stayed cold well into April. My novel bogged down and I read Percy's *Reliques,* of all things.

One day Ann Watkins called up to offer Willie a job writing the story of the Vanderbilt family for *Cosmopolitan.* He turned it down, and I was glad. On top of that, we heard at last from *The Reader's Digest.* DeWitt Wallace rejected the idea of the article on Hitler. (Since, if I remember correctly, Willie was suggesting that the rest of the world deliberately *hex* Hitler and proposed several methods by which this could be done, I can understand DeWitt Wallace's decision.)

The next Saturday Ann Watkins drove up with Colston Leigh. Ostensibly they came to discuss a new lecture contract, but Ann took the opportunity to try to persuade Willie to do the Vanderbilt piece for *Cosmopolitan*. They stayed for lunch and left in the middle of the afternoon. Ann was a small blonde bombshell and, at the time, the best literary agent in New York, and she and Willie had a deep affection for each other. But after they left, he was in a strange mood.

I had an appointment at the beauty parlor in the village, and when I came back Willie was drinking and reading over the notes he had started on the book about magic and witchcraft. He seemed unhappy, and I understood at least part of what was troubling him. More and more he was being offered financial propositions that had no relationship to literature, and with each magazine assignment, each book suggestion from his agent, such as the one to write about the Vanderbilt family, each lucrative lecture before a group of silly or pretentious women, he felt himself going farther and farther away from his goal.

We walked hand in hand down to the little pond between our place and the Langdon estate, and we watched the ducks swim around. I wrote in my Journal on Friday, April 7th: "Somehow, I am more worried about Willie in this mood than if he were violent. My darling. What can I say or do to help him? It's all so complicated and difficult and bewildering, and there is no answer, except to live and do the best we can. Maybe he takes things too seriously, too hard—himself especially."

For the Easter weekend that year we drove over to Washington, Connecticut, to visit Virginia and Phil Stong. Phil had just finished one of his "kid" books and was writing a book about horses, and Virginia was writing a novel about Kansas City in the 1880's. In the evening we played poker, as we had done in Bermuda when we first met. The next day neighbors came in—the Miltons, who had just returned from Europe and were in Munich during the crisis. There was much talk of war, and everyone was pessimistic except Willie. He was all for our getting in quickly and stopping Hitler. I was frightened, and overwhelmed by horror at what was happening to the Jews in Europe. I had a fantastic dream, as many had, of somehow shooting Hitler, myself, and preventing war. It was like waiting in the vestibule of a horror chamber; we were all of us, in that charming living room in the most beautiful of New England towns, afraid of something we could not yet even name.

Virginia, of whom I had become very fond, seemed nervous and unhappy. I knew Phil was drinking a lot, and she was worried about him and about her novel. In a way, it was like looking at ourselves in a mirror!

We drove home Monday morning, over back roads. Everything was still frozen and it was like January rather than spring. Just the same it had been Easter, of all holidays to me the most beautiful, perhaps because its message is Hope. We and the whole world needed the message that spring.

When we got home, we found that a *Reader's Digest* editor, Mr. Paine, had telephoned. Willie didn't bother to call back.

Bad news followed other worries. The Greek Orthodox Church, we learned, was bringing a suit against Willie, the *American Magazine,* and Harcourt, Brace. Sumner Blossom had given Willie an assignment to write a series of articles for the *American Magazine* about the various ethnic groups in the United States: the Germans in the Middle West, the Scandinavians in Minnesota, etc. Willie did his usual good job of reporting, embroidering facts at will to make a better anecdote and colorful writing. They were the articles subsequently published as the book called *These Foreigners.*

When Willie began work on the piece about White Russians in this country, Paul Chavchavadze took us out to Westbury, Long Island, where there was a colony of them, including exiled princes like himself, who conducted riding academies or raised cabbages, and a wonderful white bearded patriarch of the Greek Orthodox Church. We spent a good part of the day with Father Vasily and his family. Willie loved him, and wrote what we thought were laudatory remarks. He described the priest's love for little children, and told how he held an infant on his lap during the interview, and allowed it to "suck on his crucifix as if it were a lollypop."

However, in spite of the general tone of the Russian piece, which was filled with affection and praise for the colony, the members of Father Vasily's little congregation were indignant and resented the description of a baby using a cross as a pacifier. So they decided to sue for some fabulous sum of money.

Willie was sick about the fact that he had been so misunderstood, and also about the time consumed in the process. We had to go to New York for several visits to Melville Cane, and we also had to involve Prince Chavchavadze as a witness, which seemed an ungrateful thing to do. But in the end at any rate, Paul managed to convince the little colony on Long Island that Seabrook loved them all, and the lawsuit dissolved in thin air.

None of it was serious, but it came at a bad time for Willie, who was wrestling with his own soul and his own problems. I was glad he had several lecture engagements in the Middle West, because the very business of traveling about and meeting a lot of strangers would keep him from brooding—and, I hoped, from drinking.

Not long after we moved into the house of our own, I had started painting again. It filled in the periods when I was unable, for one reason or another, to concentrate on writing. I could paint in the living room, where I was available to Willie if he wanted me for anything or to the telephone or to stray callers. Willie had learned a little carpentering in Bloomingdale as physical therapy, and he made a lot of picture frames. He liked me to paint and enjoyed my pictures, which were more or less surrealistic. Although I had started out in life to be a painter and had gone to art school, I really was not very good at it, and gave it up as soon as I sold a poem to *Smart Set* while I was still in high school.

Now, with Willie gone and whole days to myself, I couldn't seem to write. I came across a poem by John Donne that seemed to me to express Willie, and so I made a large painting to illustrate various phases of Willie, and in the upper left corner, in gold leaf, I copied the poem:

A Hymn to God the Father

Wilt Thou forgive that sin where I begun,
　　Which was my sin, though it were done before?
Wilt Thou forgive that sin, through which I run,
　　And do run still, though still I do deplore?
When Thou hast done, Thou hast not done;
　　　　For I have more.

Wilt Thou forgive that sin which I have won
　　Others to sin? and made my sins their door?
Wilt Thou forgive that sin which I did shun
　　A year or two; but wallow'd in a score?
When Thou hast done, Thou hast not done;
　　　　For I have more.

I have a sin of fear, that when I've spun
　　My last thread, I shall perish on the shore;
But swear by Thyself that at my death Thy Son
　　Shall shine as He shines now and heretofore:
And having done that, Thou hast done;
　　　　I fear no more.

Willie liked it very much. The small figure of a man painted in various metamorphoses (with a few nudes and lambs scattered about) really did look like him. Some time later, when *Witchcraft* was published, Scribner's used it as a backdrop in their bookstore window on Fifth Avenue. Willie and I were in town for the publication date, and I remember our standing in front of the display, feeling proud and listening to comments from others who stopped to look. Some of the comments were indignant. Scribner's was not far from St. Patrick's Cathedral, and I remember one woman objecting to so lewd a picture being shown near the church. Perhaps it was rather shocking, but I had painted it with reverence; and besides, I had not dreamed it would ever be on public display!

It has been almost impossible for me to write about one side of Willie, possibly the side by which he is remembered, if at all. Because of a streak of prudery inherited from my mother (though heaven knows, I had broken away from her in other ways) I tried to cover up all those things that Willie was so damned exhibitionistic about. He made no secret of his sexual twist. He wanted people to know about his sadism, and to talk about it. I always felt that it was something private and horrid, to be kept out of sight like a running sore or a malignant disease. There was nothing I could do to change him, and because I couldn't run away from it (I had tried and had gone back) I lived with it, much like the proverbial ostrich, burying my face and pretending there was no sand storm at all.

That's why I never have been able to understand how it was so easy to paint that picture, or why I had so much joy doing it. Willie took great pride in it and hung it in a prominent place in his barn studio, along with a blown-up publicity still of him in the Bedouin robes he had worn when he fought with the Druses against the French. Both of those bits of biography have been lost, I suppose.

Willie came back from a successful trip. I had listened to a radio broadcast he made from Chicago and his voice sounded clear and calm, and what he had to say was interesting. He had some idea about giving a series of radio talks, but went back to writing in the barn. Tuppy, a black-and-white cat we thought was a male, gave birth to three kittens in the cellar. *The New Yorker,* which had asked to see some of my stories, turned them down but asked to see others. And I had a letter from my agent saying she had sold my story "At the Spa" to *Harper's Magazine.*

The kittens were sweet, jonquils and tulips were pushing up through the ground; the hard winter was over. But although we were enjoying a momentary spell of peace, there was to be none for the world.

The thunder in Germany was keeping us all nervous and on edge. It was a time when some people expressed an admiration for Hitler and blamed the Jews for the great trouble they were in. It was a time when anybody with Jewish blood, no matter that his reasons for obscuring the fact before, now stood up and let himself be counted. Nobody had taken religion very seriously in my family when I was a child, and in a search for something warm and near I had picked up one religion and then another. When I eloped with Stet, my first husband, his mother came to visit us and took me to Lenten services at the Episcopal Church and I thought they were simple and beautiful. I was baptized by a Father Whitehead at the very high church on 46th Street in New York, St. Mary the Virgin. Willie's in-and-out Roman Catholicism attracted me, and I kept a supply of flowers always before the little statue of the Virgin from Lourdes that Madame Tadadam had brought me from her pilgrimage. What I really came to believe was that there was one God for all of us, and that Jesus had appeared to help us understand Him.

Eugene Debs, I believe it was, said that while there was one man in prison he could not feel free. I, and millions of Jews in America, felt that while there were millions of Jews in concentration camps and in cruel exile we could not enjoy our great good fortune as Americans. We claimed kinship and fought every piece of Nazi propaganda with as much zeal and fervor as if we, too, were in that beleaguered fortress and death trap.

Just about then some friends of ours along the river had a house guest they brought over to meet us. He was a Frenchman and a writer and we welcomed him with open arms. It was good to see someone who had come recently from France and we plied him with questions about our friends, and about our beloved second country. His name was Jean Fontenoy. He was fair-haired and boyish-faced, and exceedingly brilliant. Willie had heard of him, but I had not, and so I read one book of his that Michael Pym lent me, with the setting in China, where Jean had been correspondent for a Paris newspaper. There was something about the book that aroused my misgivings, though I couldn't put my finger on it. One thing that would never have occurred to Willie or to me was that any Frenchman could be anything but fiercely patriotic and anti-German.

He dropped in to see us alone, quite frequently, always amusing and always welcome. We talked of the French authors we knew, and the places we had lived in and still loved. One day he came for lunch, which we were having on the wide terrace we'd built in front of the barn. Fontenoy was seated on a long bench next to Willie and I sat opposite them. The conversation was again on France, when, suddenly, Fontenoy faced Willie and said, earnestly, "Hit me, Seabrook. Hit me hard!"

To my amazement I saw Willie draw back his arm, and, putting all his weight behind it, deliver a punch in Fontenoy's ribs so that he doubled up with pain. Then the two men looked at each other, and the Frenchman said, "Thanks. I had it coming to me."

I was bewildered, not having followed the conversation that preceded it, but Willie understood and his face was grim.

Not long after that we gave a dinner party to which we invited Fontenoy and his hostesses, Miss Merritt and Michael Pym. Conversation at the table was general at first. And then, inevitably, as all conversation did during those years, the talk turned to Hitler. Michael began defending him. She and Miss Merritt had recently visited Germany, and she told how well run it was now, and how Germany was being restored to her role as leader in Europe. And then, to my astonishment, I heard Fontenoy agree with her.

"But you are a Frenchman," I said, from my end of the long refectory table. "You know what Hitler is threatening to do to France!"

"*Tant mieux*," he said. "It is what France needs, to be rid of the Jews. . . ."

I stood up. "I will not allow such talk at my table," I said. "Since I can't ask you to leave, I will leave." And I rushed from the barn and ran down the path to the cottage.

I stood in the middle of the living room, trembling, with tears streaming down my cheeks. I heard someone enter after me, and then felt arms around me and a kiss. It was Fontenoy. I pushed him away, and he said, "You are charming. What a

211

pity you are one of the people we must kill." I heard him laugh as he left the cottage, and I think, if I had had a knife, I would have killed him.

A little later, the guests having gone, Willie came down to the cottage. I thought he might be angry at me for leaving my own dinner party. Instead, he picked up a book, sat down, and looking over at me, said, "The poor bastard! I should have hit him twice as hard. It's what he wanted."

Much later, after the fall of France, I heard that the body of Fontenoy had been found on a side street in Paris, with a dagger in his back. Attached to the handle was a note that read: *"Ainsi meurent les traîtres!"*

The rest of the pages of my Journal for that year are blank. I suppose we both worked at writing, saw a lot of people, quarreled with each other and made up again. But we were both drinking now and that exaggerated the depths and widths of our quarrels. I loved Willie as passionately as ever, and I think he loved me, but the hurts lasted longer and so did the separations. The peace we had enjoyed together for a few lovely years was fluttering its wings, like a bird that has outgrown its nest. Fear took its place.

Chapter Twenty-one

The year 1940 began quietly for us. *Witchcraft* was finished the day after New Year's and we mailed it to Don Brace. It was a good book, well written, and we were both pleased. Although Ann Watkins had tried to sell some chapters to the magazines, she wrote Willie that the editors were afraid of his material.

Willie sent a wire to Ann saying that he wouldn't care if she didn't sell any of it, because for once in his life he'd written exactly as he pleased! But we were both secretly a little disappointed and our spirits were low. So was our bank account, although a check came to Willie out of the blue, from DeWitt Wallace, as a bonus for "his distinguished services during the year."

Entries in my Journal for this period are pleasant, but they show a kind of marking-time quality. Willie had a bridge game or two in his studio with his village cronies; Olin Dows dropped in to return some African masks he had borrowed for a lecture. I finished a painting I had started of the road to the barn, and paid some of our bills. Ed Lyons, who ran a tavern on the road to Poughkeepsie where we sometimes stopped briefly, dropped in with a little gift for Willie. He was an ex-prize fighter and Willie enjoyed talking to him. Willie liked prize fights, although I don't remember his taking much interest in baseball or football. Once, when Joe Louis was in training at a camp near us, we went over to call on him, and we had his manager over to tea one afternoon.

The weather was cold but the snow was beautiful, and we took long walks in the Montagues' woods, or the Langdons' woods, next door. We heard often from the Huxleys, who had established themselves in California, and from Golo Mann, in

Zurich, where he had gone to edit a paper written by exiles in German "to keep the real German spirit, philosophy, etc., alive."

We saw the Montagues and the Billingses and exchanged dinners with them, though there were no parties that I can remember. Willie dictated letters, which I typed for him. He played tennis on the Astors' indoor court and kept in good physical condition. But he was bored and restless and worried.

A new friend in Poughkeepsie, Simon Kaplan, was writing a book about his childhood in Russia before the Revolution. Willie was enthusiastic about its possibilities, and was helping him. It gave Willie something to do and we enjoyed evenings at the Kaplans' while new chapters were read aloud and we all made comments. We took Simon to Woodstock to call on Paul and Rosella Fiene, and Si bought one of Rosella's drawings, which pleased me because Paul and Rosella always needed money, desperately. Once, when things were going well with us, Willie gave Paul a large sum of money to have one of his pieces of sculpture cast in bronze.

My Journal for early 1940 continues with uneventful jottings. It was like the quiet we find in nature before a violent storm:

Wednesday, January 10th. To Poughkeepsie in morning with Willie, to get car fixed in the Buick garage. I bought some new paints. We had lunch in town at the Smith Brothers' restaurant, made the usual jokes about Trade and Mark, and had fun.

Deborah Dows asked us to dinner to see the new quarters she has built for herself on her mother's estate. She has an apartment over the stable where she keeps her horses and donkeys and beagle hound. It has a wall around it and reminded us of a *mas,* or wall-enclosed farm in France. Mrs. Dows and Olin were there—a pleasant dinner. Afterwards we went to the Town Hall for a "gypsy festival" at the Lutheran Church. Willie was one of the judges of costumes.

Thursday, January 11th. In the morning, Willie dictated letters, including a long one to Ann Watkins about Si Kaplan's manuscript.

Lillie Havemeyer and Louise Travers, the minister's wife, here to luncheon. Willie is very fond of Mrs. Travers and calls on her for long talks, I think because he is reminded of his mother's kind of

214

life as the wife of a minister in a small town. He is always on his very best behavior with her.

In the evening Willie played bridge in Poughkeepsie and I stayed home and read Ford Madox Ford's *It Was the Nightingale,* and discovered on page 247 that he refers to me as "a lady novelist" who told him I was disappointed the first time I heard a nightingale, and that he had asked me if I had expected "an opera loge and a box of chocolates to go with it." The conversation had never taken place, but I would have forgiven Ford anything for the beautiful review he wrote of *Mrs. Taylor* when it came out.

Although life seemed pleasant on the surface, we were still marking time. Willie worked on his friend's manuscript, and I painted, and it was a way to keep fairly busy while we waited to hear from Ann Watkins, who was still trying to sell the witchcraft book to a magazine at the usual high prices.

But it wasn't just this alone that was making Willie irritable and depressed. What was more serious was the vacuum produced by having finished one book without having a new one already sprouting shoots. What happens normally to writers is that halfway through one manuscript, an idea for a new and possibly entirely different book starts formulating and pushing its way into his consciousness. Sometimes the new idea gets so strong it has to be pushed back and told to wait. That is when a writer is happiest, when he feels productive and alive and going on all cylinders. And because this was not happening to Willie, who had rejected Ann's ideas mostly because he was looking for one of his own that would be better, he felt barren, used up, dead.

I tried to convince him that the well would fill up again, stronger and fresher than ever. But I was feeling pretty low about myself, too. I knew that my painting was of no use except for the pleasure it gave Willie. And I didn't have the heart to leave Willie to his own resources and misery while I shut myself up in my little study and started something on my typewriter.

We attended a Polish Relief concert in Poughkeepsie; we read, we took walks. Willie went fishing through the ice with some of the men from the village, and came home with a large perch and a lot of stories. He even sat down and began to write one about a ferret. He called it "The Kitten," and as I remember, it was very good. (I wish we had collected some of his short stories—those that ran in *Vanity Fair*, and a very early one called "The Salamander." They had an Ambrose Bierce quality and contained some of his best writing. I hope they aren't lost forever.)

We were drinking too much. Ann came up with a suggestion for Willie to write a book about Otto Kahn. There was a lot of money involved and I knew that Willie was tempted. But he didn't want to do it, and we discussed the whole thing thoroughly one night and in the morning he called Ann to turn it down. But not before he had drunk a bottle of whiskey in order to make the choice seem easier.

I wasn't surprised when he told me he had arranged for another "Lizzie in Chains" session in the barn studio. I had been dreading it, but by now I realized that it was his way of finding catharsis for the conflicts and the tensions. He believed them necessary, and so, I suppose, they were. But the first girl he sent for was a disappointment, and the depression deepened.

And then I found that he was brooding about something I hadn't suspected. Not long before this he had received a gift from Harrison Smith, his first editor at Harcourt, who had been visiting Haiti. The gift was a ouanga, a sort of charm used for Black Magic which Willie described at length in *The Magic Island*. The ouanga is a bag filled with various objects and sent to the person on whom a spell is to be cast. There are good ouangas and bad ones; that is, they can bring either good or bad luck, depending on the sender's intention.

In *The Magic Island* Willie described the making of a protective ouanga for him by Maman Célie, his guiding spirit on the island:

. . . a large cowhide was spread, hairy side upward, on the earthen floor, and around it in a circle sat solemnly a dozen negroes whom I knew. . . . There were eight men and four women. It was night time. The only light flickered upward from small candles arranged

216

as a geometric pentagram on the cowhide. Barring the doorsill were two crossed machetes, their broad, naked blades inscribed with white chalk symbols, the swirling serpent, the phallic staff, the enmeshed triangles.

Spread in the center of the candle pentagram, on the cowhide, was a square red cloth, like a napkin, which was to be the covering of my *ouanga* packet. Bright ribbons, red and yellow, lay beside it, and also feathers brilliantly dyed. In little, separated piles upon the cowhide were balsam leaves, leaves of the castor-bean, roots of the lime tree; a saucer of flour, a saucer of ashes, a bottle of *clairin*, a bottle of perfume, a tiny iron crucifix.

Maman Célie and I sat on one side of the circle, Papa Théodore facing us. While they chanted almost in undertones, *"Papa Legba, ouvri barrière pour li; tout Mystère gider li"* (Legba, open the gate for him and every Mystery protect him), old Théodore took some of the roots and leaves, mixed them in a brazier, charred them over a fire now kindled on a plate before him, then pounded them together in a mortar. The two machetes were taken from the doorsill and planted upright in the ground, flanking him on each side. A *bocor* (magician) filled his mouth with *clairin* and sprayed it, sputtering, over all the paraphernalia on the cowhide, to drive away evil spirits . . . the *bocor* began picking up balsam leaves and castor-bean leaves, one by one, marking each with a chalked cross and depositing it on the napkin, until a new pile was made there. Atop these leaves he now laid the crucifix, also a tuft of hair (tied together with thread) which had been cut previously from the central crown of my head; a paring from my right thumb-nail, and a small square cut from a shirt which had been worn next to my skin. . . .

Maman Célie handed me a copper coin and instructed me to place it on the packet. And now, before it was tied up, she told me to make a prayer (wish). I hesitated, then stood with both arms stretched straight out before me, palms downward, as I had seen them do and said in English:

"May Papa Legba, Maîtress Ezilée and the Serpent protect me from misrepresenting these people, and give me power to write honestly of their mysterious religion, for all living faiths are sacred."

That was a good ouanga, but there were also bad ones, to bring death or misery to an enemy. The ritual was, of course, different, and so were the contents, which were far worse than the objects the witches in Macbeth put into their nasty brew!

How much Willie believed in this magic, black or white, I was never very sure, and neither was he. But I do know that what he saw of magic in Haiti and the jungles of Africa impressed him deeply. And I know, too, that he didn't like receiving a ouanga from Hal Smith, even if it was made of red satin and tied with silk bows and was obviously done up for the tourist trade!

Once Willie and Hal had been very close friends, but something had happened to break up their friendship—perhaps so mundane a thing as Willie's refusing to leave Harcourt to go with Hal when he started a new publishing firm of his own with Jonathan Cape. They had said some bitter things about each other, and did not meet if they could help it. That is why Willie was inclined to regard Hal's present with a good deal of suspicion.

Before Willie wrote *The Magic Island,* probably nobody except the Haitians had ever heard of a ouanga, just as nobody had heard of a zombie until Willie gave those living dead to the literary world, which was so delighted it promptly invented a zombie cocktail. After Willie's book, voodoo became as much an export of Haiti as sisal and sugar or whatever else they were able to sell for money. Now nearly every visiting American brings or sends home a pretty little green or red satin bag, containing heaven knows what, and calls it a ouanga.

It was not the little bag, which Willie knew for a fake, but the *intention* that worried him, for it is the thought that can be deadly, Willie believed (and I half-believed) if the victim is made aware of it.

And so I took the ouanga out to the rubbish heap behind the barn and burned it. That afternoon, as we took a long walk in our neighbor's woods, I told Willie what I had done, and he seemed relieved.

A few days later I wrote in my Journal: "It looks as if my burning the ouanga has brought Willie what he wants—three 'Lizzies' have decided to come, one at a time! That will teach me to fool with magic! Oh, will I be glad when *this* is over.

Maybe it will clear his mind and set him back in the right direction."

It was the middle of February, and soon after Lizzie No. 1 arrived the snow began to fall, and by the next day had worked itself up into a blizzard. I kept a fire going in the big Dutch fireplace in the cottage. I started a new painting and read. I wished I were writing something that would engross me completely; but I wasn't writing at all.

Willie came down from the barn at intervals. The first Lizzie, a girl he had hired a year ago and who had returned for more, wasn't working out. She was not, he said, "the flaming thing she was last summer." She seemed tired and he felt sorry for her, so he let her go after a day or two.

The blizzard, I note in the Journal, got worse. There were drifts as high as ten feet. But Sam Wright, the kindly superintendent of the Langdon estate next to ours, came with his snowplow and cleared our road for us. And so it was cleared enough for the village taxi to bring Lizzie No. 2, who arrived on the ten P.M. train from New York.

Here are more notes from my Journal:

Friday, February 16th. The new Lizzie seems to be working out well and Willie is much more serene and confident and less depressed. No drinking!

In the morning he and I drove to the village to shop. In the afternoon we took a walk as far as the snowplow had cleared the road beyond our place. The two willow trees that Willie fought hard to preserve when the town wanted to widen the road last spring look beautiful, bowed down with snow.

Had Lizzie No. 2 down to dinner and found her rather nice.

Saturday, February 17th. Willie about his business up in the barn studio. Whatever he is doing, it seems to be going as he wants it to. He is very sweet to me, but absorbed in whatever is going on up there. As always, after it has been going on for some time, I am nervous and irritable, but hope I've succeeded in not showing my feelings. I should know by now that he has to have these sessions, but I can never understand it or *why* he has to have them, and maybe I never will be able to reconcile it with the rest of his character.

219

One thing has cheered me up a little. I've started a short story. Thought I'd never be able to sit at my typewriter for myself again.

Monday, February 19th. No matter how I pretend, or how I try, to be understanding, this Lizzie thing of Willie's worries and frightens me. I'm nervous and miserable tonight and wish to God it would soon be over and things back to normal again.

Tuesday. The Lizzie business still going on. Willie told me he drew a circle on the floor of the studio, with the letters T and F in it. Representing Bach's Toccata and Fugue. He said he would like to keep his sadism on that plane!

February 22nd. Willie's birthday. I had painted a picture for him and bought some initialed handkerchiefs he needed, and I sent them up to the barn with our little West Indian maid, Leandra, who accepts the goings-on in the barn with more equanimity than I can! (She thinks it is some ritual being performed up there, like voodoo or obeah, and since she has accepted us, she accepts that as part of us.)

I had ordered a birthday cake two days ago. I put candles on it and sent it up to the barn and made some excuse not to join them. I lunched down here in the cottage alone—and felt little and mean.

Tonight Willie went to a roast pig dinner given by some men in the village, poker afterwards. I think W. is having a happy birthday while Lizzie is suffering up in the barn—and I'm a middle-class female, ready to fly to the moon on a broomstick!

Sunday, February 25th. Willie and I had coffee early this morning and a long talk together in the bedroom. I demanded to know how long he intended to keep up this session in the barn and he said, "Well, not too long. I know she can't go on forever—neither can I." He was starting to be amusing about it, to make me smile; but I flew off the handle and said I couldn't take much more of it, either. In fact, I was ready to walk out of the house that minute and never come back.

He begged me not to go. He promised that as soon as a certain experiment he was trying for the first time had worked out, he would send this Lizzie away and would cancel the other's coming. "Then we'll do something nice together," he said. "I've just got to get this out of my system."

I looked at him and said he looked awful and I thought he was making himself sick, and that we'd all be sick if he didn't stop. But I promised not to go away, to stick it out. He was using all his charm and I couldn't stay angry with him, much as I tried. If I weren't so in love with him I'd run a thousand miles from everywhere.

Instead, took a walk by myself on the hard-crusted snow, and listened to the Philharmonic on the radio, the Brandenburg Concerto No. 2, and some Shostakovich. Some people dropped in for tea, when they left I tried to work on my story but soon gave up.

Monday, February 26th. Lizzie goes on. I hope it will be over by Thursday, as Willie promised.

Tuesday, February 27th. This thing looks pretty serious. Worried about Willie's health, and the girl's. Though I hate the whole damned stupid mucky business, I don't know what to do but wait—and try to keep sane.

Spent the day in bed with a cold and slight fever. Willie has a bad cold, too, but won't stop to pay any attention to it. Whatever is going on over there, it now consumes him entirely.

Wednesday. Had to get dressed this evening, to keep a dinner engagement with the Trenholms at the Beekman Arms. Made some excuse for Willie—that he was working on a new book and couldn't stop. After dinner Jack and Dorothy brought me back—seemed to want to visit for a while, so I took them into the cottage and left them in the living room while I went up to the barn to see if I could persuade Willie to come down and talk to them. I felt like a juggler, trying to balance the sane and the insane world on my chin!

Downstairs the barn was in darkness, but I could see a light in the studio upstairs as I walked on the path. I climbed the flight of stairs and knocked at the closed door of Willie's workroom. There was no answer, and I knocked louder. Then I said, "I'm coming in," and opened the door, which wasn't locked. I couldn't see either of them at first. Then I saw the dangling empty chain. Willie was seated in a chair, staring straight ahead of him. At his feet was the naked girl, silent and motionless. For a moment I thought my heart had stopped beating. I walked over to Willie and he looked up at me. "Call the wagon," he said. "It's all over. This is it!"

I leaned over the girl. I was so frightened for a minute I couldn't think straight. And then something told me she was only playing dead! I went into the small adjoining bedroom and from the bathroom closet took out a bottle of smelling salts. I returned and held it

221

under her nose. It was a new bottle, and strong. The way I held it, it would have revived her if she *had* been dead. In a few seconds, she opened her eyes and asked the stock question, "Where am I?" and I knew I had been right.

I didn't blame her, of course. She used probably the only means of getting out of a mess. But though I had pity on her, my only worry was about Willie and what it would have done to him if for once in his life he had gone too far!

I managed to help her get to bed, and I managed, somehow, to send the Trenholms away, saying Willie was sick. Then I hurried back to the barn and led Willie down the stairs and the path, to the cottage. I put him to bed in the guest room down here, and he went to sleep at once.

Thursday. She left on the 3 o'clock train today. Thank, oh thank God, that's over! It was the longest and most frightening siege I remember—and it might have wrecked everything.

The doctor wants Willie to stay in bed. Today he is calm and peaceful, reading a detective story, normally worried about his cold, and everything is on the road to recovery. I feel as if a steam roller had passed over me—flattened, shaky and weak—but infinitely relieved.

Friday, March 1st. Willie still in bed. Doctor says it's bronchitis. He is reading Herbert Gorman's life of James Joyce, and is being very good. He needs a lot of rest and building up after last week.

Gradually the strain is leaving us and things are coming back to normal. I will be glad to see the end of this winter. I have Henderson's *Garden Guide and Record* to look at and am planning my garden with John Lattin.

Sunday, March 3rd. Willie still in bed. He says he is determined to give up alcohol and all forms of escape. "I have twenty years left, perhaps, to write something good, and still be a great and good man," he said to me. "The truth—though it slay you," he went on. "I never knew what that meant before. Now I think I do."

When, at last, Willie got out of bed and dressed, he insisted on continuing the liquid, nonalcoholic diet, and refused to shave because he had decided to grow a beard. He read a lot of Blake and talked in a low voice. This saintlike metamor-

phosis worried me almost as much as the roaring, bad Willie
had done.

I wrote in my journal: "Sometimes I wonder just *how* mad
Willie is, and does it matter? What ought I to do about it? Do
we love each other or really hate each other? What nonsense!
But, of course, we get on each other's nerves—especially after
the strain of the past few weeks."

Chapter Twenty-two

The Otto Kahn book was definitely shelved now, and we were both relieved. Willie shaved off his beard, began to eat normally, played a few sets of tennis, and took his first drink in ten days. He was trying to write of his mystical experiences during the two weeks' session in the barn studio with Lizzie No. 2, and I could tell he was having trouble with it.

I managed to finish a short story and sent it to my agent. I didn't say anything to Willie about writing again, but decided to wait and see if my agent sold it.

People came to call and we went visiting. Willie was asked to make a speech at the Sportsman's dinner of the Rod and Gun Club, at the Beekman Arms. Herbert Gorman and Clair came to visit us and Herbert read us parts of *Finnegans Wake* and tried to explain it to us.

We all drank too much that night, and Herbert, whom I had known years before when he was married to Jean Wright and I was married to Lyman, sat on the back steps of the barn with me and suggested we run away together. Somewhere along the line, he said, we had both jumped the tracks. We sat, holding hands, and remembering.

He and Jean lived in the Village, in a nicely remodeled house between Fifth Avenue and Sixth, and Lyman and I lived in an apartment house on Waverly Place. Herbert was then one of the regular critics on the New York *Times Book Review,* and was highly regarded as a writer of both prose and poetry. A friend of mine, Geo. Theo. Hartmann, as he signed himself, was living with the Gormans, and I used to attend a sketch class there once a week. The Gormans knew everybody; they were part of the literary group of "ins" whom Burton

Rascoe mentioned almost constantly in his literary gossip column—as often as he mentioned a Van Doren! I was greatly impressed. I remembered taking Lyman's young sister, Frances, to call on Herbert one afternoon, to learn all about Padraic Colum and the Irish poets. I remembered a lot about that other life as I sat beside Herbert in the moonlight on the back steps of the Rhinebeck studio. It seemed very long ago, and in another world.

Herbert seemed to think we could get back on the rails again and find our other selves waiting for us, like a railway station with a sign saying HOME. But I shook my head.

"We'd never find it again," I said. "We'd both get lost. Besides, you love Clair and I love Willie. And I'm afraid we can't help each other. It's too late, much too late."

We sat in a mist of sadness for a little while, and then we went back into the barn for another drink.

It was about the middle of March by then. The willow trees were turning yellow, the ducks were back in the pond, and I could see the earth getting ready to let the earliest of the spring flowers send up their shoots. Willie was being very good, and he was cheerful. We took long walks together again, we listened to good music in the evenings, and to the news broadcasts by Lowell Thomas. Russia had signed a peace treaty with Finland and it looked as if the Finns might escape the fate of the Poles. We listened to Lord Haw Haw on my radio, which had a short-wave circuit, and we thought he was very silly and stupid.

Chanler Chapman came to see us, looking handsome as well as happy. He had written a book about his school and had shown us some of it in manuscript, and it was good. Now Earl Balch was going to publish it and he wanted us to know. There were letters from Maria Huxley from Llano, California, where she and Aldous had bought a ranch. She described the hardships, and the wind, which she had always hated. Every time the mistral blew at La Gorguette, the Huxleys put their house up for sale. But she said they were happy. Aldous had gone to stay for a while at Gerald Heard's "monastery" and was very much interested in the talks he was having with Krishna Murti.

There were happy days running along together. I always forgot the barn sessions when they were over, pretending to myself that there would be no more. How could there be, when life was so pleasant and Willie seemed almost happy? With the Otto Kahn book definitely shelved, Willie began to play around with several ideas of his own. There was always the chance that one of those ideas might turn into something really "great" and make the mark on the wall he so often talked about. Bills were piling up, but we decided not to worry about them. They would be met somehow.

Then one day Ann Watkins phoned to ask Willie if he would write a biography of Dr. Robert Wood, the physicist who helped establish the Palomar Observatory and was now retired. To my surprise, Willie sounded interested. Deep down underneath the layers of mysticism and fantasy, there was really a practical side to Willie. Bills had to be paid—or else. And I guess he felt that one more assignment wouldn't hurt.

Although I was glad that Willie would be at work on something again, I was somewhat dubious about this project. Having tried to write a book about Dr. Helen Montague and her career, I knew the difficulties of writing the biography of someone who was still alive. One had to please too many people.

At about this same time, Henry Morton Robinson of *The Reader's Digest* phoned Willie and asked him if, between books, he could do a piece for them on male sex hormones. And so, while Ann was straightening out some publishing tangles for the Wood biography, Willie got busy seeing the two Rhinebeck doctors and collecting preliminary material. The *Digest* sent him some books and pamphlets with sickening illustrations.

Neither of these assignments was what Willie would have chosen. They seemed so far from being up his alley, as he would say, that I was afraid of what they might do to his delicately balanced nervous system. I suggested we sell one of our houses, either the barn or the cottage, and hole up in the

226

other, and then he could start writing the autobiography he had long contemplated, and planned to call "My Brother Charlie." But Willie told me I was crazy. He said he liked having a definite assignment now and then, to keep his hand in as "a good reporter." I think maybe he was afraid to tackle the creative work he wanted to do, for fear it wouldn't be good enough to please him. That happens to a lot of writers. The longer one can put off "the great book" the longer one can feed one's soul on the possibility of its being the masterpiece one plans it to be.

The *Sunday Courier* of Poughkeepsie ran a full page about us, with photographs of us in the barn studio and outside on the terrace. And the Rhinebeck *Gazette* ran an editorial praising Willie and saying how proud they were to have us living there. It was all very flattering to our egos; but there were still low moments, and in the midst of all this, I could see and feel signs of a new "Lizzie" session shaping up. All my fine theories of what caused them were wrong, and I would have to get new theories—or stop thinking.

One morning in April Willie left to go to Baltimore for his first interview with Dr. Wood. He came back a few days later with a lot of notes and surprising enthusiasm. The Robert Woods, he said, were charming people and promised to co-operate to the hilt.

Then I discovered that Willie had asked the girl who had been with him on the long devastating session in the studio to come up again. I had been so sure he was going to get down to work right away. Everything was so wonderful when Willie was working on a new project. He was like a captain in control of a ship, he knew where he was going, his step was firm, his eyes were clear, he took care of his health. I had been waiting for that Willie to return. But now there was to be another interruption and I was sick with disappointment.

We had a long talk about it. I asked him why, when there was work to be done and the whole world was trying to keep sane in the face of terrible danger, he thought he had the right to spend days and nights in that dark section of his mind, wrestling with private demons?

I might as well have talked to the wind. It was something he had to have. But he promised to make it a short session this time, and to confine it to the barn studio.

The following day the girl arrived. But, evidently, something went wrong again. Willie sent her away and came down to the cottage in a terrible state. He talked of committing suicide. I got him into bed and sent for a doctor, a new one who had just come to town, a refugee from Hitler's Germany. He was a young man with surprisingly advanced ideas. He wanted to see the set-up in the barn, and then he came back and talked to me. He said that if this was Willie's sexual pattern there was no way to change it now. The only thing for me to do was to protect him, and wait for this to pass over. That's what I had been doing for years. That's what I would continue to do—for years—if necessary. But I had always kept some tiny thread of hope that one day Willie, who I believed could do anything, would be able to slay his evil demon before it destroyed him. Now I was told there was no basis for that sustaining hope.

That dark evening a bird flew into the house. It flew around the living room and the kitchen and then out through an open door. Willie said it meant good luck. Leandra, our little West Indian maid, said it meant somebody was going out of the house —alive or dead.

Witchcraft, Willie's book on magic, appeared with good reviews. It was now May of 1940. The Germans had invaded Denmark, then Norway, and, shortly after, the British were forced to withdraw their troops and Norway was in Hitler's possession. We were glued to our radios, shocked and indignant.

Early in June, I wrote in my Journal: "So much has happened to the world, I could not write about it. The Nazis seem to be on their incredible way to wiping out England and France. And I, in my little personal life, have almost wiped

228

out everything, or, to put it more exactly, have been almost wiped out. I am holding on as hard as I can. But I could not write about any of it."

I cannot say now, trying to look back across the bridge of years, what was happening that was too painful to write about. I could try to say that we quarreled—except, that we so seldom quarreled. Perhaps if we had, like ordinary married people, it would have been much better for us both. But I had, basically, too much respect for Willie to say those little angry things wives say, and Willie was so used to having his own way and making the laws that, if I lost my temper, he would laugh at me. But I know we were both on edge at that time, and harboring resentments that had a tremendous potential for smashing everything we had ever tried to build together.

Toward the middle of June, Willie and I spent a few days with Dr. and Mrs. Wood at their summer home in East Hampton. It was a beautiful old Long Island house with a thatched roof and gray shingles weathered by the salt spray from the beach; it was furnished in faded chintzes and wicker and smelled of furniture oil and matting and lilacs, the way summer homes of my childhood smelled. I loved it, and the Wood family too.

Dr. Robert Wood, who had invented a great many important things and contributed to the making of a powerful telescope that would help usher in the space age, was rather like a superannuated pixy, and a little hard to take unless you happened to be fond of elderly pixies, which I am not. He was forever telling about the practical jokes he had played on people, spinning them out into endless and, I thought, rather pointless anecdotes. While his family obviously respected and loved him, he must have been rather trying as a husband and father.

Gertrude Wood, his beautiful and tolerant wife, treated him as if he were an overgrown boy, and yet there was an undertone of deference that the whole family shared, or seemed to share. He really *was* an important man of science, as we found out when we visited him in the laboratory at Johns Hopkins. I don't know what his son and married daughter thought, as we

229

saw them only at dinner. They were charming and amusing, but absorbed in their own affairs like most young people.

During the days of our visit, Willie and Dr. Wood went off together to give and get data for the book, Gertrude Wood went shopping, the others disappeared, and I sketched or read. But every evening just before dinner we met on the wide veranda for cocktails that Mrs. Wood made and that were the best and strongest I have ever tasted.

The last day of our visit, at cocktail time, someone turned on the radio for the news. We had been laughing at someone's last joke; then, when the news began, there was sudden silence, and we all sat stiff and motionless, like a reel of film that has snapped off in the middle of action: Paris had fallen. The Nazis were even then entering the city.

It was unbelievable. We had always known how proud the French were, and how fiercely patriotic. With the exception of Fontenoy, we had no inkling then of those French who were friendly to the Germans and fascism. It was, to us, a fate that had befallen a most beautiful city comparable only to the rape of Troy and its magnificent women. I wept, and I am sure others wept, too, on that quiet veranda in East Hampton. I thought of my friend Choute Mirenda and of Bob Lemercier, of Monseigneur Leperq, of Kisling and Renée, and Jean Cocteau. I thought of the family at the Hôtel Place de l'Odéon, and Madame Ripperte at the corner bar in Toulon. And I ran up to our room and wrote a poem and wished them, as they had so often wished me, *"Bon Courage!"*

I became very fond of the Woods, perhaps because we had shared that news together and wept. I hoped Willie would turn out a good book, as I knew he could, although it wasn't going to be easy. And at first he seemed happy and busy with it, sorting the notes he had made and starting the first rough draft.

But it wasn't long before that initial enthusiasm disappeared. The book began to bore him before he got through the notes on Dr. Wood's boyhood. Whimsy was not William Seabrook's cup of tea, and Ann should have known that, or we should have known it. In addition to that drawback, Willie was too much of an egotist himself to write the biography of another one!

As a result, he began drinking heavily again. He would get up at five in the morning and go over to the studio, presumably to work on the book. By noon, when I called him for lunch, he was drunk. I would get some food into him and help him to bed in the cottage to sleep it off. Then, after a nap, he would return to the studio, where I would find him later, sitting in the dark, miserable and sick.

He took an office in the village, over Jake Barowsky's men's clothing store, thinking that might break up the pattern. He would go off in the car early in the morning and come back home for lunch. But one day he took me up to see the office and I noticed a bottle of whiskey on his work table, and, except for a few pages of rough draft, no evidence of progress on the biography.

I tried to help, and, between us, we got the book together and sent it to Ann Watkins. It was pretty good, but nothing that any of us was proud of. I don't remember how it sold. I think the Woods were disappointed, but they thanked us. And that was that.

But now Willie was without a project. He still rose at five in the morning, fixed himself coffee, and went over to his studio, although there was not much point in it. All he did was drink alone, and if I interfered he was abusive and mean.

Among the precepts by which Willie lived was the quotation from Epictetus which describes everything as having two handles, one by which it can be carried and one by which it cannot. I grasped the easier handle—as I had done before, in France—which was to drink enough myself so that I was not critical of or pained by Willie's drunkenness, because I would be on the same plane with him or near enough to be at least companionable! It was a mistake, of course, but it helped me to go on living with the wonderful person I loved after he had turned into an incoherent caricature of himself. I mustn't try to make excuses for myself; but I had tried with all my resources to help him, and when I failed to lift him out of hell I slid down the embankment with him.

The bitter Irish woman who had brought Fontenoy to our home made a remark about us that some friend of ours decided to tell me. It was that "Willie was drinking himself to death, and Marjorie was helping him." That came so close to the truth that I realized I must stop drinking and find the other handle.

. I sat down with Willie and tried to reason with him, tried with his help to work out some plan, as we had done before, to save him. I tried to convince him that he still had to write his best book, the one that would put him at the side of the angels, the geniuses that he worshiped. I spoke of "the mark on the wall" that he wanted to leave, and asked if he wanted that mark to be the feeble scratching of an alcoholic. I talked and talked in the dusk of that big studio among the mementos of his travels and his fame. And Willie listened.

In *Asylum* Willie said that alcoholism becomes a reality, a disease, when it interferes with a man's work. We both knew a great many people, mostly newspapermen, who were able to fill their assignments drunk or sober. And we knew a lot of so-called creative writers who were drunk most of the time. But sooner or later their work was bound to show the result of putting that into their mouth which stealeth away their brains. There was a saturation point, and Willie had reached it before, in that last summer at La Gorguette. He had reached it again, now, in Rhinebeck.

As a result of our long talk, Willie went off for a week or ten days to a farm in Woodstock, New York, to get "dried up" and back to health, and, as they say in the South of France, "to change a little one's thoughts." The farmer's wife, whom I knew from my early visits to the art colony, was a big, strapping, handsome woman who was used to artists and their ways. She agreed to rent Willie a room, give him his meals, and look after him while he tried to work on *My Brother Charlie*.

Paul and Rosella Fiene, who lived just up the hill from the

232

farm, were away in Europe on a Guggenheim Fellowship that Rosella had received. They were expected back in Woodstock that week, and I was sure they would help Willie if he needed anything. Just the same, I left for Rhinebeck with plenty of misgivings mixed up with a little bit of hope. Perhaps the complete change of environment would help—and the mountains, which on my girlhood visits to Woodstock had never failed to inspire me and make me want to do "great things." If only Willie could get back to writing something he wanted to write, I thought, everything else would clear up! I did a lot of whistling in the dark that week as I cleaned house and then got to work on a book I was trying to start.

The first letter I had from Willie, written in pencil on the rough yellow copy paper he always used, was encouraging. He wrote that all went well. He asked me to get rid of all the liquor left in the house and barn, and said that, if I agreed, we would not serve any to our guests for at least six months, until he was strong enough to have it around without drinking any of it himself.

He asked me to mail a check to Grace, the farmer's wife, and added a postscript saying he didn't know how I or anybody had put up with him recently, and that I was wonderful and he loved me.

A few days later he wrote that he was steady again. He had reached a vital turning point and later would have been too late. He said he realized he had been upsetting me terribly and wondered how I could have stood it. But he was going to be good now for a change. Everything in Woodstock helped, he wrote, even something he had read in a book about how a man who merely talks about his devils is a sham. If he really has devils, he either drives them in harness, or drinks himself to death. From now on, he said, we'd be "on the up" together. He hoped I was getting along with my novel and asked me to paint him a picture some time. And he signed the letter, "Best love, Willie."

There were several postcards and a letter which sounded as

if he were thinking of getting down to work. "Anyhow, I'm sober," he wrote and signed his name, "with all my love." The next cards were about his mail, which I had forwarded and which he hadn't received, and some mention of a package from New York that I knew nothing about. Then a card that said, "Everything here goes perfectly in all respects, love, W." And a postscript to this that said I should come over to get him on Wednesday and take him back to Rhinebeck.

Nothing in any of this correspondence prepared me for what I found when I crossed the river with some friends who had offered to drive me to Woodstock. I had missed Willie very much and was looking forward eagerly to finding him sober, healthy, and ready to start on his program of good resolutions.

When I entered the big kitchen of the farmhouse, there was someone with him. She was a tall, slender young woman, not pretty but well dressed and rather attractive. She had a brisk, offhand manner that may have been a protective mechanism, but that bordered on rudeness.

Willie introduced her and said that she had been a "foreign correspondent" and had just returned from Germany on the ship with Paul and Rosella Fiene. They had invited her to stay with them until she found something to do, and some place to live.

I don't know much about the "feminine mystique." I have always believed that women react as people—as men react—to most situations, to most phenomena. But I am sure there is some sense a woman has that lets her know when another woman means trouble. There had been a great many women in Willie's life, before and during the years I lived with him and loved him. Since there was no alternative for me except to walk out, I had to accept them as part of his life pattern. Most of them came and went, like the winter snows, without leaving anything of themselves behind. There were only a few who worried me, and each time I had been forewarned by something I might as well call intuition.

We gathered Willie's few things, and said good-bye. And on

234

the way home Willie told me that she was coming next week to stay with us for a while. A few days later, she arrived.

At least Willie had stopped drinking. But the other business was still occupying all his mind and energies. From his letters and postcards while he was in Woodstock I had been foolish enough to think that his good resolutions included a break in that pattern, too. But those devils he mentioned were riding him more than ever.

I was sick about it. I was sick about a lot of things. After a week, I found our guest giving orders to John Lattin about re-arranging the garden. It sounds silly, but often a little thing like that can detonate a bomb whose fuse has been a long time sputtering. I was furious. I told Willie, when he came down to the cottage, that she had to go.

"What makes you think she will last any longer than the others?" he asked. "It's always ended, sooner or later, and how do you know when I'll be asking you to help me get rid of her politely? Why not stick it out a little longer, please?"

I shook my head. I knew the uselessness of making an ultimatum to Willie. If I said, "Either she goes or I go," it would simply have put his back up and made it impossible for him to send her off, even if he had wanted to. He had to be handled differently. I knew that, just as I knew that I wanted desperately to help him get safely out of the nightmares. But I was at the end of my rope.

"I just can't take any more of it, Willie," I said. "Not another week or another day. I've got to get away from the whole thing. I love you, but this does something terrible to me. If I stay, I'll murder somebody. I've got to get away, now."

Of course he was sick and needed help. I would have done anything in the world to help him, if I could. But he wouldn't let me. It was as if the only world he believed in was the fantasy one he had built up in the barn. I needed help, too. And I needed perspective before I could decide where to turn.

As I always did when I needed help, I went down to my sister's house in Westchester, where there was no lack of problems; but they were the tangible problems of any healthy family. I intended to stay until I had gathered strength to face, sensibly, whatever had to be faced in Rhinebeck.

My father had died the previous year, and my mother was living with my sister and her husband, and there was my nephew who was still at college, and my young niece who was about to be engaged. It was an active household, and my troubles were of a kind they would know nothing about, so I didn't tell of them.

But at night, when I went to my own room, I thought of Willie and longed for him, for the Willie I had known, independent and strong, who knew where he was going and just how he was going to get there! A man of great talent and even greater intelligence, who could write like an angel at times and suffered anguish when he couldn't. A man who had great courage, and yet could be terribly afraid; who could make people laugh as well as cry, who could be kind and gentle and generous, who made friends and kept them—a man absolutely without prejudice or bias, who asked only that people be alive and interesting. A man for princes and princesses—and peanut venders and old cleaning women. A man with a deep thirst for life and a curiosity about "what made it tick." The Willie I had walked with over so many long and beautiful roads.

The Willie I loved was in the marrow of my bones. How could I deliberately cut myself off from him? Every night, in bed, I told myself I would take the morning train back to Rhinebeck; but I didn't. I couldn't face what I knew was still going on. Besides, if I had not dared to give an ultimatum to Willie, I had given one to myself. I would go back when Willie told me he had sent her away, and not until then.

For years, twelve at least, Willie had been dictating notes to me at intervals for the book to be called *My Brother Charlie*, an autobiography, just as *The Autobiography of Alice B. Toklas* was Gertrude Stein's. We had high hopes for that book. It was

236

to be the very best Willie could do, his masterpiece. The last time we had even discussed a new book, Willie told me he thought he was ready to start writing *My Brother Charlie*. I prayed that the urge to get started on it would be strong enough one of those days to pull him out of his sexual fantasies.

And one morning in my sister's house there was a letter for me in the mail. The handwriting was unfamiliar but the letter was from Willie, who said that after trying hard he had "fallen into the ditch again," but that he was beginning to see the light and hoped to set to work soon on the book he planned to call *My Brother Charlie*.

I couldn't make out from the letter exactly what had happened. He said that Constance Kuhr had been using every drastic, reasonable means to keep him from drinking, and that when these had failed she had dropped the reasonable means and, "with the help of Dr. Stoller," fixed things so he wouldn't be able to bend his arms for at least ten days. It was a good job, he said, because it didn't prevent sunshine or outdoor exercise, and didn't embarrass anybody. The hardest aspect of it was being deprived of cigarettes, which he enjoyed—he'd always hated alcohol. A postscript, written by Willie himself in large childish block letters, said that although it would be some time before he could use a typewriter he was already dictating part of *My Brother Charlie*. He ended by begging me to come up soon, because John wanted to consult with me about the garden. And he told me that I could call him anytime—Miss Kuhr could hold the phone for him—and that he was happy, and that he loved me.

I was sick with apprehension, with fear at what might have happened to Willie. For so long I had been shielding him, and now I had run away and let him get into what sounded like real trouble. I put in a call immediately to Dr. Stoller in Rhinebeck. When I finally got him he told me that Miss Kuhr had plunged Willie's elbows, both of them, into a basin of boiling water and kept them there until they were badly scalded. Then they had called the doctor and he had had the burns dressed at the hospital. Willie was no longer in danger of infection, but of course both arms were bandaged and he would not be able to do anything for himself for several weeks.

"I'll be up on the first train I can get," I said.

There was silence, and then Dr. Stoller said, "Don't come back, Mrs. Seabrook," and hung up the phone.

There was a late afternoon train, and I took it. All the way up along the Hudson I looked out of the dirty train window and thought, "I will kill her!"

Chapter Twenty-three

It was after I returned and had a chance to size up the situation that I realized Willie had probably made Miss Kuhr do what she had done. Instead of entertaining melodramatic ideas of murder, I had to overcome a feeling of revulsion. What it came down to was the fact that Willie was sick; but I didn't know how sick, or whether there was any way to help him.

I talked to Dr. Stoller, who reassured me about Willie's recovery from the scalding but not about the extent of his aberration. Just as the doctors at Bloomingdale had told me, the pattern was so fixed there was little if any hope of changing it. Sadism and masochism were two sides of the same coin. Willie had what he believed he needed at the present moment. It was something I couldn't give him. Once again, Dr. Stoller advised me to go away.

But it wasn't so easy. Willie asked me to stay. He came down to the cottage one morning and asked me if I couldn't go on living there, near him. He loved me, he said. And who could tell how long this arrangement would last?

I tried to stay. I honestly didn't care what the situation might look like to other people. They say. What do they say? Let them say. In the United States of America a wife doesn't live next door to her husband and another woman. I don't think in my distressed mind I gave a hoot in hell what other women did or didn't do. But I hated this woman for what she had willingly or unwillingly done to Willie. And although I have never been able to bring myself to kill a fly or a spider, I was quite capable of killing her. In some way I confused her with my nightmares of Hitler and everything German. We were all more or less hysterical at that time. The threat of a powerful enemy made us suspicious of a lurking shadow behind a tree—or under our beds. I'm afraid I was like that. I saw a Hitler salute in a raised arm and a Nazi sympathizer in a common pretzel. I was not alone in this; but added to my personal emotional imbalance in those days, I can see why I may not have been able to make any careful or detached decisions.

Willie sent me notes by Miss K. and John Lattin. I have kept some of them all these years, and I wonder if I had read them then in the same light as I do now whether I would have made the same decision?

One night, while I was still living in the cottage, I made a big pot of stew and sent some of it up to the barn. The next morning John brought me a note from Willie, saying that the stew had been so wonderful he'd gobbled it and licked the plate and hummed about eels and eel broth. (There were a lot of old ballads, French or English, that Willie liked, and one of them was about Lord Randall, who returns to his mother after a night with the girl he loves but of whom his mother disapproves. The boy is dying, and his mother asks him what she fed him, and his reply is "eels and eel broth, mother.")

Another note had a postscript describing two dreams he'd had. In one, I had spanked "the Rose Myra part of me," by which he meant the prudery that was like my mother's and his mother's, and become humanly friendly with Miss Kuhr because she seemed to be doing such a good job with the gorilla-ape side of him; but of course that was only a dream. The other dream had been of a different sort, he said; he knew he had told me, over and over again, that from now on things would be different, but he asked me, underlining the words, just what it was that made me think the present arrangement was going on forever.

But it was going on for a long time, and I hated every minute of it—and myself, too. There was a heroine in the Canterbury Tales known as Patient Griselda, whose husband tries her by submitting her to various cruel tests, including divorcing her and sending her home and telling her he is about to marry another. Finally her patience is rewarded by his love. I had found her as hard to believe and as unpalatable as any modern woman would, and yet . . . Well, Griselda was dead. Chaucer in the envoy to the "Clerk's Tale" wrote:

> Griselde is dead, and eke her pacience,
> And both at once buried in Italie.

And I decided to leave, and bury her in Rhinebeck, too.

I told Dr. Montague, and she, like Dr. Stoller, advised me to go away and try to start a new life of my own. If they had asked me to stay, I might have. But they didn't. And besides, something else must have happened. I have forgotten what, but I blew up finally, packed my bags, and, with my dog, went to New York. I was really through this time. I knew it. I had closed the door. Later I could pick up the pieces of what was broken.

I spent a week in a hotel and then began a series of visits to friends, including the Stongs, who were going away on a trip for the magazine *Holiday* and invited me to stay in their house in Connecticut. I was utterly miserable wherever I went. And the letters from Willie that reached me, those that I have miraculously preserved over the years, were of no help in my search for peace of mind.

There is a long one, dated March 10, 1941, in which he said he knew I loved him and that I considered his work as the very soul of him—something far more important than his happiness or comfort. He also knew, he said, that I feared or disliked some aspects of his nature not because they were fantastic or had erotic overtones, but because I understood that they were an effort to "go back"—to childhood, to the mother's womb, in extreme instances to what he called the cosmic womb. I believed they could never lead forward; they were a form of escape, what Freud calls regression. But he could not agree about this, he told me; he had always felt that the regressions renewed in him the power to move forward, but because this was a feeling, divorced from reason, he'd always had trouble explaining it to me.

He said he'd been reading a forthcoming book by Malcolmson, *Ten Heroes,* that Cap Pearce had sent him. It was about sources of creativeness in writing, and he begged me to read it. It was Malcolmson's theory that the going back, the so-called regression, was not only not sterile but was as true a way forward as any— that for some choked but potentially creative writers it was the *only* way. And the three examples from modern literature analyzed by Malcolmson were Proust, Thomas Wolfe—and William Seabrook!

In writing *My Brother Charlie* he had to go back, Willie said, and he did not believe this was accidental. He believed that life was like a jigsaw puzzle: when one neglected piece suddenly fits in its right place, all the others begin to collect and fit and round out the pattern. He assured me that drink played no part in the process that was now going on for him; and because of the letters I'd written to him he was confident that I'd be driving up soon, to help John start the garden and give all sorts of other advice and help, to thank Miss Kuhr for having done so well the job she had unselfishly taken on, and to prepare to return and be happy with him as soon as possible. He and John and I were all a part of the place; but so, too, he said—and if I could not understand this from his letter, surely I would when I came up—was something he'd looked for all his life in vain, and which was bigger than any individual. He begged me to believe that it was of ultimate importance to the real creative work he hoped to do and that other people were kind enough to believe he would do. But if I was unwilling to come up, and help about the place, and try to understand what he meant— that, he said, would surely be bad for both of us.

So much of the letter was Willie, and so much of it was not. I was on a rack of indecision—but I didn't go back. He had something he needed, but that I could no longer be a part of. Perhaps if he had not included that line about Miss Kuhr I might have fooled myself into thinking I was a necessary piece in that jigsaw puzzle he wrote about. The decision was about as easy as hacking off one's own arm to keep from dying of poison.

But I did it, in spite of the fact that at the time I really didn't care if I lived or died.

A month later, on April 17th, Willie wrote me another letter, in which he said he'd made a miraculous discovery, as if a clear light had shone out in what had been a long darkness. He had suddenly perceived what albatrosses we had become around each other's necks, and how profoundly we had hurt each other's writing. He said he was now alive and writing in a way that was not my way, and he was convinced that my best way to be alive and writing, which was not his way, was to be free of the "nightmare-incubus" he had become to me in trying to force me to participate in his way. But he missed me, and he truly loved me in whatever way could make sense in the new clear light.

He went on to say that he believed there was a strange parallel between the eating of human flesh and the burning of his arms. In both cases, the compulsion had been absolute, and vital if he was to continue to function as a writer: if he hadn't done the first he could never have written *Jungle Ways* and if he had not accepted the second he would not be writing *My Brother Charlie*. In terrible things of that sort, of which, he said, he was not proud, I could never help him. We were different sorts of animals, he and I, and all he could hope was that I might understand.

"Albatross." "Incubus." If I had known then all that I know now, I would have gone back and waited again for a phase to be over, if it was just a phase. But I *didn't* know and one does only what one is capable of doing at a certain moment in time. And I no longer had the strength, physically or morally, to go back and face what I knew, in spite of Willie's fine words, I would find. Instead I kept on running through a dark tunnel, running away from my love, running toward an escape hole I didn't know about or care about or really want to find.

When I was very young I memorized a lot of poetry, some of it good, some of it bad. One of the verses that remain, without a memory of who wrote it or where it came from, is this:

243

The sins that ye do,
Two by two . .
Ye pay for
One by one.

I divorced Willie, all alone, in Newburgh, N.Y., before a
decrepit old judge who was hard of hearing. It was a nightmare
through which I walked like an automaton. It was a major
operation with no anesthetic. After it was over I signed papers
in a lawyer's office in Poughkeepsie. I felt as if I had died, as if
my ghost walked out of that office and got on a bus to nowhere.

Everyone was kind. The Huxleys asked me to come out to
California and live near them. Maria had even found a little
house for me and I was to come quickly, as it was all ready and
waiting. Alfred Harcourt took me to lunch at the Algonquin
and advised me to go West and start an entirely new life among
people who didn't know me. He suggested Arizona. It was good
advice and I should have taken it, but I didn't. I lacked the
energy and the desire to strike out into new lands or to have
new adventures. I wanted only to crawl off somewhere until the
wounds were healed.

My sister asked me to come to live with them, putting it on
the grounds that she needed me to look after mother, who wasn't
well. I accepted, gratefully. It was a busy household, and soon
we were all engaged in war work, so-called. I worked all morning in the Mayor's office, filing cards with information about
all the citizens for Civilian Defense purposes. Two afternoons
a week my sister and I sat in the basement of the high school
as part of the air-raid-warning system, listening for the signals
that, happily, never came. At night, during blackouts, I walked
all over the neighborhood with my sister and her husband,
checking on people who left their lights on. It was all rather
exciting and made us feel we were doing something—which was
a help to us if not to the world at war.

Between these activities, I wrote. Stories came rushing in to
fill the vacuum that was the place where I once had a cottage,

a garden, and Willie. At first I sold them to *Harper's* and the other "quality" magazines that paid me two hundred dollars or so. Then, on a visit to the Stongs, I met their agent, Harold Matson, who had been with Ann Watkins and was now in business for himself. I gave him a story about Toulon during the Occupation of France and a spy who got his "comeuppance." I called it "Black Market" and Hal sold it to *Collier's*; so I broke into the "slicks," which paid fantastic prices, much more than any story was worth, it seemed to me.

That summer I went to Massachusetts with the family, to my sister's summer place on top of a hill in Ashby, with ninety acres to walk in. On a clear day we could see the State House in Boston, and at night we could see a million stars and sometimes the Northern Lights. But these were things I could hardly bear to look at more than an instant at a time. Along with my sister's riotous garden, these beautiful things were somehow mixed up in a crazy way with thoughts of Willie and Rhinebeck. So I didn't look much, but kept on working in a large square room with sprigged wallpaper. I turned out a novelette that Hal sold to *Cosmopolitan,* and a short story he sold to *McCall's*; and at the end of the summer I felt rich enough to be able to live alone in New York.

I took an apartment overlooking the East River, furnished it with some of the things I had salvaged from the cottage, and wrote more stories. And one night, when I was taking my dog for a walk, I stopped at a newsstand and bought a *Daily News.* That was how I learned that Willie had married Miss Kuhr. Up to that moment I don't think I actually believed my separation from Willie was a reality. Now, in one cold black-and-white fact, I realized what I had done.

I had to learn to stand up and stop crying for something that was supposed to be bad for me but that I still wanted, with all my heart and soul and body. My life was my own now. I could throw it away as I wished. And I started trying to fall in love, having affairs, persuading myself that this man or another meant something to me. If I could fall in love again, I assured myself,

I could forget Willie. But it didn't work very well. I bought a lot of pretty clothes that pleased me, not the kind Willie liked me to wear. And I worked hard at my typewriter, turning out stories that kept selling to *Cosmopolitan, McCall's,* and the rest as soon as I finished them. I dined at Voisin or at "21" every night, and wore orchids that an admirer sent to me twice a week. And all my good friends were happy because I was so successful.

Willie's book came out. It was no longer called "My Brother Charlie." The title was *No Hiding Place.* Alfred Harcourt had turned it down and so it was published by Lippincott.

Willie sent me a copy. On the flyleaf he had written:

> To Marjorie Worthington
> —pages 396–397
> are good, maybe.

So I read those pages first:

When your eyes are open again after such a blind landing, they are keen with a clear vision that doesn't necessarily last. It's like the religious experience known as being born again. People used to get born again on the Glory Trail at the Billy Sunday revivals with the help of Homer Rodeheaver's trombone if they were white, and with the help of Holy Roller howling and Egypt Walking if they were black, but most of them were drunk and in the ditch again a few days later. You have to be reborn with each new dawn. On days when your sun doesn't rise, the days are awful. You are like a dead man walking. The awfulest part is that you know it.

I'd begun to write again, stiff-armed, with pad and pencil—not hack work now but stuff I'd wanted to do for years and never dared tackle—feeling it was now or never—and there were days when all the horrid fears came back that nothing I had ever done, might ever do, was any good or ever would be.

At times when I was struggling to make my mother or my dead brother Charlie come alive again, I felt that in a fleeting phrase I'd almost done it. But never for long. It came sometimes in spurts and rushes most of which had to be crossed out later, but the times when a phrase or sentence seemed to remain alive came rarely and faded quickly.

How they come and how they fade—whether the writer be good, bad, great or small—nobody knows. Least of all the writer . . . Your decision has no value anyway. On some tomorrow after you are dead, others will decide. If nobody reads you after you are dead, your words are dead, but if some living people continue to read your words, your words remain alive.

And you remain alive. And there is your mark on the wall, Willie, I thought. But I could not judge that book of his. I tried in all fairness to read it impersonally, and that was impossible.

I saw Willie a number of times after the book came out. He was doing some pieces for his old outfit, King Features Syndicate, whose offices were just a few blocks away from my apartment building. He would drop in for lunch, usually just cottage cheese and milk, which we would eat on trays sitting opposite each other in chairs by the window, while along the gray river even grayer ships slid past, on their way to or from Europe.

We talked mostly of trivial, safe things, both of us afraid to touch the places that were painful. Although once he said, "What has happened to me since you left shouldn't happen to a dog—or should it?" and he looked at me with the smile I knew so well, sly, mischievous, and rueful.

I saw him after his son was born, and I sentimentally went with him to Schwarz's toy store and sent a stuffed animal toy to Rhinebeck, without a card. I saw him again when he was given an assignment to go overseas. He asked me to go to Brooks Brothers with him while he was fitted for a correspondent's uniform. And after he had the uniform, I went to dinner with him to "21" at his request. It was, I felt, a farewell dinner. I remembered how, soon after we had met for the first time, he brought me, among other treasures, the paper he had received with the Croix de Guerre, citing him for bravery in the First World War. I knew he was enormously proud to think that he was going to have some part in this one. He was at his best that night, almost like the old Willie. I

247

remember he forgot his officer's cap in the restaurant and we had to go back for it, and laughed. But it wasn't much of a celebration. The clock had moved too far ahead, and it was very late.

Willie didn't get overseas. The rest of what happened to him came to me only by hearsay. Something blew before he actually got his assignment, and he was sent to Rockland State Hospital, from which he was subsequently discharged. The rest was a going in and coming out of asylums.

I heard that he and Constance had taken a little apartment in the Village as a *pied-à-terre,* and that Willie was trying to interest Dali in a ballet based on the sadistic games that seemed to have completely absorbed him by then. Nothing came of it, although Dr. Helen Montague told me he had come to see her and shown her photographs he had taken that were, she said, "very beautiful."

Did she try to help him again, as she had helped him once before? I don't know. Perhaps she thought there was no use trying, as other doctors had felt. I was busy, with some war work I was doing, with writing for a living, with the thousand and one little things I made fill my life.

And one evening my telephone rang, and at the other end was a woman who had loved Willie, too. She told me he had been found in his bed that morning, dead from what seemed to be an overdose of sleeping pills.

Two things Willie lived by were quotations from Epictetus, whom he loved: "A mark is not set up for the purpose of missing the aim," and "Everything has two handles, one by which it can be carried, and one by which it cannot." I had often heard him say, "In the end, it is not good." I had also heard him say he would never be really happy until he was dead. But I never thought he would take his own life. I suppose that, at the end, he couldn't find the handle by which his life could be carried.

For the moment, he and his books are forgotten; a whole generation has come into being whose members have never even heard his name. But other writers have gone through periods of neglect and been rediscovered. I was too close to him, too caught up in that powerful personality, to be a good judge of him as a writer. I only know that he wrote some illuminated passages of prose, and that he was, in his own peculiar way, a dedicated artist. A mark on the wall is something a man must make for himself. Posterity is the only real judge, and sometimes, I feel, it makes mistakes.

William B. Seabrook contributed a lot to the world's knowledge of primitive people. His books on Arabia and Haiti and the African jungle, although they may not have been literal truths, were better than that. As one critic said, he traveled "deeply" as well as widely. *Asylum* was one of the first books to suggest the treatment of alcoholism as a disease for which people need not be ashamed to seek help. And it was a book that helped a great many people, even if he could not help himself.

In spite of the sexual pattern that he let dominate his life, he was no Marquis de Sade. He was a fine, intelligent, and lovable man, with a touch of genius as well as madness: a man capable of inspiring deep and indestructible love, not only mine, but that of friends who survived him, those who tried to help but were not successful.

He was a minister's son. He had made a profound study of all religions. He was deeply religious himself, though often blasphemous. He never lost a childlike belief that he was "a lamb of God." As such, I hope, I have presented him.

Fort Lauderdale,
Florida
May, 1965

Books by William B. Seabrook

Adventures in Arabia, 1927

The Magic Island, 1929

Jungle Ways, 1931

Air Adventure, 1933

The White Monk of Timbuctoo, 1934

Asylum, 1935

These Foreigners, 1938

Witchcraft, 1940

Dr. Wood, 1941

No Hiding Place, 1942